PVRCHASED WITH THE INCOME OF THE

COLONEL MASON WHITING TYLER FVND

PLAINFIELD PVBLIC LIBRARY

Morgan Colt.

Mary

H. Clay

John Hancock

Dwight D. Eisenhower

D. P. Madison

D1411607

A Treasury of
GREAT
AMERICAN
LETTERS

The Great Letters

With Descriptions of

the Circumstances, Surroundings

and Significance of Each

At the Time of Its Writing

Along With the Sequels and

Repercussions

Which Made History

From

1493

to

1961

With Illustrations from Various Historical Periods

A Treasury of GREAT AMERICAN LETTERS

OUR COUNTRY'S LIFE & HISTORY
IN THE LETTERS OF ITS
MEN AND WOMEN

BY CHARLES AND ELEANOR HURD

☆

HAWTHORN BOOKS, INC., *Publishers, New York*

PUBLIC LIBRARY, PLAINFIELD, N. J.

816
H 93

Copyright © 1961 by Hawthorn Books, Inc., 70 Fifth Avenue, New York 11, New York. Copyright under International and Pan-American Copyright Conventions. All rights reserved, including the right to reproduce this book or portions thereof, in any form except for the inclusion of brief quotations in a review. This book was manufactured in the United States of America and published simultaneously in Canada by McClelland & Stewart, Ltd., 25 Hollinger Road, Toronto 16. Library of Congress Catalogue Card Number: 61–11994. Suggested Dewey Decimal Classification: 816.00.

FIRST EDITION
1961

Title page illustration—Bettman Archive

ACKNOWLEDGMENTS

THE compilers of this book are greatly indebted to a host of individuals, libraries and publishers for cooperation in gathering the letters included in this work, and while every effort has been made to assign proper credits and obtain appropriate releases, some credits may have been omitted where they are due. If so, these will be included in subsequent editions.

Christopher Columbus letter, by permission of the Rare Book Room, the New York Public Library.

Dr. William Douglass letter, by permission, from *Letters and Papers of Dr. Cadwallader Colden* (first volume 1711–1729), the New York Historical Society, 1917.

John Hancock letter, by courtesy of the Rare Book Room, the New York Public Library.

Daniel Carroll letters, 1775 and 1787, from manuscript collection of *Letters of Daniel Carroll,* in editorial custody of Sister M. Virgina, S.S.N.D., College of Notre Dame of Maryland.

B. Freeman letter, by permission, from the personal family papers of Miss Bertha A. Marshall, Northbrook, Pa.

George Washington letter, 1776, from a privately published transcription of the original in 1777, by courtesy of the New York Public Library.

Thomas Jefferson letters, from the Library of Congress, with the editorial assistance of James A. Bear, Jr., curator, Thomas Jefferson Memorial Foundation, Charlottesville, Va.

Fabius (John Dickinson) excerpts, from 1797 edition of *Collected Letters of Fabius,* edited by W. C. Smith, by courtesy of the New York Public Library.

5

Rudolph Van Dorsten letter, from Clarence W. Bowen's *History of the Centennial Celebration of the Inauguration of George Washington,* New York, 1892.

George Washington letter, 1793, and John Jay letter, by courtesy of the Elkins Collection, the Free Library of Philadelphia.

Mason Locke Weems letter, from *The World of Washington Irving,* by Van Wyck Brooks, copyright 1944, E. P. Dutton & Co., New York, N.Y.

Noah Webster (Aristides) letter, from a copy of the original 1800 printing, by courtesy of the New York Public Library.

Alexander Hamilton letter, from original manuscript, by courtesy of the Elkins Collection, the Free Library of Philadelphia.

Washington Irving letter, 1802, from original book publication by Effingham Wilson, London, 1824, courtesy of the New York Public Library.

William Wirt letter, 1805, by permission, from original manuscript, Alderman Library, University of Virginia, Charlottesville, Va.

William Wirt letter, 1822, and Henry Clay letter, from manuscript in Hampton L. Carson Collection, the Free Library of Philadelphia.

Henry Wadsworth Longfellow letter, from *Authors and Friends,* by Annie M. Fields, copyright 1896, Houghton Mifflin & Co., Inc., Boston, Mass.

Marquis de Lafayette letter, from privately printed collection, the Rare Book Room, the New York Public Library.

Ellen Bigelow letter, from the *Journal of the Illinois State Historical Society,* 1929.

Abraham Lincoln letter, *circa* 1835, by courtesy of the United States Post Office Department.

James Bowie and William B. Travis letters, from original manuscript, Western Americana Collection, Yale University Library.

Richard Rush and James Kent letters, from manuscript, by permission, the Hampton L. Carson Collection, the Free Library of Philadelphia.

William Strickland letter, by courtesy of the Society of Architectural Historians.

W. B. Wade letter, from manuscript, by courtesy of the Yale University Library.

James Fenimore Cooper letter, 1846, from *James Fenimore Cooper,* by Henry Walcott Boynton, copyright 1931, Appleton-Century-Crofts, New York, N.Y.

Emily Dickinson letter, owned by Mt. Holyoke College, and published in *A Hundred Years of Mount Holyoke College,* by Arthur C. Cole, copyright 1940, Yale University Press, New Haven, Conn.

Oliver Wendell Holmes, Sr. letter, 1851, from *Authors and Friends,* by Annie M. Fields, copyright 1896, Houghton Mifflin & Co., Inc., Boston, Mass.

Dame Shirley letter, from *Pioneer Magazine,* San Francisco, 1854.

Ralph Waldo Emerson letter, by special permission of letter's owner, Charles E. Feinberg, Detroit, Mich.

Brigham Young letter, from manuscript, by permission of the Yale University Library.

Abraham Lincoln letter, 1858, from the Library of Congress.

Frank Hall letter, from the Frank Hall Collection, Denver Public Library, by special permission of his family.

"Monitor" letter, from *Chicago History,* Vol. III, Chicago Historical Society.

Gro Svendsen letter, by special permission of the Norwegian-American Historical Association, Northfield, Minn.

Carl Schurz letter, from *The Intimate Letters of Carl Schurz, 1841–1869,* Joseph Schafer, trans. and ed. (Wisconsin Historical Publications, *Collections,* v. XXX, Madison, 1928, 304–311).

Ulysses S. Grant letter, by permission of the Elkins Collection, the Free Library of Philadelphia.

Charles W. Eliot letter, from *Life and Letters of Charles W. Eliot,* by Henry James, Houghton Mifflin Company, Boston, Mass.

William Henry Jackson and George A. Custer letters, from manuscript, by permission of the Yale University Library.

Horace Greeley letter, from manuscript, by permission of the Denver Public Library.

Susan B. Anthony letter, from Ida Hustes Harper Collection, Henry E. Huntington Library: *Susan B. Anthony: Rebel, Crusader, Humanitarian,* by Alma Lutz, copyright 1959, Beacon Press, Beacon Hill, Mass.

Bernard J. McQuaid letter, from collection in custody of the Rev. Robert F. McNamara, professor of church history, St. Bernard's Seminary, Rochester, N.Y.

W. T. Sherman letter, from manuscript, courtesy of the Yale University Library.

Mark Twain form letter, from *Mark Twain, A Biography,* by Albert Bigelow Paine, copyright 1912, Harper & Brothers, New York, N.Y.

P. T. Barnum letter, from *Barnum's Own Story,* copyright 1927, Viking Press, Inc., New York, N.Y. All rights reserved.

William Randolph Hearst, letter, by personal permission of William Randolph Hearst, Jr.

James Cardinal Gibbons and Roger Brooke Taney letters, from *Documents of American Catholic History,* by the Right Rev. John Tracy Ellis, copyright 1956, Bruce Publishing Company, Milwaukee, Wis.

Thomas A. Edison letter, by courtesy of the Edison Laboratories National Monument, West Orange, N.J.

Mary Baker Eddy letter, from *Miscellaneous Writings,* copyright 1896, renewed 1924, by permission of the custodian, Archives of the Mother Church.

Theodore Roosevelt letter, from the Theodore Roosevelt Collection, the Library of Congress.

Maxwell E. Perkins letter, from *The Letters of Maxwell E. Perkins,* edited by John Hall Wheelock, copyright 1950, Charles Scribner's Sons, New York, N.Y.

William E. Borah letter, from *Borah of Idaho,* by Claudius O. Johnson, copyright 1936, Longmans, Green & Co., Inc., New York, N.Y.

Sherwood Anderson from Story Magazine (Anderson Memorial Issue) copyright 1941; reprinted by permission of Story Magazine, Inc.

Louis Dembitz Brandeis and Oliver Wendell Holmes, Jr., letters, from *Brandeis: A Free Man's Life,* copyright 1946, by A. T. Mason, reprinted by permission of The Viking Press, Inc., New York, N.Y.

E. M. House letter, from *The Intimate Papers of Colonel House,* edited by Charles Seymour, copyright 1928, Houghton Mifflin Company, Boston, Mass.

John Foster Dulles letter, by permission of his estate.

Woodrow Wilson letter, from *Borah of Idaho,* by Claudius O. Johnson, copyright 1936, Longmans, Green & Co., Inc., New York, N.Y.

Will Rogers letter, from *Letters of a Self-Made Diplomat to His President,* by Will Rogers, copyright 1927, Albert and Charles Boni, Inc., New York, N.Y.

Bartolomeo Vanzetti letter, from *The Letters of Sacco and Vanzetti,* edited by Marion Denman Frankfurther and Gardner Jackson, copyright 1928, 1956, by The Viking Press, Inc., New York, N.Y.

Thomas Wolfe letter, by special permission of the Thomas Wolfe Collection, Pack Memorial Library, Asheville, N.C.

F. Scott Fitzgerald letter, from *The Crackup,* edited by Edmund Wilson, copyright, New Directions Publishing Co., New York, N.Y.

George C. Marshall letter, from original manuscript, by permission of the George C. Marshall Research Foundation, Arlington, Va.

John Barrymore letter, from *Good Night Sweet Prince,* copyright 1944 by Gene Fowler, The Viking Press, Inc., New York, N.Y.

Franklin D. Roosevelt letter, from published public letters, selected with the assistance of Miss Grace Tully.

Irvin S. Cobb letter, from privately published pamphlet, by permission of the Irvin S. Cobb Memorial Committee, Paducah, Ky.

Robert Frost letter, from *Steeple Bush,* copyright 1947, by Henry Holt & Co., Inc., reprinted by permission of Holt, Rinehart and Winston, Inc.

Robert Oppenheimer letter, by permission, from the writer's own files and heretofore unpublished.

Ogden Nash letter, by permission of the author, © 1958 by The Family Circle, Inc.

Herbert Hoover letter, by permission of the author, and by copyright holder's permission, copyright 1959, by the Reader's Digest Association, Inc.

Francis Pharcellus Church letter, by permission of the World-Telegram and Sun, New York, N.Y.

Robert E. Lee letter to his wife, from *The Wartime Papers of Robert E. Lee,* edited by Clifford Dowdey and Louis H. Manarin, copyright 1961, Little, Brown & Co.

Maxwell E. Perkins letter to Van Wyck Brooks, reprinted with the permission of Charles Scribner's Sons from *Editor to Author: The Letters of Maxwell E. Perkins* (pp. 10–14), edited by John Hall Wheelock, copyright 1950, Charles Scribner's Sons.

Jane Addams letter, from *Jane Addams, a Biography,* by James Weber Linn, copyright 1935, D. Appleton-Century Co., Inc.

Edna St. Vincent Millay letter, from *Letters of Edna St. Vincent Millay,* edited by Allan Ross MacDougall, copyright 1952 by Harper & Brothers.

Alan Seeger letter from *Letters and Diary of Alan Seeger,* copyright 1917 by Charles Scribner's Sons.

John F. Kennedy letter, by express permission of the White House.

FOREWORD

THIS work represents the first attempt to assemble in one volume a selection exclusively of letters from or by Americans, which contribute a third dimension to the proud story of our country spanning three centuries—or almost five if one starts with the date of the first letter in this book.

In these letters are the privately expressed aspirations and hopes, fears, and triumphs, of a heterogeneous people. Many of the letters are the intimate revelations of persons great in our history—some are letters written in youth by those who were later to become great—many are by individuals who lived out their lives in anonymity, but who, in some brief inspired moment, wrote a footnote to our history almost as important as our laws and famous victories.

Whole libraries of notable writings and speeches by Americans exist—speeches which frequently seem to have been written with a dramatic eye to the audience of the moment. However, the letters in this volume are private, confidential and self-revealing, with the delightful exception of a few that were written for publication in periods of great debate (before the so-called press interview was invented).

These letters illuminate the heart of America, not just the publicly expressed mind. For example, a Boston physician tells a New York colleague of the difficulties of his practice in 1720; John Jay writes an affectionate note to his wife, informing her that he must go abroad to negotiate a treaty; John Hancock postpones signing George Washington's army commission, while he writes a note to his fiancée; George Washington, from winter headquarters, gives affectionate advice to his stepson; Abraham Lincoln sympathizes with a mother whose five sons have been reported lost in the Civil War; a Norwegian immigrant on the Prairies writes home, in 1863, that "the land is our own"; John Brown and Bartolomeo Vanzetti tell their families their thoughts on the eve of execution; Will Rogers pens a report from London as Calvin Coolidge's "unofficial ambassador"; and the elder Oliver Wendell Holmes expresses ecstasy over an offer of $100 to write a poem.

Twenty years of stimulating experience with the recorded words of American history gave no hint of the problems involved in assembling a volume of "great" American letters. It was relatively easy to list some "classic" letters for inclusion and many more letters were suggested by the perusal of memoirs by and biographies of outstanding Americans. This left at least half of the contents still to be selected, a job involving research and winnowing impossible for the editors working alone. Consequently, this book represents a venture based on the generous and selfless assistance of a group of experts, to whom really adequate thanks can never be rendered.

In response to requests for help in the quest for letters, a number of newspapers gave assistance, most notably The New York Times and the Christian Science Monitor. Several hundred individual letters were sent to metropolitan libraries and to the listed historical societies most likely to have collections either unpublished or in print only in privately circulated editions. These appeals resulted in something very similar to a major national project.

The Yale University Library became the first focal point of research, when David R. Watkins, head of the Reference Department, made available the Yale Collection of American Literature and the Historical Manuscripts Collection. Guidance through this invaluable collection was freely given by Donald Gallup, in charge of American Literature; Robert Metzdorf, archivist; Howard Gottlieb, librarian of Historical Manuscripts, and Archibald Hanna, curator of the Collection of Western Americana. Their valuable assistance saved months of research.

In Philadelphia, Pa., the Free Library made their priceless Americana collection available to us. Emerson Greenaway, the director, went to great pains to list possibly suitable material spanning a great era both in time and in diverse personalities, particularly from the Coe and Elkins Collections.

Francis L. Berkeley, Jr., associate librarian of the Alderman Library, at the University of Virginia, recommended materials from that collection and suggested other letters to be found elsewhere.

Louis M. Nourse, director of the St. Louis Public Library, led us to the Carl Schurz letter on Abraham Lincoln, which is in the possession of the Illinois State Historical Society.

The New York Public Library gave us access to its files and indexes in the Rare Book Room (based on the former Lenox Library) and its Department of Americana, plus giving every requested staff assistance, as did the New York Society Library, one of the oldest and largest private subscription libraries in the United States.

In Denver, Colo., Mrs. Alys Freeze, head of the Western History Department of the Denver Public Library, produced the Horace Greeley and Frank Hall letters, among others.

Many other librarians suggested letters which could not be included in this work, but which helped greatly in developing perspective and making comparisons.

James A. Bear, Jr., curator of the Thomas Jefferson Memorial Foundation at Charlottesville, Va., suggested a wide range of Jefferson letters, out of his knowledge of this great file in the Library of Congress.

The Right Reverend John Tracy Ellis, a biographer of note in his own right and secretary of the American Catholic Historical Association, volunteered his assistance and that of some thirty church scholars currently specializing on biographical projects, ranging from Frey Serra to Cardinal Gibbons and including such lay notables as Chief Justice Taney and Daniel Carroll. Particular thanks are due to Sister M. Virgina, of the College of Notre Dame of Maryland and the Rev. Robert F. McNamara, professor of church history, St. Bernard's Seminary, Rochester, N.Y.

Two outstanding scholars interrupted work on current biographical projects to contribute suggestions: Louis H. Manarin, associate editor of the R. E. Lee Papers, and Forrest C. Pogue, director of the Research Center of the George C. Marshall Foundation.

Special thanks go to Miss Myra Champion, librarian of the North Carolina Collection in the Pack Memorial Public Library, Asheville, N.C., for suggesting and arranging release of the Thomas Wolfe letter; to Charles E. Feinberg, of Detroit, Mich., for the contribution from his collection of the Emerson letter to Walt Whitman; to Miss Bertha Marshall, of Northbrook, Penn., for the letter to John Bartram, an ancestor; to Mrs. John L. Gilchrist, of the Historical Society of Pennsylvania, for suggesting the Strickland letter; and to the Public Library at Stonington, Conn., for the letter describing how a 20-year-old sea captain from that port became the first man to sight Antarctica.

Unfortunately, space does not permit acknowledgment of help and suggestions from many others.

Finally, we acknowledge with special gratitude the patient assistance of Miss Elizabeth C. Kelley, in correspondence and manuscript preparation.

—CHARLES AND ELEANOR HURD

CONTENTS

Should include Chas & Anne Lindbergh if copyright allows.

LIST OF ILLUSTRATIONS

CHRISTOPHER COLUMBUS
At the Court of Barcelona, center of a magnificent reception in honor of his supposed discovery of a new route to China and India.

CAPTAIN JOHN SMITH
When he was leader of the Jamestown colony.

THOMAS JEFFERSON
The young author-patriot drafting the Declaration of Independence.

JOHN HANCOCK
As painted by J. S. Copley.

BENJAMIN FRANKLIN
As painted by Charles Wilson Peale.

GEORGE WASHINGTON *and* **GENERAL LAFAYETTE**
A farewell at Mt. Vernon.

ALEXANDER HAMILTON *and* **AARON BURR**
Their famous duel.

COMMODORE PERRY
During the battle of Lake Erie.

JAMES BOWIE
Firing his last shots before death, as Santa Anna's troops overwhelm the Alamo.

MRS. JAMES (DOLLY) MADISON
A courageous first lady.

A Treasury of
GREAT
AMERICAN
LETTERS

CHRISTOPHER COLUMBUS

"Because my undertakings have attained success . . ."

IT is an ironic paradox of history that the first known letter written from or about America was composed by a man who thought he had discovered another continent and was not aware that he had seen only the outer fringe islands of his unknown discovery.

Christopher Columbus sailed from Palos, Spain, as Admiral commanding the three famous ships, the Santa Maria, the Pinta and the Niña, on August 3, 1492. On October 12, he sighted land—an island he named San Salvador, "the name of the blessed Saviour"—now generally thought to be Watling Island in the Bahamas, although this is still a matter of debate. He actually thought he might have discovered "Cipango" (Japan) or islands off the coast of "Cathay" (China).

Columbus wrote a letter of report to Gabriel Sanchez, Treasurer of King Ferdinand of Spain, filled with pious phrases, some excellent description, and an underlying note of apology and excuse for not accompanying the letter with the riches expected from his voyage. The following excerpts from that letter (dated March 14, 1493, and published in Barcelona a month later) are from the version edited in 1893 for the Lenox Library, by Wilberforce Eames.

BECAUSE my undertakings have attained success, I know that it will be pleasing to you: these I have determined to relate, so that you may be made acquainted with everything done and discovered in this our voyage. On the thirty-third day after I departed from Cadiz, I came to the Indian sea, where I found many islands inhabited by men without number, of all which I took possession for our most fortunate king, with proclaiming heralds and flying standards, no one objecting.

To the first of these I gave the name of the blessed Saviour, on whose aid relying I had reached this as well as the other islands.

But the Indians called it Guanahany. I also called each one of the others by a new name. For I ordered one island to be called Santa Maria of the Conception, another Fernandina, another Isabella, another Juana, and so on with the rest.

As soon as we had arrived at that island which I have just now said was called Juana, I proceeded along its coast towards the west for some distance; I found it so large and without perceptible end, that I believed it to be not an island, but the continental country of Cathay; seeing, however, no towns or cities situated on the seacoast, but only some villages and rude farms, with whose inhabitants I was unable to converse, because as soon as they saw us they took flight.

I proceeded farther, thinking that I would discover some city or large residences. At length, perceiving that we had gone far enough, that nothing new appeared, and that this way was leading us to the north, which I wished to avoid, because it was winter on the land, and it was my intention to go to the south, moreover the winds were becoming violent, I therefore determined that no other plans were practicable, and so, going back, I returned to a certain bay that I had noticed, from which I sent two of our men to the land, that they might find out whether there was a king in this country, or any cities. These men traveled for three days, and they found people and houses without number, but they were small and without any government, therefore they returned . . .

This island is surrounded by many very safe and wide harbors, not excelled by any others that I have ever seen. Many great and salubrious rivers flow through it. There are also many very high mountains there. All these islands are very beautiful, and distinguished by various qualities; they are accessible, and full of a great variety of trees stretching up to the stars; the leaves of which I believe are never shed, for I saw them as green and flourishing as they are usually in Spain in the month of May; some of them were blossoming, some were bearing fruit, some were in other conditions; each one was thriving in its own way. The nightingale and various other birds without number were singing, in the month of November, when I was exploring them.

There are besides in the said island Juana seven or eight kinds of palm trees, which far excel ours in height and beauty, just as all the other trees, herbs, and fruits do. There are also excellent pine trees, vast plains and meadows, a variety of birds, a variety of honey, and a variety of metals, excepting iron. In the one which was called Hispaña, as we said above, there are great and beautiful mountains, vast fields, groves, fertile plains, very suitable for planting and cultivating, and for the building of houses.

The convenience of the harbors in this island, and the remarkable number of rivers contributing to the healthfulness of man, exceed belief, unless one has seen them. The trees, pasturage, and fruits of this island differ greatly from those of Juana. This Hispaña, moreover, abounds in different kinds of spices, in gold, and in metals.

On this island, indeed, and on all the others which I have seen, and of which I have knowledge, the inhabitants of both sexes go always naked, just as they came into the world, except some of the women, who use a covering of a leaf of some foliage, or a cotton cloth which they make themselves for that purpose.

All these people lack, as I said above, every kind of iron; they are also without weapons, which indeed are unknown; nor are they competent to use them, not on account of deformity of body, for they are well formed, but because they are timid and full of fear. They carry for weapons, however, reeds baked in the sun, on the lower ends of which they fasten some shafts of dried wood rubbed down to a point; and indeed they do not venture to use these always; for it frequently happened when I sent two or three of my men to some of the villages, that they might speak with the natives, a compact troop of the Indians would march out, and as soon as they saw our men approaching, they would quickly take flight, children being pushed aside by their fathers, and fathers by their children. And this was not because any hurt or injury had been inflicted on any one of them, for to every one whom I visited and with whom I was able to converse, I distributed whatever I had, cloth and many other things, no return being made to me; but they are by nature fearful and timid.

Yet when they perceive that they are safe, putting aside all fear, they are of simple manners and trustworthy, and very liberal with everything they have, refusing no one who asks for anything they may possess, and even themselves inviting us to ask for things.

They show greater love for all others than for themselves; they give valuable things for trifles, being satisfied even with a very small return, or with nothing. . . .

In all these islands there is no difference in the appearance of the people, nor in the manners and language, but all understand each other mutually; a fact that is very important for the end which I suppose to be earnestly desired by our most illustrious king, that is, their conversion to the holy religion of Christ, to which in truth, as far as I can perceive, they are ready and favorably inclined. . . .

In all these islands, as I have understood, each man is content with only one wife, except the princes or kings, who are permitted to have twenty. The women appear to work more than the men. . . .

Truly great and wonderful is this, and not corresponding to our merits, but to the holy Christian religion, and to the piety and religion of our sovereigns, because what the human understanding could not attain, that the divine will has granted to human efforts. For God is wont to listen to his servants who love his precepts, even in impossibilities, as has happened to us on the present occasion, who have attained that which hitherto mortal men have never reached.

For if anyone has written or said anything about these islands, it was all with obscurities and conjectures; no one claims that he had seen them; from which they seemed like fables. Therefore let the king and queen, the princes and their most fortunate kingdoms, and all other countries of Christendom give thanks to our Lord and Saviour Jesus Christ, who has bestowed upon us so great a victory and gift. Let religious processions be solemnized; let sacred festivals be given; let the churches be covered with festive garlands. Let Christ rejoice on earth, as he rejoices in heaven, when he foresees coming to salvation so many souls of people hitherto lost. Let us be glad also, as well on account of the exaltation of our faith, as on account of the increase of our temporal affairs, of which not only Spain, but universal Christendom will be partaker. . . .

Christopher Columbus, admiral of the Ocean fleet

The sequel:

In the following decade Columbus made three other voyages to America. A bold and vain explorer, but a miserable governor and administrator, both his honors and disgraces at the hand of Spain were extreme. He died in an atmosphere of tragedy and despondency; it remained for others to mark his success and to reap the financial rewards of his adventures.

JOHN SMITH

A "True Relation" from Jamestown, Virginia

ON May 13, 1607, English colonists landed at Jamestown, on the James River, Va., to form the first permanent English colony in the New World. (Two earlier attempts at English colonization in North America ended in failure.) The English were far behind the Spanish, who had already colonized parts of what are now the United States and Mexico, and the French, established on the St. Lawrence River.

This new group was the London Company (later known as the Virginia Company), and it included 28-year-old Captain John Smith as its military commander. He was part of a colony of 144 men, women and children who had cruised for six months in three small ships: the Susan Constant (100 tons) under Captain Christopher Newport, who also commanded the squadron; the Godspeed (40 tons) under Captain Bartholomew Gosnold, and the Discovery (20 tons) under Captain John Ratcliffe.

In the care of Captain Newport also was "the Box," a chest given to the colonists by the Virginia Company of London, which financed the venture. When "the Box" was opened, as related hereafter, it was found to contain the names of those who were to govern the colony.

A year later, probably as the result of the many conflicting reports sent back to London, Captain Smith assayed a report designed to set the facts straight. He called his letter a "True Relation."

KINDE SIR, commendations remembred, &c. You shall understand that after many crosses in the downes by tempests, wee arrived safely uppon the Southwest part of the great Canaries; within
foure or five daies after we set sail for Dominica, the 26. of Aprill:
the first land we made, wee fell with Cape Henry, the verie mouth
of the Bay of Chissiapiacke, which at that present we little
expected, having by a cruell storme bene put to the Northward. Anchoring in this Bay twentie or thirtie went a shore with the Captain and in coming aboard, they were assalted with certaine Indians which charged them within Pistol shot; in which conflict
Captain Archer and Mathew Morton were shot: whereuppon
Captaine Newport seconding them, made a shot at them, which
the Indians little respected, but having spent their arrows retyred
without harme. And in that place was the Box opened, wherein
the Counsell for Virginia was nominated; and arriving at the
place where wee are now seated, the Counsell was sworn, and the
President elected, which for that yeare was Maister Edm Maria
Wingfield, where was made choice for our Scituation, a verie fit
place for the erecting of a great cittie, about which some conten-
tion passed between Captaine Wingfield and Captaine Gosnold;
notwithstanding, all our provision was brought a shore, and with
as much speede as might bee went about our fortification . . .

Captaine Newport having set things in order, set saile for England the 22d of June, leaving provision for 13. or 14 weeks. The
day before the Ships departure, the King of Pamaunke sent the
Indian that had met us before in our discoverie, to assure us
peace; our fort then being palisaded round, and all our men in
good health and comfort, albeit, that through some discontented
humors, it did not so long continue, for the resident and Captain
Gosnold, with the rest of the Counsell, being for the moste part
discontented with one another, in so much, that things were
neither carried with that discretion nor any business effected in
such good sort as wisdome would, nor our owne good and saftie
required, whereby, and through the hard dealing of our President,
the rest of the counsell beeing diverslie affected through his auda-
cious command; and for Captaine Martin, albeit verie honest,
and wishing the best good, yet so sicke and weake; and myself
so disgrac'd through others mallice; through which disorder God

(being angrie with us) plagued us with such famin and sickness, that the living were scarce able to bury the dead: our want of sufficient and good victualls, with continuall watching, foure or five each night at three Bulwarkes, being the chiefe cause: onely of Sturgion wee had great store, whereon our men would so greedily surfet, as it cost manye their lives: the Sack, Aquavite, and other preservatives for our health, being kept onely in the Presidents hands, for his owne diet, and his few associates. Shortly after Captaine Gosnold fell sicke, and within three weeks died, Captaine Ratcliffe being then also verie sicke and weake, and my selfe having also tasted of the extremities theof, but by God's assistance being well recovered, Kendall about this time, for divers reasons deposed from being of the Councell; and shortly after it pleased God (in our extremity) to move the Indians to bring us Corne, ere it was halfe ripe, to refresh us, when we rather expected when they would destroy us; about the tenth of September there was about 46. of our men dead, at which time Captaine Wingefield having ordered the affaires in such sort that he was generally hated of all, in which respect with one consent he was deposed from his presidencie, and Captaine Ratcliffe according to his course was elected.

Our provision being now within twentie dayes spent, the Indians brought us great store both of Corne and bread ready made: and also there came such aboundance of Fowles into the Rivers, as greatly refreshed our weake estates, whereuppon many of our weake men were presently able to goe abroad. As yet we had no houses to cover us, our Tents were rotten and our Cabbins worse than nought: our best commoditie was Yron which we made into little chissels. The president and Captaine Martins sickness, constrayned me to be Cape Marchant, and yet to spare no paines in making houses for the company; who notwithstanding our little misery, little ceased their mallice, grudging, and muttering. As at this time were most of our chiefest men with sicke or discontented, the rest being in such dispaire, as they would rather starve and rot with idleness, then be perswaded to do any thing for their owne reliefe without constraint; our victualles being now within eighteene dayes spent, and the Indian trade decreasing, I was sent to the mouth of the river, to Kegquouhtan an Indian Towne, to trade for Corne, and try the River for Fish, but our fishing we could not effect by reason of the stormy weather. The Indians thinking us neare famished, with carelesse kindness, offered us little pieces of bread and small handfulls of beanes or wheat, for a hatchet or a piece of copper: In like manner I entertained their kindness, and in like scorne offered them like commodities, but the Children, or any that shewed extraordinary kindness, I liberally contented with free gifte, such trifles as wel contented them. Finding this colde comfort, I anchored before the Towne, and the next day returned to trade, but God (the absolute disposer of all heartes) altered their conceits, for now they were no less desirous of our commodiites than we of their Corne; under colour to fetch fresh water, I sent a man to discover the Towne, their Corne, and force, to trie their intent, in that they desired me up to their houses: which well understanding, with foure shoat I visited them. With fish, oysters, bread, and deere, they kindly treated with me and my men, being no lesse in doubt of my intent, then I of theirs; for well I might with twentie men have freighted a Shippe with Corne.

The Towne containeth eighteene houses, pleasantly seated uppon three acres of ground, uppon a plaine, halfe invironed with a great Bay of the great River, the other part with a Baye of the other River falling into the great Baye, with a little Ile fit for a Castle in the mouth thereof, the Towne adjoyning to the maine by a necke of Land of sixtie yards. With sixteene bushells of Corne I returned towards our Forte: by the way I encountered wih two Canowes of Indians, who came aboord me, being the inhabitants of Waroykoyack, a kingdome on the south side of the river, which is in breadth 5. miles and 20 miles or neare from the mouth: With these I traded, who having but their hunting provision, requested me to return to their Towne, where I should load my boat with corne; and with neare thirtie bushells I returned to the fort, the very name whereof gave great comfort to our desparing company.

The sequel:

As time passed, Captain Smith assumed strong leadership of the Jamestown Colony. In the following year his famous contribution to romance was made, with his recounting of the manner whereby Pocahontas saved his life (only to turn later to John Rolfe, whose bride she became). Pocahontas wrote no letters but, as Captain Smith noted later in his Generall Historie of Virginia, Pocahontas became "the first Christian ever of that Nation, the first Virginian ever spake English, or had a childe in mariage by an Englishman."

WILLIAM DOUGLASS

"I reckon this place no better than a factory . . ."

FROM the earliest days, medical practitioners have labored under the dual handicap of performing an essential public service while at the same time pursuing a business, in the sense that their work must provide their livelihood.

Dr. William Douglass illustrated this dilemma almost two and a half centuries ago in a frank letter to Dr. Codwallader Colden, in New York, a colleague who like himself had emigrated to the American colonies from Scotland.

Boston, Feb. 20, 1720

. . . You complain of the Practice of Physic being undervalued in your parts and with good reason; we are not much better in that respect in this place; we abound with Practioners tho no other graduate than my self, we have 14 Apothecary shops in Boston, all our Practioners dispense their own medicines, my self excepted being the first who hath lived here by Practice without the advantage of advance on Medicines . . .

I have resolved to fix here and ramble no more. I can live handsomely by the income of my Practice, and save some small matter. I reckon this place at present no better than a factory as to my interest, for here we have a great trade and many strangers with whom my business chiefly consists. I have here practice among four sorts of People. Some familys pay me 5 £ per annum each for advice sick or well, some few fee me as in Britain, but for the Native New Englander I am obliged to keep a day book of my

Consultation advice and Visits and bring them in a Bill, others of the poorer sort I advise and Visit without any expectation of fees . . .

The sequel:

Dr. Douglass did very well, practicing happily in Boston until his demise in 1752, at the then venerable age of 59 years. But his plaint lingers on.

BENJAMIN FRANKLIN

". . . prefer old Women to young ones."

THOUGHTS that are vulgarities when expressed by base minds often become classics from the pens of sages competent to discuss them.

Such a sage was Benjamin Franklin, who could go out into the rain to fly a kite in his quest for knowledge about electricity or—unhampered by scruples—discuss the virtues of women, through long experience that appears to have been unexcelled for his day.

There is satisfactory evidence that when in Paris in 1776, as a Commissioner for the American Colonies in the Revolution, he still remained active, at 70, in his researches into romance, just as he was still a leader in philosophical, economic and political thought.

One of Franklin's classic letters was written thirty-one years earlier, addressed to an inquirer whose name has disappeared, but who apparently had asked for advice of a kind not then dispensed as extensively through the press as it is today. Franklin counseled marriage, first and foremost, but failing that . . .

June 25, 1745

My Dear Friend;—

I know of no Medicine fit to diminish the violent natural inclination you mention; and if I did, I think I should not communicate it to you. Marriage is the proper Remedy. It is the most natural State of Man, and therefore the State in which you will find solid Happiness. Your Reason against entering into it at present appears to be not well founded. The Circumstantial Advantages you have in View by Postponing it, are not only uncertain, but they are small in comparison with the Thing itself, the being married and settled. It is the Man and Woman united that makes the complete human Being. Separate she wants his force of Body and Strength of Reason; he her Softness, Sensibility, and acute Discernment. Together they are most likely to succeed in the World. A single Man has not nearly the Value he would have in that State of Union. He is an incomplete Animal. He resembles the odd Half of a Pair of Scissors.

If you get a prudent, healthy wife, your Industry in your Profession, with her good Economy, will be a Fortune sufficient.

But if you will not take this Counsel, and persist in thinking a Commerce with the Sex is inevitable, then I repeat my former Advice that in your Amours you should prefer old Women to young ones. This you call a Paradox, and demand my reasons. They are these:

1 Because they have more Knowledge of the world, and their Minds are better stored with Observations; their Conversation is more improving, and more lastingly agreeable.

2 Because when Women cease to be handsome, they study to be good. To maintain their Influence over Man, they supply the Diminution of Beauty by an Augmentation of Utility. They learn to do a thousand Services, small and great, and are the most tender and useful of all Friends when you are sick. Thus they continue amiable. And hence there is hardly such a thing to be found as an old Woman who is not a good Woman.

3 Because there is no hazard of children, which irregularly produced may be attended with much inconvenience.

4 Because through more Experience they are more prudent and discreet in conducting an Intrigue to prevent Suspicion. The Commerce with them is therefore safer with regard to your reputation; and regard to theirs, if the Affair should happen to be known, considerate People might be inclined to excuse an old Woman, who would kindly take care of a young Man, form his manners by her good Councils, and prevent his ruining his Health and Fortune among mercenary Prostitutes.

5 Because in every Animal that walks upright, the Deficiency of Fluids that fill the Muscles appears first in the highest Part. The Face first grows lank and wrinkled; then the Neck; then the Breast and Arms; the lower parts continuing to the last as plump as ever; so that covering all above with a Basket, and regarding only what is below the Girdle, it is impossible of two Women to know an old from a young one. And as in the Dark all Cats are grey, the pleasure of Corporal Enjoyment with an old Woman is at least equal and frequently superior; every Knack by Practice capable by improvement.

6 Because the sin is less. The Debauching of a Virgin may be her Ruin, and make her for Life unhappy.

7 Because the Compunction is less. The having made a young Girl <u>miserable</u> may give you frequent bitter Reflections; none of which can attend making an old Woman <u>happy</u>.

8th & lastly. They are so Grateful!!!

Thus much for my Paradox. But still I advise you to marry immediately; being sincerely

Your Affectionate Friend,
Benj. Franklin

JOHN HANCOCK

"I dearly love you should be particular . . ."

THE Continental Congress, sitting in Philadelphia in the early summer of 1775, was indeed a busy one, and among the busiest of its busy members was John Hancock, member from Massachusetts and chairman of the Committee on Military Affairs.

On June 21, 1775, Hancock sat before his desk with 500 officer commissions to be signed for officers in the just-formed Continental Army, but he pushed these aside to write a hasty note to Dorothy Quincy—hasty for a reason explained in the note.

Congress Room, 21st June, 1775

My Dear Dolly

Last Evening I had the pleasure of your Letter. You must not, my Dear, think hard of any earnest Expressions to you & of my Notice of the shortness of your Letters & omission in writing, when I tell you it arises from the greatness of my Regard & my Anxiety when absent from you. You do not tell whether the little things I sent you by Doct Church suited, did the Shoes & Stockings fit, I dearly love you should be particular, pray write me one long Letter, fill the whole paper, you can do it if you only set about it. I verily think now we shall adjourn to Connecticut, as the Seriousness of the Times seems to Call for it. I shall let you know in Time, I heartily wish for it. My Regard to all Friends. I Refer to Mr. Henshaw for every thing about me, I am greatly hurried, have Five hundred Commissions to Sign for the Officers of our Army. I am now going to Sign General Washington's Commiss'n he will pass thro' Fairfield in 4 or 5 days,

My Love to my Dr Aunt, & believe me My Dear, what I profess to be,

Yours for ever
JOHN HANCOCK

The sequel:

George Washington duly got his commission and two months later John Hancock married "Dorothy Q." On July 4, 1776, as first signer of the Declaration of Independence, John Hancock firmly wrote his name that all the world might read it and all Americans remember it.

DANIEL CARROLL

*". . . their Conduct justified the
recommendations . . ."*

AMONG the members of the Carroll family of Maryland noted for their patriotism and humane undertakings, the name of Daniel Carroll has been overshadowed by that of his more famous brother, Charles Carroll of Carrollton, but Daniel holds in his debt the great body of Americans of Irish descent.

It was through his encouragement, financial assistance and "follow-through" on their behalf that the first oppressed farmers from Ireland settled in the United States, even before it became a country.

In 1775, Daniel Carroll wrote his views to George Washington, coupled with a gentlemanly understatement of his own part in the plan to provide a haven from the oppressions of his former homeland.

Sept. 1, 1775

. . . In the Winter of 1771 I received a letter from a Mercht of my acquaintance in Galway in Ireland, strongly recommending some Irish families who had embarked for America. These poor people, finding they could not live under the exaction of their landlord . . . were able to pay their passages, and bring with them some family goods and working utensils . . . They have had room and firing on my land since their arrival. The men have worked abroad and by their Conduct justified the recommendations given of them and I am certain will be of Singular Service, wherever they settle, particularly in working meadows . . . It would not, I apprehend, be bad policy in those who may possess large bodys or tracts of land to lay out a Glebe for a Clergyman. This would have considerable weight with many Irish Catholicks who would probably bring their own Clergymen with them. I intend myself taking a trip into these new Countries, as they are called and purchasing some lands if the terms and title were agreeable, in hopes of making it turn to advantage as my connections are in Ireland . . . Should matters be settled time enough this fall, I shall put my resolution into execution.

B. FREEMAN

To John Bartram—on pensions and politics

JOHN BARTRAM was the pioneer botanist of the American Colonies, native born, but honored with the rank of "botanist to King George III." In 1776, he was 77 years old and had virtually completed work in his special-study field of mosses listed in today's textbooks under BARTRAMIA. After fifty years of study and travel he now devoted most of his time to receiving visitors from the other colonies and from abroad, who came to see his world-famous gardens at his home near Philadelphia.

The aging man was deeply concerned over the impending revolution in the Colonies, as well as worried about some delays or hitches in the transmission from London of his pension.

He wrote an inquiry (now lost) about both to an official of the Royal Treasury, B. Freeman, whose brief, cordial reply illuminates the feelings of many thinking, but unofficial, persons on both sides of the Atlantic, in the middle of 1776:

Lond 5 mo 4th 1776

Dear Fd
    John Bartram
    An opportunity offering wch we hope will reach thee Icod not but embrace it to express my Wishes that under that anxiety, thy feeling Mind, that the distressing situation both you that are Natives of America & many of our Countrymen must be in, that thou and thy family may be in Health and Safety and also to transmit the Acct. whereby thou'l find thy Pension has been most punctually paid, but it will be proper in future for me to receive at least a few lines from thee to be with me a week or two, before the

usual times of receiving the pension, viz. Ladyday to Michaelmas, of they own handwriting.

I am wth respect they F^d

B. Freeman

The sequel:

The account that was enclosed is now illegible. The good intentions of the letter were probably thwarted, and Bartram's worries increased, by other onrushing events. Long before the next paydays, Michaelmas (September 29, 1776), and Lady Day (March 25, 1777), England and America were at war. And by Michaelmas in 1777 John Bartram was dead.

GEORGE WASHINGTON

". . . with a soldier, success alone is merit . . ."

ON June 18, 1776, George Washington wrote what was—to him—one of the most important letters of his life. In this letter, he poured out his innermost thoughts about himself, discussing his pride, his dignity, his lack of military experience, and his fear of disgrace should he not achieve victory, as Commander-in-Chief of the small colonial army.

He had already experienced two phases of war: first in his victory at Dorchester, Mass., that forced the evacuation of Boston in the prior March, and afterward his now present task of attempting to defend New York against the greatly superior and more experienced forces of Sir William Howe; he seemed then to know that this fight would be lost.

On the day previous to the one on which he wrote he had received a shocking surprise; a letter from his adored stepson, John Parke Custis, relating his intention to join the army. This handsome, but ineffectual, young man, without previous military experience, tied devotedly to his mother and a young wife, upset Washington with this news, starting a train of thought which resulted in the following profound letter.

June 18, 1776

My Very Dear Jack,

You have exceedingly obliged me by your letter which I received by yesterday's post. It discovers an attention to the great affairs now carrying on, and an information concerning them, which I own to you I had not given you credit for. Your youth and inexperience pleaded your excuse: and though you gave me no opportunity to praise you for any active exertions, I paid you no ordinary compliments, in my own mind, for your modesty in forbearing to meddle with things which it was no reproach to you to confess, were out of your reach. Considering your rank, fortune, and education, whenever it is proper for you to come forward on the theatre, it must not be any underpart that you act. You are, therefore, certainly, in the right to decline taking any part at all, till you are fit for a first and leading character. And you have my full and perfect approbation of your resolution to persist in your purpose, not to accept of any rank, either civil or military . . . The momentous enterprise, in which our country is engaged, is not to be accomplished in this, or that year. If, in no longer a period than the siege of Troy, we bring all our mighty schemes to bear, it will be the greatest work that ever was perfected in so little a time.

You have set your heart, you tell me, on a military employment. This is the usual bent of young men; and, as it was my own, it will be with an ill grace, that I reproach it in you . . . I love arms, I am married to my sword, as well as to your most amiable mother; and, herein is my witness, that I am in earnest when I say, death alone shall divorce me from either.

I am not so blindly devoted, however, to my profession, as not to see by how frail a tenure I hold the little reputation I have in it. As a statesman, as a senator, it is in the general, sufficient that you mean well, that you are careful to qualify yourself to form a right judgment of the true interests of your country, and that, with the honest impartiality of a free man, you have still exerted your best endeavours to promote those interests. But, with a soldier, success alone is merit; and there is nothing that can atone for the want on it. The world is a worse judge of military matters, than of any other. It would astonish you, to find, on a minute comparison, how very little difference there was in the skill and spirit which guided Braddock and Wolfe in the last actions of their lives. But, how different has been their fate!—I think I am not without some talents for the line of life, which has fallen to my lot. But, opposed as I must be by men, probably, of infinitely superior skill, and encompassed moreover with such hosts of other difficulties and discouragements as I am, it is not mine to command success. And, when either my contemporaries, or future historians, shall sit in judgment on my conduct, if, haply, ill fortune should overtake me, seeing our miscarriages only, and having neither curiosity nor ability to investigate the thousand causes which led to them, am I not too well warranted in concluding, that they will be attributed to mis-management?

Have I not then reason to wish that your choice had fallen on the quieter but not less important calling of a private gentleman; in which, as a senator, you might have given proof of your abilities in a way, in which fortune would not have had so great a share? But, notwithstanding all this, and if after all, you be irretrievably determined to try your fortune in the field, and you can gain your mother's and your wife's consent, I here give it to you, under my hand, that you shall not want mine. Most certainly there cannot be a more honourable employment: and if (which heaven avert!) Fortune should declare against you, my consolation will be that, I can assure myself, you will deserve to be successful. I will on the opening of the next campaign, procure you an appointment to the command of a regiment, either here, or in the southern wing . . .

Meanwhile, permit me to press you to persevere in your attention to military matters. The manual exercise, which you were so justly diligent to learn, whilst I was with you, is but the A, B, C, of your profession. Neither will you profit so much as you might reasonably expect, from the study of those authors, who have written professedly on the art of war. This is like the learning of the game of Whist by reading Hoyle. I have been witness of the mischievous effects of it. A man, book-learned only, does very well in the still scenes of marchings and encampments. But when, in the various bustles of actual war, a cause arises, as must often be the case, not described in his books, he is utterly at a loss . . .

. . . the main and most essential qualification is an high sense of honour, an elevation of sentiment, and a certain dignified stile of behaviour, that distinguishes, or should distinguish, a soldier from every other man. It is a shame, indeed, if he who undertakes to command others, has not first learned to command himself . . . I am not solicitous to pay you compliments, even by implication; but, I may certainly be permitted to say, that if I had not known you to be a gentleman, you never should have had my consent to your becoming a soldier . . .

The sequel:

"Jack" Custis' military career was undistinguished. He began and ended it with the titular command of a regiment (a gentleman's prerogative), while other youths such as young General Alexander Hamilton, the Marquis de Lafayette, and James Monroe (later President of the United States), won renown. When Jack Custis died in 1781, two of his four young children were adopted by George and Martha Washington as their own children and heirs. One of these, George Washington Parke Custis, born in 1781, almost coincident with his father's death, became a planter and a well known playwright, and father of the girl who married Robert E. Lee.

GEORGE WASHINGTON

". . . banish these thoughts from your mind . . ."

WHAT would have been the history of the United States had George Washington become its king? Impossible?

A cabal of hero-worshipping officers made this suggestion, and communicated it to him in proposals sent by a Colonel Nichola, whose identity otherwise is so unclear that his first name has been forgotten.

On the spring-green heights about Newburgh, N.Y., where he was superintending the discharge of the Continental Army, seven months after the surrender of Lord Cornwallis, the "Father of His Country" took pains to squelch such thoughts in a letter to the proposer of the project.

The clear and concise expression of sentiments in this dramatic letter underline the more mature conclu-sions that in later years would form the basis for Washington's celebrated First Inaugural Address and the even more paternal Farewell Address.

Newburgh May 22^d '82

Sir,

With a mixture of great surprise & astonishment I have read with attention the Sentiments you have submitted to my perusal.– Be assured Sir, no occurrence in the course of the War, has given me more painful sensations than your information of there being such ideas existing in the Army as you have expressed, & I must view with abhorrence, and reprehend with severity–For the present, the communication of them will rest in my own bosom, unless some further agitation of the matter shall make a disclosure neces-sary.–

I am much at a loss to conceive what part of my conduct could have given encouragement to an address which to me seems big with the greatest mischiefs that can befall my Country.– If I am not deceived in the knowledge of myself, you could not have found a person to whom your schemes are more disagreeable–at the same time in justice to my own feeling I must add, that no man possesses a more sincere wish to see ample justice done to the Army than I do, and as far as my powers & influence, in a constitution, may extend, they shall be employed to the utmost of my abilities to effect it, should there be any occasion– Let me conjure then, if you have any regard for your Country–concern for yourself or posterity–or respect for me, to banish these thoughts from your mind, & never communicate, as from yourself, or any one else, a sentiment of the like nature.–

With esteem I am Sir
Yr Most Obed Ser
G. Washington

The sequel:

We often overlook the fact that although the Revolution officially ended in victory on October 19, 1781, General Washington spent more than two more years in the field, attempting to procure recognition and benefits for his ragged troops, from the lackadaisical Continental Congress.

He resigned his commission at Annapolis, Md., on December 23, 1783, and returned a few weeks to Mt. Vernon, anticipating permanent retirement from public life. But with the passing years, his prestige brought him to a succession of duties culminating in his becoming the first President of the United States.

Washington died, on December 14, 1799, at Mt. Vernon—where he had enjoyed a few years of relatively peaceful retirement—reportedly as the result of complications following a chill he caught in riding into Washington to observe progress on the construction of the new Capital buildings.

THOMAS JEFFERSON

". . . let your clothes be clean, whole and properly put on."

SO many famous roles were played by Thomas Jefferson that our contemporary image of him virtually ignores the roles of father and husband, to which he devoted himself as assiduously as to the writing of the Declaration of Independence.

On December 22, 1783, Jefferson was in Annapolis, Md., for a most important occasion. He was attending a special session of the Continental Congress, convened in the Maryland Statehouse, where, on the following day, George Washington would resign as Commander-in-Chief of the American Army he had led to victory in the Revolution.

So many problems faced this Congress that adjournment for the Christmas holidays was out of the question, and Jefferson must have been one of the busiest among a group of busy men. Somehow, during the crowded hours he found time to write a letter to his eleven-year-old daughter, Patsy, at Monticello.

This letter was about something most important—Jefferson's concern that Patsy was not as meticulous about her appearance as she might have been.

Annapolis Dec. 22, 1783.

My dear Patsy

I hoped before this to have received letters from you regularly and weekly by the post, and also to have had a letter to forward from you to one of your aunts as I desired in my letter of November 27th. I am afraid you do not comply with my desires expressed in that letter. your not writing to me every week is one instance, and your having never sent me any of your copies of mr Simitiere's lessons is another. I shall be very much mortified and disappointed if you become inattentive to my wishes and particularly to the directions of that letter which I meant for your principal guide. I omitted in that to advise you on the subject of dress, which I know you are a little apt to neglect. I do not wish you to be gayly clothed at this time of life, but that what you wear should be fine of it's kind; but above all things, & at all times let your clothes be clean, whole, and properly put on. do not fancy you must wear them till the dirt is visible to the eye. you will be the last who will be sensible of this. some ladies think they may under the privileges of the dishabille be loose & negligent of their dress in the morning. but be you from the moment you rise till you go to bed as cleanly and properly dressed as at the hours of dinner or tea. a lady who has been seen as a sloven or slut in the morning, will never efface the impression she then made with all the dress and pageantry she can afterwards involve herself in. nothing is so disgusting to our sex as a want of cleanliness and delicacy in yours. I hope therefore the moment you rise from bed, your first work will be to dress yourself in such a stile as that you may be seen by any gentleman without his being able to discover a pin amiss, or any other circumstance of neatness wanting.

By a letter from mr Short I learn that your sisters are well. I hope I shall soon receive a letter from you informing me you are so. I wrote a letter to Polly lately, which I supposed her aunt would read to her. I dare say it pleased her, as would a letter from you. I am sorry mrs. Trist has determined to go at so inclement a season, as fear she will suffer much more than she expects. present my compliments to her and the good family there, as also very particularly to mrs. Hopkinson whose health and happiness I have much at heart. I hope you are obedient & respectful to her in every circumstance and that your manners will be such as to engage her affections. I am my Dear Patsy

Yours sincerely & affectionately

Th: Jefferson

BENJAMIN FRANKLIN

". . . It appears . . . to be a discovery of great
   importance . . ."

IN 1784, Benjamin Franklin's interests, while he lived in France, ranged through a wide list of subjects, from those involving his governmental position as Minister to France for the American Colonies to scientific and philosophical subjects in which he was looked upon as a master.

To him came an inquiry from a Dr. Ingenhauss, of Vienna, concerning the intricacies of the newly invented balloon. In reply, Franklin not only described this formidable invention as it then existed, but projected his thinking into its possible tactical and military value.

A Monsieur . .
Monsieur Le Dʳ. Ingenhauss
Medicin de Sa Majesté Imperiale á Vienne
   en Autriche

                                                           Passy, Jan. 16, 1784

Dear Friend,
I have this Day received your Favour of the 2d Instant. Every Information in my Power respecting the Balloons I sent you just before Christmas, contain'd in Copies of my Letters to Sir Joseph Banks. There is no Secret in the Affair, and I make no doubt that a Person coming from you would easily obtain a Sight of the different Balloons of Mongolfier & Charles, with all the Instructions wanted; and if you undertake to make one, I think it extreamly proper and necessary to send an ingenious Man here for that purpose: otherwise for want of Attention to some particular Circumstance, or of being acquainted with it, the Experiment might miscarry, which being in an Affair of so much public Expectation, would have bad Consequences, draw upon you a great deal of Censure, and affect your Reputation. It is a serious thing to draw

out from their Affairs all the Inhabitants of a great City & its Environs, and a Disappointment makes them angry. At Bourdeaux lately, a Person who pretended to send up a Balloon & had received Money of many People, not being able to make it rise, the Populace were so exasperated that they pull'd down his House, and had like to have kill'd him.—

It appears as you observe, to be a Discovery of great Importance, and what may possibly give a new Turn to human Affairs. Convincing Sovereigns of the Folly of Wars, may perhaps be one Effect of it: since it will be impracticable for the most potent of them to guard his Dominions. Five Thousand Balloons capable of raising two Men each, would not cost more than Five Ships of the Line: And where is the Prince who can afford so to cover his Country with Troops for its Defence, as that Ten Thousand Men descending from the Clouds, might not in many Places do an infinite deal of Mischief, before a Force could be brought together to repel them?—It is a pity that any national Jealousy, should, as you imagine it may, have prevented the English from prosecuting the Experiment, since they are such ingenious Mechanicians, that in their Hands it might have made a more rapid Progress toward Perfection, & all the Utility it is capable of affording.—The Balloon of Messrs Charles & Robert, was really fill'd with inflammable Air. The Quantity being great it was expensive, & tedious in filling, requiring two or three Days & Nights constant Labour. It had a Soupape near the Top, which they could open by pulling a String, and thereby let out some Air when they had a mind to descend; and they discharg'd some of their Ballast of Sand, when they would rise again. A great deal of Air must have been let out when they landed, so that the loose Part might envelope one of them; yet the Car being lightned by that one getting out of it, there was enough left to carry up the other rapidly. They had no Fire with them. That is us'd only in Messrs Mongolfier's Globe, which is open at Bottom, and Straw constantly burnt to keep it up. This kind is sooner & cheaper fill'd; but must be much bigger to carry up the same Weight; since Air rarify'd by Heat is only twice as light as common Air, & inflammable Air ten times lighter. M. de Morveau a famous Chemist at Dijon, has found an inflammable Air that will cost only a 25th part of the Price of what is made by Oil of Vitriol pour'd on Iron Filings. They say it is made from Sea Coal. Its comparative Weight is not mentioned.—

I dispatch'd your Letters by the petit Poste to day as soon as I receiv'd them.—

As the Pacquet of German Papers & Almanacs were 18 Months in getting to your hands, I begin to fear for my last Packet, since it was trusted to the same Conveyance, being sent to the Ambassador's, who promis'd to take care of it. I therefore send a Copy of my Letter with this Post, but I cannot copy the other Papers (they being too long) so as to go by this Courier.—Nor can I now add farther but that I am, as ever, my dear Friend,

Yours most affectionately
B. FRANKLIN.

I have still some Letters of yours to answer.

DANIEL CARROLL

". . . the best form of government . . .
ever . . . offered to the world."

IN the harsh debates over adoption of the Constitution, two of its framers, Charles Carroll of Carrollton and Daniel Carroll (brothers), became among the most eloquent of its defenders.

Daniel Carroll became so exasperated with the opposition that his initially lukewarm support grew into that of an ardent advocate.

The passage here quoted is from an open letter to the press, published under the pseudonym, "A Friend to the Constitution," in reply to no less a figure than Samuel Chase, who was bombarding the press with opposition letters, signed "Caution."

October 16, 1787

It is neither extraordinary nor unexpected, that the Constitution offered to your consideration should meet with opposition . . .

I will confess indeed that I am not a blind admirer of this plan of government, and that there are some parts of it, which if my wish had prevailed, would certainly have been altered. But when I reflect how widely men differ in their opinions, and that every man . . . has an equal pretension to assert his own, I am satisfied that anything nearer to perfection could not have been accomplished. If there are errors, it should be remembered, that the seeds of reformation are sown in the work itself, and the concurrence of two-thirds of the Congress may, at any time, introduce alterations and amendments . . . Regarding it, then, in every point of view with a candid and disinterested mind, I am bold to assert, that it is the best form of government which has ever been offered to the world.

A FRIEND TO THE CONSTITUTION

JOHN DICKINSON

". . . soundness of sense and honesty of heart."

FOR almost three centuries, men with causes to espouse have used letters to newspapers to propound their arguments and lay them before the public. Frequently, these letters are signed by fictitious names, either to conceal the writer's identity or to cloak the written word with modesty.

The "Letters of Fabius" which appeared in a long series in the Delaware Gazette, published at Wilmington, in the hectic political year of 1788, were of the latter type.

The Fabius letters were from the pen of John Dickinson, 68 years old. Dickinson was a weatlhy lawyer in Philadelphia. A conservative, he had begun his political career in 1760, and notably opposed Benjamin Franklin's efforts to abolish the Pennsylvania proprietorship of the Penn family. He had refused, as a member of the First Continental Congress, to sign the Declaration of Independence, aligning himself both against the British Crown and the American "radicals" led by Samuel Adams; but by 1787 he was a vigorous supporter of the Constitution.

Thus, in 1788 he was using his forceful pen, under the pseudonym of Fabius, to support this keystone of the new Federal establishment. Fragments of his letters, later collected by W. C. Smith, are here pieced together.

Letter I

What concerns all should be considered by all; and individuals may injure a whole society, by not declaring their sentiments. It is therefore not only their right, but their duty, to declare them. Weak advocates of a good cause or artful advocates of a bad one, may endeavor to stop such communications, or to discredit them by clamour and calumny. This, however, is not the age for such tricks of controversy. Men have suffered so severely by being deceived upon subjects of the highest import, those of religion and freedom, that truth becomes infinitely valuable to them, not as a matter of curious speculation, but of beneficial practice—a spirit of inquiry is excited, information diffused, judgment strengthened . . .

Heaven grant! that our countrymen may pause in time–duly estimate the present moment–and solemnly reflect–whether their measures may not tend to draw down the same distractions upon us, that desolated Greece.

They may now tolerably judge from the proceedings of the Federal Convention and of other conventions, what are the sentiments of America upon her present and future prospects. Let the voice of her distress be venerated–and adhering to the generous declaration, let them resolve to "cling to Union as the political Rock of our Salvation."

Fabius

Letter II

. . .

How varied, balanced, concordant, and benign, is the system proposed to us? To secure the freedom, and promote the happiness of these and future states, by giving the will of the people a decisive influence over the whole, and over all the parts, with what a comprehensive arrangement does it embrace different modes of representation from an election by a country to an election by an empire? What are the complicated ballot, and all the refined devices of Venice for maintaining her aristocracy, when compared with this plain-dealing work for diffusing the blessings of equal liberty and common prosperity over myriads of the human race?

All the foundations before mentioned, of the federal government, are by the proposed system to be established, in the most clear, strong, positive, unequivocal expressions, of which our language is capable. Magna charta, or any other law, never contained clauses more decisive and emphatic. While the people of these states have sense, they will understand them; and while they have spirit, they will make them to be observed.

Fabius

Letter III

. . .

We may with reverence say, that our Creator designed men for society, because otherwise they cannot be happy. They cannot be happy without freedom; nor free without security; that is, without the absence of fear; nor thus secure, without society. The conclusion is strictly syllogistic—that men cannot be free without society.

Fabius

Letter IV

. . .

Trial by jury and the dependence of taxation upon representation, those corner stones of liberty, were not obtained by a bill of rights, or any other records, and have not been and cannot be preserved by them. They and all other rights must be preserved, by soundness of sense and honesty of heart. Compared with these, what are a bill of rights, or any characters drawn upon paper or parchment, those frail remembrances? Do we want to be reminded, that the sun enlightens, warms, invigorates, and cheers? or how horrid it would be, to have his blessed beams intercepted, by our being thrust into mines or dungeons? Liberty is the sun of society. Rights are the beams . . .

Fabius

RUDOLPH VAN DORSTEN

Describing the First Inaugural of President Washington

AFTER the ratification of the Constitution by the requisite number of states in 1788, the election of George Washington as President, despite his evidently sincere hesitancy, was automatic.

He was inaugurated in New York City on April 30, 1789, delivering his address from the steps of the temporary Capitol, a building on Wall Street, facing directly into Broad Street. (The old building has long since disappeared, being succeeded by a massive Greek revival building that for many years housed the sub-Treasury offices. Today, the building is a museum, forming a background for a bronze statue of George Washington as he appeared there almost two centuries ago.)

One of the many thousands of people who witnessed that Inaugural was a young Dutch diplomat, Rudolph Van Dorsten, Secretary of the United Netherlands Legation, who wrote the following letter as part of his report to his homeland.

New York, May 4, 1789

Your Right Noble Worship:

Since I wrote to you, on April 7th, both the President and Vice-President arrived here and took charge of their respective offices. Mr. Vice-President John Adams entered this city on the 20th of April, and was received fifteen miles from the city by Brigadier-General Malcom and the officers of the brigade, besides a company of uniformed citizens on horseback, and sundry notable personages in coaches, as well as gentlemen of Congress and residents of New York. They accompanied his Excellency to the residence of Mr. Jay, where he alighted. When passing the Battery, thirteen shots were fired as a salute. Immediately after his Excellency received the congratulations of the gentlemen of the committee of Congress on his safe arrival. The next day, April 21st, the gentlemen of the committee of Congress escorted his Excellency to the Senate-chamber, and, after being seated in the presidential chair, his Excellency delivered a speech, of which I enclose a copy.

President George Washington made his entry into New York on Thursday, April 23rd. On the previous day a barge left this city. The barge was built expressly by the citizens of New York, and was rowed by thirteen pilots, all dressed in white. A committee of three Senators and five Representatives on behalf of Congress, and three of the first officers on behalf of New York, went to Elizabethtown in New Jersey, to welcome the President, and to await his arrival there. His Excellency was also accompanied by some well-equipped sloops and by a multitude of small craft with citizens of New Jersey and New York on board. A Spanish royal packet-boat, happening to be anchored at the entrance of the harbor, at sight of the barge, on board of which was the President, fired a signal-shot, whereupon that vessel was dressed at once with the flags of all nations. When the presidential barge passed, the Spanish vessel saluted his Excellency by firing thirteen guns, which was repeated by the Battery, and again thirteen guns were fired by the fort when the President landed. His Excellency was received by Governor George Clinton, the mayor of the city and other officers, and, after a procession had formed, consisting of some companies of uniformed citizens and the merchants and other citizens of the city, the President walked with his escort, and Governor Clinton at his side, to the house prepared by Congress for his use. Shortly afterward his Excellency was called for in a coach by Governor Clinton, without any ceremony. At Governor Clinton's residence he took a midday meal, though a magnificent dinner had been prepared for his Excellency at his own residence. Both these personages were on that day dressed very plainly in civilian clothes, without any display.

The rush of the people to see their beloved General Washington was amazing, and their delight and joy were truly universal and cordial. At night the whole city was illuminated. No accident occurred, and everything passed off well and quietly.

On Thursday, April 30th, General Washington was inaugurated President of the United States. New York was represented by the same companies of citizens under arms as on his arrival . . . After the President, pursuant to the new Constitution, had publicly taken the oath of office, in presence of an innumerable crowd of people, his Excellency was led into the Senate-chamber and there delivered an oration . . . By this address this admirable man made himself all the more beloved. The coaches, in which were seated gentlemen of Congress, were drawn by two horses and the presidential coach by four. His Excellency was dressed in plain brown clothes, which had been presented to him by the mill at Hartford, Connecticut. At night there was a display of fireworks at the State-House. Moreover, the houses of the Comte de Moustier, the minister of France, and of Senor de Gardoqui, of Spain, were illuminated. The next day the President received congratulations. The President adopts no other title than simply President of the United States. He receives visits twice a week, Tuesdays and Fridays, from two to three o'clock, and not at other times. It is further stated that his Excellency returns no visits, nor will he accept invitations to attend banquets or other entertainments, for the reason that his Excellency, as head of the Executive Department of the new Government, has his time fully occupied. This gentleman alone, by his courteous and friendly demeanor and still more so by his frugal and simple mode of living, is able to unite the parties in America and to make the new Government effective and regular in execution, if such be possible.

THOMAS JEFFERSON

". . . it is not for an individual to chuse his post."

IN November and October, 1789, Thomas Jefferson, the American Ambassador to France, received two urgent letters from George Washington, who on April 30 of that year had been inaugurated as the first President of the United States.

Washington, already plagued by the disagreements between "conservatives" and "liberals" in American politics, wanted as his Secretary of State the arch-liberal and author of the Declaration of Independence, Thomas Jefferson, to balance his appointment of Alexander Hamilton, of New York, an arch-conservative, as Secretary of the Treasury.

Jefferson was reluctant, after enjoying four years of European life and the rousing excitement of first-hand observation of the French Revolution. However, in the best tradition of his view of public service, he could not well refuse, although he anticipated future circumstances that would force his resignation. Jefferson's mixed reactions are reflected in his reply to Washington's letters.

Chesterfield, Dec. 15, 1789.

Sir

I have received at this place the honour of your letters of Oct. 13. and Nov. 30. and am truly flattered by your nomination of me to the very dignified office of Secretary of state; for which permit me here to return you my humble thanks. could any circumstance seduce me to overlook the disproportion between it's duties & my talents it would be the encouragement of your choice. but when I contemplate the extent of that office, embracing as it does the principal mass of domestic administration, together with the foreign, I cannot be insensible of my inequality to it: and I should enter on it with gloomy forebodings from the criticisms & censures of a public, just indeed in their intentions, but sometimes misinformed & misled, & always too respectable to be neglected.

I cannot but foresee the possibility that this may end disagreeably for one, who, having no motive to public service but the public satisfaction, would certainly retire the moment that satisfaction should appear to languish. on the other hand I feel a degree of familiarity with the duties of my present office, as far at least as I am capable of understanding it's duties. the ground I have already passed over enables me to see my way into that which is before me. the change of government too, taking place in the country where it is exercised, seems to open a possibility of procuring from the new rulers some new advantages in commerce which may be agreeable to our countrymen. so that as far as my fears, my hopes, or my inclination might enter into this question, I confess they would not lead me to prefer a change.—but it is not for an individual to chuse his post. you are to marshal us as may best be for the public good: and it is only in the case of it's being indifferent to you that I would avail myself of the option you have so kindly offered in your letter. if you think it better to transfer me to another post, my inclination must be no obstacle: nor shall it be, if there is any desire to suppress the office I now hold, or to reduce it's grade. in either of these cases, be so good only as to signify to me by another line your ultimate wish, & I shall conform to it cordially. if it should be to remain at New York, my chief comfort will be to work under your eye, my only shelter the authority of your name, & the wisdom of measures to be dictated by you, & implicitly executed by me. whatever you may be pleased to decide, I do not see that the matters which have called me hither will permit me to shorten the stay I originally asked; that is to say, to set out on my journey Northward till the month of March. as early as possible in that month I shall have the honor of paying my respects to you in New York. in the mean time I have that of tendering you the homage of those sentiments of respectful attachment with which I am Sir

> Your most obedient
> & most humble servant
> Th: Jefferson

The sequel:

In 1793, after a stormy and contentious term as Secretary of State, Jefferson left the Cabinet, not to fight Washington's leadership but to serve as standard bearer against the conservative trend of the Federalist leadership under Washington.

In 1797 his followers made him Vice President under John Adams and in 1801 he toppled Adams and the conservatives and won the Presidency himself.

GEORGE WASHINGTON

". . . at the expense of some sacrifices of inclinations . . ."

IN the hot and sultry days of August, 1793, President George Washington remained in Philadelphia, rather than retreating to Mount Vernon, in an effort to hold together the differing factions of what had been the Federalist Party. But irreconcilable enmities were developing, particularly between the conservatives led by Alexander Hamilton and John Adams and the liberals led by Thomas Jefferson.

As Secretary of State, Jefferson held the President's highest regard, but President Washington felt equally loyal to—and bound to— Alexander Hamilton, his Secretary of the Treasury. Even the venera-tion both felt for Washington could not bring these two into agreement, whether on the question of a strong central government in domestic affairs, or on acceptable treaty terms to settle differences with Great Britain.

Jefferson finally told President Washington that he must leave the government. The conversation was not recorded, but a few days later, on August 12, 1793, the President, who so recently had been accustomed to commanding, sat down and wrote in his own hand a short note addressed on the back: To Mr. T. Jefferson, Sec. of State.

Philadelphia, Augt. 12th 1793

Dear Sir,

I clearly understood you on Saturday—and, of what I conceive to be two evils, must prefer the least—that is—to dispense with your temporary absence in autumn (in order to retain you in office till January) rather than part with you altogether at the close of September.—

It would be an ardent wish of mine that your continuance in office (even at the expense of some sacrifice of inclinations) could have been through the winter of the ensuing session of Congress —for many many many weighty reasons which present themselves to my mind; one of which, and not the least is, that in my judgment the affairs of this Country as they relate to sovereign powers—Indian disturbances—and internal policy—will have to take a more decisive, and I hope agreeable form, that they can bear before that time—when perhaps other public servants might also indulge in retirement. —If this cannot be, my next wish is, that your absence from the Seat of Government in autumn, may be as short as your convenience can make it.

    With much Truth and regard
    I am—Your Obed. & Aff. Servt.
        G°. Washington

The sequel:

    Jefferson would not relent. He resigned.

JOHN JAY

"A thousand Reflections crowd into my mind . . ."

ON the evening of April 15, 1794, John Jay sat down in his apartment in Philadelphia to write a short letter, which he then addressed to:

    Mrs. Jay
    Broadway
    New York

John Jay was then Chief Justice of the United States, and at 49 years of age, an elder statesman whose services had included assistance in bringing his new country into being and helping Benjamin Franklin to negotiate the Treaty of Paris in 1781, in settlement of the problems with Great Britain following the Revolution.

This day, Justice Jay had been called into conference with President George Washington; the country and the peace were seriously challenged. Misunderstandings over the Treaty of Paris had prompted Great Britain, still smarting under defeat by her former colonies, to take sharp reprisals against American shipping. Washington decided that Jay—despite his previously announced intention never to undertake another diplomatic mission—must go abroad and finish what the Treaty of Paris had begun.

So Jay notified his wife, in a letter whose gentle terms reveal the deeper emotions of an otherwise austere and coldly analytical mind.

Tuesday Ph.ª 15 July 1794

My dear Sally

I was this Evg fav^d with your's of the 14th post—it is now between 8 and 9 oc^k. and I am just returned from court—as yet I am uninformed whether the Miss Allens are arrived.

I expect my dear Sally to see you sooner than was expected. There is here a serious Determination to send me to England, if possible to avoid a War. The object is so interesting to our Country and the Combination of Circumstances such, that I find myself in a Dilemma between personal considerations and public ones—nothing can be much more distant from every wish on my own acc^t. —I feel the Impulses of Duty strongly, and it is probable that if on the Investigation I am now making, my mind should be convinced that it is my Duty to go, you will join with me in thinking that on an occasion so important I ought to follow its Dictates and commit myself to the care and kindness of that Providence in which we have both the highest Reason to repose the most absolute Confidence—this is not of my seeking—on the contrary I regard it as a measure not to be desired but to be submitted to.

A thousand Reflections crowd into my Mind, and a thousand emotions into my heart—I must remember my motto Deo Duce perseverandum—the Knowledge I have of your Sentiments on these subjects affords me consolation.

If the nomination sh^d. take place it will be in the Course of a few days, and then it will appear in the papers—in the meantime say nothing on the Subject, for it is not improbable that the Business may take another Turn, tho' I confess I do not expect it will.

My dear dear Sally, this letter will make you as grave as I am myself—but when we consider how many Reasons we have for Resignation and acquiescence, I flatter myself that we shall both become composed.

If it should please God to make me instrumental to the continuance of peace and in preventing the Effusion of Blood and other Evils and Miseries incident to War we shall both have Reason to rejoice whatever may be the Event, the Endeavour will be virtuous and consequently consolatory— Let us repose unlimited

Trust in our Maker— It is our Business to adore and to obey—
My Love to the Children . . .

With very sincere and tender Affection I am

my Dear Sally ever yours

John Jay

P.S. It is supposed that the object of my mission will be completed
in Time to return in the fall.

The sequel:

Jay went to London. The result of his mission has come down in history under the name of Jay's Treaty. He resigned from the Supreme Court, to serve two terms as Governor of New York, 1795–81. Jay never took another diplomatic assignment; he also declined proffered reappointment to the Supreme Court. Through twenty-eight years of retirement, he devoted his attention exclusively to his farm north of New York City, in Westchester County, and to his "dear dear Sally."

MASON LOCKE WEEMS

"Millions are gaping to read about him."

SOME events evolve so strongly into legend, that even if they were not initially true, it is dangerous to question their veracity. A most notable example is the American story of George Washington and the cherry tree. Neither the most scholarly research nor the most biting questions by "realistic" biographers have been able to shake this report.

For it, and a thousand other reports from a prolific wandering pen, we are indebted to "Parson Weems," itinerant bookseller, preacher, prolific writer, tale bearer, and collector of anecdotes.

With his trunks of books, he roved the south, indifferent as to where he lodged and whether he sold his wares in a tavern or in the churches in which he preached. He was the principal salesman for, and most prolific contributor to, Matthew Carey, the Philadelphia publisher, and termed himself the "ragged Mother Carey's chicken."

Thus, it was natural, early in 1800, that Weems, with his nose for topical interest, should dash off the following note to his publisher.

Washington, you know, is gone! Millions are gaping to read about him. I am nearly primed and cocked for 'em. Six months ago I set myself to collect anecdotes about him. You know I live conveniently for that work.

The sequel:

This note led to the *Life of Washington,* the first popular work about the Father of His Country. Hack writing it might be, but Weems, the gifted story teller, wrote for his readers, not for critical acclaim.

He wrote many other volumes in his lifetime, with success that only a few years later would have made him wealthy from royalties. But it is doubtful that he would have wished to live otherwise than he did —as a vagabond of the road.

NOAH WEBSTER

". . . your conduct on this occasion will be deemed little short of insanity."

NOAH WEBSTER not only organized the modern English language universally used by Americans, but in his lifetime he was one of its most prolific users. We remember his tremendous fifty years of work in compiling the grandfather of American dictionaries, his textbooks which by their royalties made him wealthy, and his fight for copyright laws to protect authors.

Little is recalled, however, of the Noah Webster who as writer and editor first proposed in 1785 (he contended) the principles that were written into the Constitution, who founded a newspaper in New York to support George Washington and the Federalist cause, and who crossed swords in angry political debate with his erstwhile friends when Federalism splintered into factions, an inevitable occurence under all single-party governments.

In 1800, with Washington dead a year, the dream of the "Father of His Country" for a single party was smashed completely. President John Adams, finishing out his first and only term, was angrily denouncing those who would unseat him. Opposition ranged from Thomas Jefferson, whose new Republican (later the Democratic) Party would defeat John Adams, to other Federalists, themselves opposed to Jefferson but who also were sniping at Adams, notably Alexander Hamilton and

Aaron Burr. (It was Burr who would be Vice President in Jefferson's first term, and who a few years later would kill Hamilton in a duel.)

To express his opinion of this confused political tangle, Noah Webster wrote a pamphlet, addressed to Hamilton and signed, after the fashion of the day, with the pseudonym "Aristides," although every reader knew the author's real identity.

From that open letter, written by the master of the English language when he was 42 years old, exactly midway through his life, the final three blistering paragraphs are here presented.

. . .

It avails little that you accuse the President of vanity, for as to this, there is less difference between men, in the degree of the quality possessed, than in the manner of showing it—and were it an issue between Mr. Adams and yourself, which has the most, you could not rely on an unanimous verdict in your favour. The same remark is applicable to the charge of self-sufficiency. That the President is unmanageable, is, in a degree, true; that is, you and your supporters cannot manage him; but this will not pass in this country for a crime. That he is unstable is alleged—pray, sir, has he been fickle and wavering in his opposition to your policy? If he has, the sound part of the American people will join in reproaching him. Did he waver during the revolutionary war? Did he waver at the negotiations of 1783? There is a wide difference, Sir, between a hasty declaration in familiar conversation and instability in a system of policy.

But it is an opinion formed on thirty years of public service, that Mr. Adams is a man of pure morals, of firm attachment to a republican government, of sound and inflexible intergrity and patriotism—and by far the best read statesman that the late revolution called into notice. Opposed to these qualifications for the station of Chief Magistrate, his occasional ill-humour at unreasonable opposition, and hasty expressions of his opinion, are of little weight; and when to these considerations we add the extreme hazard of affording a triumph to the opposition, your conduct on this occasion will be deemed little short of insanity.

Whatever apologies you may make for this step, and whatever apparent candor may be indicated by your declaration that you would not divert a vote from Mr. Adams, the world will duly appreciate the tendency of your letter and the views of the author. The world will find the difference between candor and jesuitism —and in an attempt to defend the honor and interests of the United States, by censuring the President for the embassy to France, the citizens of America will see the deep chagrin and disappointment of a military character, whose views of preserving a permanent military force on foot, have been defeated by an embassy which has removed the pretext for such an establishment.

ARISTIDES.

ALEXANDER HAMILTON

"He is as unprincipled and dangerous a man as any country can hold."

THE enmity between Alexander Hamilton and Aaron Burr is well known, but the depth of the roots of this hatred come forth as fresh as today's news in letters of the period.

In 1800 Hamilton was working as hard to destroy Burr as he was to defeat Thomas Jefferson in the latter's effort to unseat President Adams. Being a practical politician, he polled sentiment in the northern states on the upcoming Presidential election, three months before the balloting.

Then in a letter in his own hand, not dictated and therefore highly confidential, Hamilton sent his views to Charles Carroll of Carrollton, the aging Federalist and Maryland political leader, who was campaigning on the same side of the day's issues.

New York, Aug. 7, 1800

Dear Sir

In the present critical state of public affairs, it is desirable that the influential friends of the Government in different states should communicate with each other and give mutual information. With this view I shall now offer you a short sketch of the state of things north of Maryland according to the advices I have received–and in return I shall beg you for the substance of your information concerning the southern Quarter particularly the state of Maryland.

In New Hampshire there is no doubt of Federal Electors–but there is a decided partiality to M^r. Adams and a pretty general satisfaction with his conduct and administration. I took pains to [tell] Governor Gilman, whose influence is very preponderating, of the defects and errors of M^r. Adams and of the danger that no candidate could be carried in by the mere Federal strength; consequently of the expediency & necessity of unanimously voting for General Pinckney (who in the south might get some Antifederal votes) as the best means of excluding M^r. Jefferson. The Governor appeared convinced of the soundness of this view and gave me to expect that he would second the plan.

Yet I do not count upon New Hampshire for more than two things—an unanimous vote for M^r. Adams and no vote for any Antifederalist.

In Massachusetts almost all the leaders of the first class are dissatisfied with M^r. Adams & enter heartily into the policy of supporting General Pinckney– But most of the leaders of the second class are warmly attached to M^r. Adams and fearful of jeopardizing his election by promoting that of General Pinckney. And the mass of the people are well affected to him & to his administration.

Yet I have very good hopes, by the exertions of the principal Federalists, that Massachusetts will unanimously vote for Adams & Pinckney.

Rhode Island is in a state somewhat uncertain. Scisms have grown up from personal . . . which have been improved by the Antifederalists to strengthen their interest. Governor . . . expresses a hope that there will be two Antifederal Electors. Our friends reject the idea as wholly improbable.

But I am not perfectly convinced that they know the ground. In any event however I believe M^r. Adams will have there a unanimous vote. I think nothing can be relied upon as to General Pinckney.

Connecticut will, I doubt not, unanimously vote for General

Pinckney; but being very much displeased with M^r. Adams, it will require the explicit advice of certain Gentlemen to induce them to vote for him. No Antif- has any chance there.

About Vermont I am not as yet very accurately informed; but I believe Adams & Pinckney will both have all her votes.

In New York all the votes will certainly be for Jefferson & Burr.

New Jersey does not stand as well as she used to do. The Antif. hope for the votes of this state. But I think they will be disappointed. If the Electors are Federal, Pinckney will certainly be voted for and Adams will or will not be as leading friends shall advise.

It is a question whether there will be any Election in Pennsylvania, but I rather suppose there will be one by Districts which will give a Majority of three in that state to the Anti-federal Candidates, according to my calculations.

Everybody takes it for granted that Delaware will give all federal Electors; who will certainly vote for General Pinckney & for Adams or not as they shall be advised.

Hence you will perceive that our prospects are not brilliant—and that there is too much probability that Jefferson or Burr will be President. The latter is intriguing with all his might in New Jersey, Rhode Island & Vermont. There is a possibility of some success to his intrigues— He counts positively on the unanimous support of the Antifederalists & that by some adventitious aid from our quarter he will overtop his friend Jefferson. If he does he will certainly attempt to reform the Government a la Buonaparte— He is an unprincipled and dangerous a man as any country can hold.

As between Pinckney & Adams I give a decided preference to the first. If you have not heard enough to induce you to agree in this opinion I will upon your request enter into my reasons. M^r. Adams has governed & must govern from impulse and caprice, under the influence of the two most mischievous of Passions for a Politician, to an extreme that to be portrayed would present a caricature—Vanity and Jealousy. He has already disorganized & in a great measure prostrated the Federal Party. Under his auspices the Government can scarcely fail to decline & with him the federal party will be disgraced. This is my anticipation on mature reflection.

Will not Maryland vote by her Legislature? I am aware of many objections to the measure; but if it be true as I suppose that our Opponents aim at Revolution & employ all means to secure success that Content must be very unequal if we <u>not only</u> refrain from <u>unconstitutional</u> and <u>criminal</u> measures but even from such as may offend against the <u>routine of</u> strict decorum.

With very great esteem & regard I have the honor to be Dᵣ. Sir

Your Obed Servant
A Hamilton

ABIGAIL ADAMS

". . . I deign to be pleased."

IN the late and dreary fall of 1800, President John Adams moved out of the comfortable President's House in Philadelphia to the new Executive Mansion in Washington.

A dozen years earlier, with establishment of the new Republic, it had been agreed that Washington, D.C., should be created as the permanent capital of the United States. On October 12, 1892 (the four hundredth anniversary of the discovery of America) a cornerstone had been laid for the Mansion. (It was not to be called the White House until after 1816, when the burned and rebuilt edifice was painted to conceal the scars of the British firing of it in 1814.)

President and Mrs. Adams were bitter, because their required move came after the Republican revolt against the Federalist Party had already made it clear that John Adams could not be re-elected to a second term. Consequently, he must spend a contentious winter in Washington only to see his successor inaugurated the following March.

In that atmosphere, Abigail Adams sat down to write a letter to her daughter, in Braintree, Mass. All her compliments are irony, and her jests are bitter. But there is no doubt as to her accuracy.

Washington, November 21, 1800

My dear child,

I arrived here on Sunday last, and without meeting any accident worth noticing, except losing ourselves when we left Baltimore, and going eight or nine miles on the Frederick road, by which means we were obliged to go the other night through woods, where we wandered two hours without finding a guide, or the path. Unfortunately a straggling black came up with us, and we engaged him as a guide, to extricate us out of our difficulty; but woods are all you see, from Baltimore until you reach the city, which is only so in name. Here and there is a small cot, without a glass window, interspersed amongst the forests, through which you travel miles without seeing any human being. In the city there are buildings enough, if they were compact and finished, to accommodate Congress and those attached to it; but as they are, and scattered as they are, I see no great comfort for them. The river, which runs up to Alexandria, is in full view of my windows, and I see the vessels as they pass and repass.

The house is upon a grand and superb scale, requiring about thirty servants to attend and keep the apartments in proper order, and perform the ordinary business of the house and stables; an establishment very well proportioned to the President's salary. The lighting of the apartments, from the kitchen to parlors and chambers, is a tax indeed; and the fires we are obliged to keep to secure us from daily agues is another very cheering comfort. To assist us in this great castle, and render less attendance necessary, bells are wholly wanting, not one single one being hung through the whole house, and promises are all you can obtain. This is so great an inconvenience, that I know not what to do, or how to do. The ladies from Georgetown and in the city have many of them visited me. Yesterday I returned fifteen visits,–but such a place as Georgetown appears,–why, our Milton is beautiful. But no comparisons;–if they will put me up some bells, and let me have wood enough to keep fires, I deign to be pleased. I could content myself almost anywhere three months; but, surrounded with forests, can you believe that wood is not to be had, because people cannot be found to cut and cart it! Briesler entered into a contract with a man to supply him with wood. A small part, a few cords only, has he been able to get. Most of that was expended to dry the walls of the house before we came in, and yesterday the man told him it was impossible for him to procure it to be cut and carted. He has had recourse to coals; but we cannot get grates made and set. We have, indeed, come into a new country.

You must keep all this to yourself, and, when asked how I like it, say that I write you the situation is beautiful, which is true. The house is made habitable, but there is not a single apartment finished, and all withinside, except for the plastering, has been done since Briesler came. We have not the least fence, yard, or other convenience, without, and the great unfinished audience-room I make a drying-room of, to hang up the clothes in. The principal stairs are not up, and will not be this winter. Six chambers are made comfortable; two are occupied by the President and Mr. Shaw; two lower rooms, one for a common parlor, and one for a levee-room. Up stairs there is the oval room, which is designed for the drawing-room, and has crimson furniture in it. It is a very handsome room now; but, when completed, it will be beautiful. If the twelve years, in which this place has been considered as the future seat of government, had been improved, as they would have been if in New England, very many of the present inconveniences would have been removed. It is a beautiful spot, capable of every improvement, and, the more I am delighted with it.

Since I sat down to write, I have been called down to a servant from Mount Vernon, with a billet from Major Custis, and a haunch of venison, and a kind, congratulatory letter from Mrs. Lewis, upon my arrival in the city, with Mrs. Washington's love, inviting me to Mount Vernon, where, health permitting, I will go, before I leave this place.

MRS. SAMUEL HARRISON SMITH

*". . . an address . . . sentiments the most
liberal . . ."*

SOON after Thomas Jefferson was elected President, he invited an old and trusted friend, Samuel Harrison Smith, to move from Philadelphia to Washington and there found a newspaper to bespeak the principles of Jefferson's new Republican Party.

Smith responded and established the *National Intelligencer,* which continued for almost half a century as Washington's leading newspaper, and for a large part of that period served as the official reporter of Congressional debates.

Mrs. Smith, an indefatigable letter writer, despite some exaggerations and mistakes, left a priceless descriptive record of the early days of the National Capital. She was everyone's friend, and as her husband prospered, affairs at their estate, named Sydney, established her as Washington's first hostess.

In the following letter, she describes Jefferson's Inaugural to her sister, with a typical curve at the end suggesting a potential romance.

March 4, 1801

Let me write to you my dear Susan, e'er that glow of enthusiasm has fled, which now animates my feelings; let me congratulate not only you, but all my fellow citizens, on an event which will have so auspicious an influence on their political welfare. I have this morning witnessed one of the most interesting scenes, a free people can ever witness. The changes of administration, which in every government and in every age have most generally been epochs of confusion, villainy and bloodshed, in this our happy country take place without any species of distraction, or disorder. This day, has one of the most amiable and worthy men taken that seat to which he was called by the voice of his country. I cannot describe the agitation I felt, while I looked around on the various multitude and while I listened to an address, containing principles the most correct, sentiments the most liberal, and wishes the most benevolent, conveyed in the most appropriate and elegant language and in a manner mild as it was firm. If doubts of the integrity and talents of Mr. Jefferson ever existed in the minds of any one, methinks this address must forever eradicate them. The Senate chamber was so crowded that I believe not another creature could enter. On one side of the house the Senate sat, the other was resigned by the representatives to the ladies. The roof is arched, the room half circle, every inch of ground was occupied. It has been conjectured by several gentlemen whom I've asked, that there were near a thousand persons within the walls. The speech was delivered in so low a tone that few heard it. Mr. Jefferson had given your Brother a copy early in the morning, so that on coming out of the house, the paper was distributed immediately. Since then there has been a constant succession of persons coming for the papers. I have been interrupted several times in this letter by the gentlemen of Congress, who have been to bid us their adieus; since three o'clock there has been a constant succession. Mr. Claiborn, a most amiable and agreeable man, called the moment before his departure and there is no one whose society I shall more regret the loss of. You will smile when I tell you that Gouveneur Morris, Mr. Dayton and Bayard drank tea here; they have just gone after sitting near two hours.

Mr. Foster will be the bearer of this letter; he is a widower, looking out for a wife; he is a man of respectable talents, and most amiable disposition and comfortable fortune. What think you my good sister Mary of setting your cap for him? As for you, Susan, you are rather too young, and I have another in my eye for you.

WASHINGTON IRVING

"Jonathan Oldstyle, Gent." on "modern times"

AMONG the treasured "Letters" of America are many that are openly fakes when judged by the standards of bona fide personal messages between individuals, but nonetheless are considered letters in the deeper sense of the word. Writers discovered that satire, in particular, could best be written for readers as personal communications printed for open distribution, with a false signature to establish verisimilitude.

Such a letter writer, who kindled wide popular reaction in 1802–03, was "Jonathan Oldstyle, Gent.," an easily-pictured, elderly fussbudget willing and ready to comment on "modern" social custom through kindly, barbed comparisons with earlier days of his recollection.

These letters were actually written by a young man, a law student, in his nineteenth and twentieth years. A young student named Washington Irving, who created a writing character thirty or forty years older than himself.

Sir,

Nothing is more intolerable to an old person than innovation on old habits. The customs that prevailed in our youth become dear to us as we advance in years; and we can no more bear to see them abolished, than we can bear to behold the trees cut down under which we have sported in the happy days of infancy.

Even I myself, who have floated down the stream of life with the tide—who have humoured it in all its turnings—who have conformed in a great measure to all its fashions,—cannot but feel sensible of this prejudice. I often sigh when I draw a comparison between the present and the past; and though I cannot but be sensible that, in general, times are altered for the better, yet there is something even in the imperfections of the manners which prevailed in my youthful days, that is inexpressibly endearing.

There is nothing that seems more strange and preposterous to me, than the manner in which modern marriages are conducted. The parties keep the matter as secret as if there was something disgraceful in the connection. The lady positively denies that anything of the kind is to happen; will laugh at her intended husband, and even lay bets against the event, the very day before it is to take place. They sneak into matrimony as quietly as possible, and seem to pride themselves on the cunning and ingenuity they have displayed in their manoeuvres.

How different is this from the manners of former times! I recollect when my Aunt Barbara was addressed by 'Squire Stylish; nothing was heard of during the whole courtship, but consultations and negotiations between her friends and relatives; the matter was considered and re-considered, and at length the time set for a final answer. Never, Mr. Editor, shall I forget the awful solemnity of the scene. The whole family of the Oldstyles assembled in awful conclave: my aunt Barbara, dressed out as fine as hands could make her—high cushion, enormous cap, long waist, prodigious hoop, ruffles that reached to the end of her fingers, and a gown of flame-coloured brocade, figured with poppies, roses, and sunflowers. Never did she look so sublimely handsome. The 'Squire entered the room with a countenance suited to the solemnity of the occasion. He was arrayed in a full suit of scarlet velvet, his coat decorated with a profusion of large silk buttons, and the skirts stiffened with a yard or two of buckram: a long pigtailed wig, well powdered, adorned his head; and stockings of deep blue silk, rolled over the knees, graced his extremities; the flaps of his vest reached to his knee-buckles, and the ends of his cravat, tied with the most precise neatness, twisted through every button-hole. Thus accoutred, he gravely walked into the room, with his ivory-headed ebony cane in one hand, and gently swaying his three-cornered beaver with the other. The gallant and fashionable appearance of the 'Squire, the gracefulness and dignity of his deportment, occasioned a general smile of complacency through the room; my aunt Barbara modestly veiled her countenance with her fan; but I observed her contemplating her admirer with great satisfaction through the sticks.

The business was opened with the most formal solemnity, but was not long in agitation. The Oldstyles were moderate—their articles of capitulation few: the 'Squire was gallant, and acceded to them all. In short, the blushing Barbara was delivered up to his embraces with due ceremony. Then, Mr. Editor—then were the happy times: such oceans of arrack—such mountains of plumcake

—such feasting and congratulating—such fiddling and dancing:— ah me! who can think of those days, and not sigh when he sees the degeneracy of the present: no eating of cake nor throwing of stockings—not a single skin filled with wine on the joyful occasion —nor a single pocket edified by it but the parson's.

It is with the greatest pain I see those customs dying away, which served to awaken the hospitality and friendship of my ancient comrades—that strewed with flowers the path to the altar, and shed a ray of sunshine on the commencement of the matrimonial union.

The deportment of my aunt Barbara and her husband was as decorous after marriage as before; her conduct was always regulated by his—her sentiments ever accorded with his opinions; she was always eager to tie on his neckcloth of a morning—to tuck a napkin under his chin at meal time—to wrap him up warm of a winter's day, and to spruce him up as smart as possible of a Sunday. The 'Squire was the most attentive and polite husband in the world; would hand his wife in and out of church with the greatest ceremony—drink her health at dinner with particular emphasis, and ask her advice on every subject—though I must confess he invariably adopted his own:—nothing was heard from both sides, but dears, sweet loves, doves, &¢. The 'Squire could never stir out of a winter's day, without his wife calling after him from the window to button up his waistcoat carefully. Thus, all things went on smoothly; and my relations Stylish had the name, and, as far as I know, deserved it, of being the most happy and loving couple in the world . . .

The sequel:

Irving considered his early writings, including these "letters," to be merely a schoolboy's whim. He went on to be a lawyer, businessman, and soldier, serving as Minister to Spain from 1842 to 1846.

He never stopped writing and will always be remembered as America's first "classic" author, acknowledged even in his own time as a literary giant, for such works as *The Sketch Book of Geoffrey Crayon* and *The Legend of Sleepy Hollow*.

As a commentator of his period wrote, "His pen and his ledger are exchanged for his pencil and his sketch-book; and Geoffrey's drafts are more highly honored, than those of any merchant in the land."

AARON BURR

"I have the honor to be Yours respt . . ."

ON the evening of June 22, 1804, an otherwise undistinguished New York gentleman, by name Mr. Van Ness, carried through the narrow streets a letter whose contents, expressing bitter hatred couched in the courtly formalities of the "code of honor," was a preface to a flaming chapter in history.

Its contents would lead to the murder, or martyrdom, of Alexander Hamilton, the "bastard of Barbadoes," who had risen to the post of Washington's personal aide in the Revolution, had been the first Secretary of the Treasury, and was the founder of New York's first bank. This killing would consign to permanent shame Aaron Burr, Hamilton's bitter financial and political rival, and former Vice President of the United States.

Hamilton himself had poured salt in the wounds of Burr's injured vanity, calling him untrustworthy, selfish and profligate, as if goading him.

Burr finally wrote Hamilton as follows.

N. York June 22^d 1804

Sir

Mr. V. Ness has this evening reported to me verbally that you refuse to answer my last letter, that you consider the course I have taken as intemperate and unnecessary and some other conversation which it is improper that I should notice.

My request to you was in the first instance prepared in a form the most simple in order that you might give to the affair that course to which you might be induced by your temper and your knowledge of facts. I relied with unsuspecting faith that from the frankness of a soldier and the candor of a gentlemen I might expect an ingenuous declaration; that if, as I had reason to believe, you had used expressions derogatory to my honor, you would have had the spirit to maintain or the magnanimity to retract them, and, that if from your language injurious inferences had been improperly drawn, sincerity and decency would have pointed out to you the propriety of correcting errors which might then have been widely diffused.

With these impressions, I was greatly disappointed in receiving from you a letter which I could only consider as evasive and which in manner, is not altogether decorous. In one expectation however, I was not wholly deceived, for at the close of your letter I find an intimation, that if I should dislike your refusal to acknowledge or deny the charge, you were ready to meet the consequences. This I deemed a sort of defiance, and I should have been justified if I had chosen to make it the basis of an immediate message: Yet, as you had also said something (though in any opinion unfounded) of the indefiniteness of my request; as I believed that your communication was the offspring, rather of false pride than of reflection, and, as I felt the utmost reluctance to proceed to extremities while any other hope remained, my request was repeated in terms more definite. To this you refuse all reply, reposing, as I am bound to presume, on the tender of an alternative insinuated in your letter.

Thus, Sir, you have invited the course I am about to pursue, and now by your silence impose it upon me. If, therefore your determinations are final, of which I am not permitted to doubt, Mr. Van Ness is authorized to communicate my further expectations either to yourself or to such friend as you may be pleased to indicate.

I have the honor to be
Yours respt
A. Burr

The sequel:

Hamilton accepted the challenge and met Burr at dawn on the morning of July 11, 1804, at a spot on Weehawken Heights, in New Jersey. They fired at 10 paces from each other; Burr was unscathed, while Hamilton fell mortally wounded and died the following day.

On July 14, in the cemetery of Trinity Church, New York City, Hamilton was buried and eulogized by Gouverneur Morris in an oration that gave the speaker enduring fame, and which concluded:

"You all know how he perished. On this last scene I cannot, I must not dwell. It might excite emotions too strong for your better judgment. Suffer not your indignation to lead to an act which might again offend the insulted majesty of the laws. On his part as from his lips, though with my voice—for his voice you will hear no more—let me entreat you to respect yourselves. And now, ye ministers of the everlasting God, perform your holy office and commit these ashes of our departed brother to the bosom of the grave."

By this time, Burr was in hiding, hunted both in New York and New Jersey. He undertook an abortive filibustering expedition to Mexico, tried to conspire to make himself head of a secessionist state in the Mississippi Valley, and lived on for thirty-two years, a symbol of shame until his death in 1836.

WILLIAM WIRT

"Matrimony is not like a ball . . ."

ELSEWHERE in this collection, the penetrating views of William Wirt, the lawyer, are set forth in a communication to a young man desiring to "read law" with him. There we see the professional side of a towering figure in American jurisprudence.

Wirt was also whimsical, serious and deeply concerned with human relationships, as shown by a letter to his niece, Eliza, in 1805. Eliza was an orphan and Wirt's ward.

While in Norfolk, Va., on legal business, Wirt received word from Eliza Johnston that she soon would marry Dabney Minor, of Gale Hill.

Wirt's concern was not with the husband Eliza had chosen, but with what he feared were the romantic conceptions that filled young girls' heads at the beginning of the 19th century.

Norfolk January 25
1805

My Dear Eliza

. . . The occasion of your letter of the 5th is indeed an important one. You call it important, because perhaps you have heard that it was so–but I fear you have not taken the time to consider how very important it is to yourself, to the gentleman, and to those who may follow you. In this serious point of view you ought to sit down and consider it in all its bearings with a heart composed and at rest and a mind perfectly calm and collected. If you suffer your mind merely to glance towards the subject and that at times when it is giddy, perhaps by the whirl of pleasure and while your heart is fluttering and bounding high with hope and expectation–if it is only at times and in a disposition and frame of mind like this that you have thought of matrimony, you are very unfit as yet to enter into it. Let me, although it may not be very pleasant to you, suggest a few of those serious considerations which it is proper that you should have before you take this awful step.

Matrimony is not like a ball, where every body goes to be merry, where you may dance or not as you please, and where if you have a disagreeable partner it is but for an evening, & in the meantime you can relieve your mind by the gay & sprightly conversation of others– Yet most girls consider matrimony in this point of view, as a frolic, a joyous revolution, the era of independence, a kind of Christmas festival, when all is to be liberty and gaiety and bliss. What is the consequence? Almost every girl is disappointed, they find that there is very little frolic in the superintendence and management of a family of servants, perhaps of bad servants, very little of gaiety ensuing to scouring the house, rubbing the furniture, attending to the clothing of the white & black family, giving out breakfast & dinner and supper &c—very little like a ball in sitting all silence and solitude knitting or sewing while the husband is out on the plantation day after day, or gone perhaps for weeks on business, and when he comes home perhaps fretted out of humour, something gone amiss with him, everything is not right about the house, dinner is not ready in time, the victuals not well cooked–you are to be . . . . . .–and this to last not for one day, not for a week, not for a month, not for a year, nor two years–but perhaps for 40, 50 or 60–certainly for the life of one of you. Let us suppose that you are married and carried home–perhaps Lucy, or Susan or some of your other friends go with you & they stay there for some days–but as it would not be proper for them to live there, they will return to their respective homes after a few days and you will be left alone, or with your husband only. You will probably have a cry at this separation from your friends, and this cry will not be very like a Christmas festival. Well, your husband, if he is amiable, will comfort you, caress you and after a few hours compose your mind entirely & dry up your tears. Well, what then–he can't stay court- ing you–he must go out & see how the people are coming on, or he must go to Charlottesville or perhaps to Fredericksburg, for he is an industrious man & a man engaged in business which requires his mind & body to be pretty constantly employed in it. Well, he goes out on some one of these occasions, and then how little will you find the death-like silence of a country house to resemble the jocund notes of the fiddle, the sound of the dancers' feet, the lively good humoured conversation and the loud careless laugh, then you will sit all alone, thinking of Maryland, your Aunt there, your Uncle in Norfolk, when will you see them again; then you will think of the parties of pleasure which you are now engaged in, they are all gone & never again to return, for altho' you may go to dances again you will remember that you are married & will no longer be Eliza Johnston talking with the beaux but will be treated with distant formal respect as the wife of another man. Then you will think perhaps of Rockingham again & think round & round of all your friends and all the gay occasions of your life, & it is ten to one as you look around upon the gloomy & silent walls of your house, but you have another cry, then there will be no hus- band there to comfort you, none of your female friends, and you will remember that this is to be the case day after day for a long, long life. Bye and bye your husband comes home, he no longer advances towards you bowing & smiling with the polite & tender solicitude of a lover, but gravely and coldly hangs up his hat and asks if dinner is ready, if not he frowns, asks whether such & such a thing which he orders has been done, if not asks "Why," rather angrily. You get warmed and tell him "he need not make such a fuss about it," He looks at you with amazement, asks himself can this be Eliza Johnston, makes no reply to you but sighs, puts on his hat and walks out again, perhaps instead of this forbearance, he answers you that "he has a right to make a fuss when his orders are disobeyed, that he has not been used to have his business neglected & would not"–You look glum, he thinks you look ugly & frowns still more, you think he is horribly ugly, that besides his clothes are rusty and dirty, such as you never saw him wear, he thinks you look sluttish, wishes he had not married you, you wish so too, but it is too late. You quarrel, cry, perhaps kiss & make up, but you fancy that he has ceased to love you, that he is cold & indifferent about you, that he disapproves of everything you do, and then you get to crying by yourself, fancy that you are the most unfortunate and miserable girl in the world, ask yourself "where all your golden dreams of matrimonial bliss are flown? Where is the romantic tenderness, the soft, unceasing assiduity, the life of ease of pleasure and delight that you expected, if this is matrimony, say you, I be bound I will advise all my acquaintances against it." Trust me, my dear Eliza this is the experience of nine girls out of ten. They may not all acknowledge it with equal candor, and indeed it might be imprudent in them to do so, but there are very few who will not own that they are disappointed in matrimony, and the disappointment proceeds from the unreasonable, foolish & romantic expectations which they entertain of it.

It is not the era of liberty, but of servitude, the mistress of a family has a more various, more troublesome and perplexing servitude than any servant about the house. The cook has her separate duties, the chambermaid is satisfied when she has made up the beds & swept out the house & so every servant in their particular departments, but the mistress of the house has all these departments to attend to, & if she withdraws her attention from any one, that one is sure to be neglected. Thus so far from having ease & liberty she has her cares constantly upon her mind, & will be in almost constant thought & anxiety about these duties & so have ease, & . . . . . enough, but this would be the ready way to banish your husband from his house, and yourself from his heart. Do not marry then, my dear, with the silly expectation that a married life is a life of ease, pleasure, gallantry & amusement, if you do you will be certainly disappointed.

I have not said all this, my dear Eliza, to dissuade you from the resolution which you seem to have taken, but only to give you a true view of the subject and prevent the mortification which you would experience at finding the brilliant pictures of fancy all reversed by matter of fact. I beg you therefore once for all, not to expect that a matrimonial life is a life of perpetual sunshine. You will find the sky frequently overcast with clouds, and not a little of dark, dismal rainy & squally weather, but this you must expect and prepare your mind to encounter it.

The gentleman whom you mention is well known to me: and I think there can be no manner of objection to him. But if you are going to marry him, "to rid me of a trouble" as you call it, you are going to act from a very improper motive. I have never thought it a trouble, my dear Eliza, to do any thing for you that I could . . . Whatever I have had in my power to do for you, I have done cheerfully and with pleasure, the same I shall still be ready and happy to do, and I beg therefore that this motive may not enter into the consideration of the subject.

If you love the gentleman, if you think you can make him happy by displaying in your life & . . . . . the attention, the thoughtfulness, the industry, the neatness, the management, the systematic arrangement & order of a housewife, with the pure and rational love of a wife: if you marry him without any romantic & exorbitant expectations of raptures and ecstasies and never-clouded bliss; but merely with the expectation of comfort and tranquil enjoyment which I hope you may safely expect, the marriage will make me and your Aunt happy . . .

Yrs affectionately
Wm. Wirt

JAMES MONROE

". . . the feelings of humanity . . . so often outraged . . ."

WHILE James Monroe is best remembered as a President of the United States and author of the Monroe Doctrine, he cut his diplomatic teeth in an unsuccessful mission to London planned by President Jefferson, to stop the actions inevitably leading toward the second war fought by this country and England.

Monroe was in London in company with William Pinckney, dealing with Lord Mulgrave, Secretary of State for Foreign Affairs. In the course of that mission he demonstrated the toughness of fiber that led President Madison to name him Secretary of State and which eventually carried him to the Presidency.

Monroe wrote a letter to Lord Mulgrave, which so succinctly stated the cause of this country in its protests against British disregard of American shipping rights and the rights of the seamen who manned our ships, that President Jefferson sent a copy to the Congress and had it published.

Great Cumberland Place,
September 23, 1805

My Lord,

I flattered myself, from what passed in our last interview, that I should have been honored before this with an answer from your lordship to my letters respecting the late seizure of American vessels . . .

I cannot conclude this note without adverting to the other topics depending between our governments, which it is also much wished to adjust at this time . . . With a view to perpetuate the friendship of the two nations, no unnecessary course of collision should be left open. Those adverted to are believed to be of this kind, such as the case of boundary, the impressment of seamen, &c . . . In the topic if impressment, however, the motive is more urgent. In that line the rights of the United States have been so long trampled under foot, and the feelings of humanity in respect to the sufferers, and the honor of their government, even in their own ports, so often outraged, that the astonished world may begin to doubt, whether the patience with which those injuries have been borne, ought to be attributed to generous or unworthy motives . . . I have only to add, that I shall be happy to meet your lordship on these points, as soon as you can make it convenient to you.

I have the honor to be,
With high consideration,
Your lordship's most obedient servant,
James Monroe

GOUVERNEUR MORRIS

". . . pure democracy is rare."

THE private correspondence of many great American patriots shows occasional doubts about the revolutionary American social and political experiment, doubts that were carefully screened from their public speeches.

Gouverneur Morris furnishes an extraordinary example, through correspondence carefully cloaked in anonymity at the time, even though published in the press—as in "Gazette 1806."

In 1806, when he set forth the views quoted here, Morris was a retired statesman, living on ancestral property at Gouverneur, N.Y., named in honor of the then-45-year-old Morris, who had been a member of the Constitutional Convention of 1787, U.S. Minister to France and Senator from New York. Morris made no secret of his loyalist sympathies, his dallying with the idea of a monarchy as the best ultimate form of government, or his participation in a plot to rescue Louis XVI during the French Revolution.

Monday morning, 17th Nov. 1806

My dear sir,

In answer to your inquiries respecting the United States of America, I send you the enclosed notes which you may communicate to any of your friends who may be prompted by curiosity or interest to seek information on the subjects to which you referred. You will, however, take notice, that I do not aspire at the character of an author, and therefore the hints now sent are not to be published.

I am,
With esteem and respect,
Your obedient servant

Between the high coloring of exaggeration and the dark shade of detraction, it may be difficult to discern the truth in what relates to America . . . It seems proper to remark, that when strangers undertake to delineate the character of a nation from what they meet with in trading towns, great parts of whose inhabitants are like (themselves) strangers, the portrait, however excellent in colour and expression, will hardly possess the merit of a good likeness . . . It is easy to conceive that one bred in the politer circles of London might not be pleased with the manners of Amsterdam, Hamburgh, or Philadelphia. The inhabitants of those towns have the humility to believe they want that high polish which courts alone can give . . . When the Count de Laraguis was asked, on his return from England, his opinion of its produce and inhabitants, he exclaimed . . . "Tis the strangest place you can conceive. They have twenty religions and but one sauce. All their liquors are sour except the vinegar. They have no ripe fruit but baked apples, and nothing polished but steel."

It would be well that this speech were printed on the title page of some books of travels in America which Englishmen have published . . . The American who claims for his country a proud exemption from the ills attached to humanity is less to be applauded for his zeal than pitied for his folly . . .

This sketch has run to such length, that one important subject must remain almost untouched. Still, however, a few words on the government of America cannot be dispensed with. It is the fashion at present to decry republicks, and so far as democracies are concerned, no discreet man will object to the censure. But pure democracy is rare, and is rather a destruction than a form of republican government, It is the passage to monarchy. It never did, and never can exist, but for a moment, and that too is a moment of agony . . . That America, when fully peopled, may become a monarchy, is not improbable, but in the meantime she is free, prosperous, and happy . . . The British monarchy, if monarchy it must be called, is certainly a good government, well suited to that country. Whether it would suit America, would be known only by experiment . . . If we inquire by what power it is sustained in England, we shall find it is the good sense and mild spirit of Englishmen . . . A similar spirit, with a fair portion of common sense, induced the Americans to adopt that system under which they live, and it may reasonably be expected, that a continuance of the same mind and temper will preserve to them, for a long time, the blessings of order, liberty, and law.

ALBERT GALLATIN

*". . . we have been too happy and too
prosperous . . ."*

WHEN Thomas Jefferson became President in 1801, his Secretary of the Treasury was a younger man, Albert Gallatin, one of the first of a new generation of cultured Europeans who migrated to the United States soon after the Revolution. Swiss born orphan of a prominent family, he had completed his formal education when he arrived in the United States in 1780, at the then-mature age of 19 years.

Gallatin had established an estate in Pennsylvania, plunged into politics, and become a member of Congress in 1794. There, he had been a leader of the minority opposing the Federalists, advocating financial reform and fighting agitation for a war with France.

As Secretary of the Treasury, displacing the die-hard Federalist, Alexander Hamilton, he reduced the national debt and backed Jefferson's foreign policy of moderation. However, he looked wryly on the mounting material prosperity of the United States, fearing its soporific effect on national thinking.

One day he set down a summarization of his thoughts in a note to his wife.

Washington, July, 1808

I enclose a National Intelligencer (the Washington daily newspaper), one paragraph of which, together with the Bayonne decree, contains the substance of the intelligence. The last we have not officially. I think the aspect of affairs unfavorable. England seems to rely on our divisions and on the aggression of France as sufficient to force us into a change of measures, perhaps war with France, without any previous preparation or relaxation on her part. Of the real views of the French Emperor nothing more is known than what appears upon the face of his decrees and in his acts; and these manifest, in my opinion, either a deep resentment because we would not make war against England, or a wish to seek a quarrel with us.

Between the two our situation is extremely critical, and I believe that poor limited human wisdom can do and will do but little to extricate us. Yet I do not feel despondent, for as long as we adhere strictly to justice toward all, I have a perfect reliance on the continued protection of that Providence which has raised us and blessed us as a nation.

But we have been too happy and too prosperous, and we consider as great misfortunes some privations and a share in the general calamities of the world. Compared with other nations, our share is indeed very small.

The sequel:

In 1812, the calamity of war did come, but with England over her stubborn impressment of American sailors, and not with France. Gallatin was blamed somewhat for unpreparedness because of his fiscal policies. However, in 1812 he was sent by President Madison to Russia on a mission seeking support, and when Britain showed willingness to negotiate peace, Gallatin served on the mission to Ghent.

Ironically, in later years, Gallatin served, at different periods, as Minister to both France and Great Britain.

OLIVER HAZARD PERRY

"We have met the enemy; and they are ours!"

LITTLE victories in war often make big victories, and dramatic little messages often make historic reports. So it is with Commodore Perry's famous cryptic message to General William Henry Harrison, his superior officer in the campaign to wrest Lakes Erie and Ontario from the British, in 1813.

Born in 1785, Perry became a midshipman in 1799 (through the usual use of political assistance) and served in the war with the Barbary pirates. He won a lieutenancy (then a command rank) in 1807, but since there were no wars he turned to shipbuilding. Thus he was both an officer of the line and an experienced ship constructor in 1812, although only 27 years old. He was sent to Lake Erie to build and command a small force to oppose a British naval mission.

Eventually he had two brigs and four or five schooners in the water. The British had two ships slightly larger than brigs, two brigs, one schooner and one sloop. Perry flew his flag from the brig Lawrence. The other brig under his command was the Niagara.

The two forces clashed on the morning of September 10, 1813. Perry's brave crews were largely landsmen hastily trained as sailors and gunners, augmented by a troop of Kentucky riflemen who, manning the rigging, were credited with picking off practically every British officer on the decks of the enemy ships.

In the afternoon of that famous day, Perry sent his message to General Harrison.

U.S. Brig Niagara, Off the Western Sister, Lake Erie
Sept. 10, 1813.

Dear General,

We have met the enemy; and they are ours! 2 ships, 2 brigs, 1 schooner, and 1 sloop.

Yours with great respect and esteem,

Gen. Harrison   O. H. Perry

Three days later, with his wounded cared for as well as possible, and the dead buried, Perry sent a more detailed report (but one that still gave very little hint of his own gallantry) to William Jones, Secretary of the Navy.

U.S. Schooner Ariel, Put-in-Bay, Sept. 13, 1813

Sir,

In my last I informed you that we had captured the enemy's fleet on this lake. I have now the honour to give you the most important particulars of the action. On the morning of the 10th instant, at sunrise, they were discovered from Put-in-Bay, where I lay at anchor with the squadron under my command. We got under way, the wind light at S.W. and stood for them. At 10 A.M. the wind hauled to S.E. and brought us to windward: formed the line and bore up. At 15 minutes before 12, the enemy commenced firing; at 5 minutes before 12, the action commenced on our part. Finding their fire very destructive, owing to their long guns, and its being mostly directed at the Lawrence, I made sail and directed the other vessels to follow for the purpose of closing with the enemy. Every brace and bow-line being shot away, she became unmanageable, notwithstanding the great exertions of the sailing master. In this situation she sustained the action upwards of 2 hours within cannister distance, until every gun was rendered useless, and the greater part of her crew either killed or wounded. Finding she could no longer annoy the enemy, I left her in charge of Lieut. Yarnall, who I was convinced, from the bravery already displayed by him, would do what would comport with the honour of the flag. At half past two, the wind springing up, Capt. Elliott was enabled to bring his vessel, the Niagara, gallantly into close action: I immediately went on board of her, when he anticipated my wish by volunteering to bring the schooners which had been kept astern by the lightness of the wind, into close action. It was with unspeakable pain, that I saw, soon after I got on board the Niagara, the flag of the Lawrence come down, although I was perfectly sensible that she had been defended to the last, and that to have continued to make a show of resistance would have been a wanton sacrifice of the remains of her brave crew. But the enemy was not able to take possession of her, and circumstances soon permitted her flag again to be hoisted.

At 45 minutes past 2, the signal was made for "close action." The Niagara being very little injured, I determined to pass through the enemy's line, bore up and passed ahead of their two ships and a brig, giving a raking fire to them from the starboard guns, and to a large schooner and sloop from the larboard side at half pistol shot distance. The smaller vessels at this time having got within grape and cannister distance, under the direction of Capt. Elliott, and keeping up a well directed fire, the two ships, a brig and a schooner surrendered, a schooner and sloop making a vain attempt to escape. . . .

Very respectfully, I have the honour to be,
Sir, your obedient servant,

Hon. William Jones   O. H. Perry
Sec'y of the Navy.

The sequel:

With the British naval forces destroyed, the way was open for General Harrison to win the Battle of the Thames, with Perry's help in securing his water transport.

In 1819, Perry was sent on a mission to Venezuela, where he contracted yellow fever and died, at the age of 35. He was buried in Trinidad, but as his fame grew, his body was transferred to Newport, R.I.

MRS. JAMES (DOLLY) MADISON

" . . . where I shall be tomorrow, I cannot tell!!"

ON August 24, 1814, during the hottest, steamiest Washington, D.C. weather, one housewife, stripped by war of all the trappings of her position as wife of the President, occupied herself in hectic activity, with the calm of a determined woman.

From her roof, through a spy glass, she watched a battle and the rout of her husband's little army on the dusty roads to the northeast. She worked to select and pack, from all the Mansion's papers and treasures, what little could be placed in a single carriage for removal, helped only by her chef. She also managed to write a piecemeal letter to her sister in Philadelphia.

When Dolly Madison wrote this letter, there was no "happy end-ing" in sight. Out on Bladensburg Road, the militiamen personally commanded by President Madison were routed. In the early afternoon, the 4,000 British troops set fire to the Capitol, a mile from the Executive Mansion. Only their looting of houses along Pennsylvania Avenue gave Dolly Madison time for packing and writing. All the while, American refugees were hurrying westward toward Maryland and jamming the single narrow bridge to the south and safety of Virginia. The Mansion slaves were sent along by Dolly, and the token guard of 100 soldiers assigned to the Mansion under Daniel Carroll had been fruitlessly summoned to the battlefield, as reinforcements.

Wednesday morn^g twelve o'clock

Dear Sister . . .

Since sunrise I have been turning my spyglass in every direction, with unwearied anxiety, hoping to discover the approach of my dear husband and his friends; but also, I can descry only groups of military wandering in all directions, as if there were a lack of arms or of spirit to fight for their own fireside . . .

Three o'clock.—Will you believe it, my sister? We have had a battle, or skirmish, near Bladensburg, and I am still here within sound of the cannon! Two messengers, covered with dust, come to bid me fly; but I wait for him . . .

At this late hour a wagon has been procured; I have had it filled with the plate and most valuable portable articles belonging to the house; whether it will reach its destination, the Bank of Maryland, or fall into the hands of British soldiers, events must determine.

Our kind friend, Mr. Carroll, has come to hasten my departure, and is in a very bad humor with me because I insist on waiting until the large picture of George Washington is secured, and it requires to be unscrewed from the wall. This process was found to be too tedious for these perilous moments; I have ordered the frame to be broken and the canvas taken out; it is done—and the previous portrait placed in the hands of two gentlemen from New York for safe keeping. And now, dear sister, I must leave this house, or the retreating army will make me a prisoner in it, by filling up the road I am directed to take. When I shall again write to you, or where I shall be tomorrow, I cannot tell!!

The sequel:

Dolly Madison's later journals tell us that, as she rode unescorted, with the White House treasures and records, a coachman did get her safely across the Georgetown bridge to Virginia, where President Madison joined her in Alexandria, two days later.

The "gentlemen from New York" saved the "large picture of General Washington" (the famous Lansdowne by Stuart), which today hangs in a place of honor in the White House.

British soldiers ate and drank the ample supplies kept in the Mansion by Dolly, and then set the house afire, along with the French furniture and yellow damask hangings, all so recently installed by Dolly, herself.

LITTLE PRINCE

". . . as you are our friend and father . . ."

WHEN General Andrew Jackson invaded Florida in 1818 in his campaign against the Seminole Indians, one of his loyal followers was Little Prince, a minor chieftain among the Indians in what is now Alabama.

Little Prince returned to find that undisciplined soldiers had attacked and burned the village of Chehaw, killing several of the inhabitants, including the aged chief, who was called "Major Howard."

Little Prince thereupon wrote a letter to the Indian Agent, General Mitchell, who sent the letter to General Jackson.

My Great Friend:

I have got now a talk to send to you. One of our friendly towns, by the name of Chehaw, has been destroyed. The white people came and killed one of the head men and five men, and a woman, and burnt all their houses. All our young men have gone to war with General Jackson, and there is only a few left to guard the town, and they have come and served us this way. As you are our friend and father, I hope you will try and find out, and get us satisfaction for it. You may depend upon it that all our young men have gone to war but a few that are left to guard the town. Men do not get up and do this mischief without there is someone at the head of it, and we want you to try and find them out.

The sequel:

On hearing of the massacre, General Jackson—always a just man—was filled with anger. He had Captain Wright, the officer in charge of the men who had attacked Little Prince's village, put in irons to await a decision on the case by President Monroe himself.

Eventually, Captain Wright was tried and, in effect, acquitted, but indemnity of $8,000 was paid to the Chehaw Indians.

THOMAS JEFFERSON

*". . . too feeble indeed to walk much, but riding
without fatigue 6 or 8 miles a day, and sometimes
30 or 40."*

IN the spring of 1819, Thomas Jefferson was rounding out the 75th year of his life, a sturdy age in any epoch, but markedly venerable for his generation.

To him was addressed a clinical inquiry from a physician, Dr. Vine Utley, as to his health and habits.

The Sage of Monticello sat down and wrote a frank reply concerning his energies and habits, adding a postscript requesting that the letter not be made public. It was not made public for many years, eventually ending up in the Library of Congress.

Monticello Mar. 21, 1819

Sir:

Your letter of Feb. 18. came to hand on the 1st. instant; and the request of the history of my physical habits would have puzzled me not a little, had it not been for the model, with which you accompanied it, of Dr. Rush's answer to a similar enquiry. I live so much like other people, that I might refer to ordinary life as the history of my own. like my friend the Doctor, I have lived temperately, eating little animal food, & that, not as an ailment so much as a condiment for the vegetables, which constitute my principal diet. I double however the doctor's glass and a half of wine, and even treble it with a friend; but halve it's effect by drinking the weak wines only. the ardent wines I cannot drink, nor do I use ardent spirits in any form. malt liquore & cyder are my table drinks, and my breakfast, like that also of my friend, is of tea & coffee. I have been blest with organs of digestion which accept and concoct, without ever murmuring whatever the palate chuses to consign to them, and I have not yet lost a tooth by age. I was a hard student until I entered on the business of life, the duties of which leave no idle time to those disposed to fulfill them; & now, retired, and at the age of 76, I am again a hard student. indeed my fondness for reading and study revolts me from the drudgery of letter writing, and a stiff wrist, the consequence of an early dislocation, makes writing both slow and painful. I am not so regular in my sleep as the Doctor says he was, devoting to it from 5. to 8. hours, according as my company or the book I am reading interests me; and I never go to bed without an hour, or half hour's previous reading of something moral, whereon to ruminate in the intervals of sleep. but whether I retire to bed early or late, I rise with the sun. I use spectacles at night, but not necessarily in the day, unles in reading small print. my hearing is distinct in particular conversation, but confused when several voices cross each other, which unfits me for the society of the table. I have been more fortunate than my friend in the article of health. so free from catarrhs that I have not had one, (in the breast, I mean) on an average of 8. or 10. years thro' life. I ascribe this exemption partly to the habit of bathing my feet in cold water every morning for 60. years past. a fever of more than 24. hours I have not had abot 2. or 3. times in my life. a periodical head ach has afflicted me occasionally, once perhaps in 6. or 8. years, for 2 or 3 weeks at a time, which seems now to have left me; and, except on a late occasion of indisposition, I enjoy good health; too feeble indeed to walk much, but riding without fatigue 6 or 8 miles a day, and sometimes 30. or 40. I may end these egotisms therefore, as I began, by saying that my life has been so much like that of other people, that I might say, with Horace, to every one, 'Nomine mutato, narratur fabula de te.' I must not end however without due thanks for the kind sentiments of regards you are so good as to express towards myself, and, with my acknolegements for these, be pleased to accept the assurance of my respect and esteem.

Th: Jefferson

P.S. a great unwillingness to be obtruded on the public notice on any occasion, but especially on one so little worthy of it, induces me to request that this letter may not be permitted to find it's way into the public papers. Doctr. Vine Utley

The sequel:

This was no dying testament, as Jefferson lived another seven vigorous years among his books, agricultural projects and not-inconsiderable family, at Monticello.

FREDERICK BUSH

"*. . . you have discovered . . . Palmers land.*"

IN 1820, a 21-year-old Yankee captain, commanding the tiny sloop *Hero,* sailed blindly into the mists of the South Atlantic to a point more than 800 miles south of the tip of South America—in a discouraging quest for seals. However he found land never before seen by man, and thereby started an international controversy not yet concluded, over rights in Antarctica.

The youth, Nathaniel B. Palmer, out of Stonington, Connecticut, first became aware of his find when he was intercepted by a unit of the Russian Navy later on the same voyage. Of all the accounts of his discovery, one of the most engaging was written years later in a letter by Hon. Frederick Bush, for many years United States consul at Hong Kong. An abstract of Bush's letter was published in 1882.

It was at the time of his (Palmer's) second voyage to China. He was in a Clipper Ship the "Houqua." A vessel of his own designing and owned by A. A. Lou and Brothers and himself. He was my guest at dinner in Hong Kong, and after much persuasion I heard him repeat to Admiral Sir John Francis Austin (to whom he was presented by myself as the discoverer of "Palmers Land," the southern point of the globe) the following. I pass over his account of the voyage of the Hero to the South Shetland, the scarcity of seals there and his determination to seek better hunting grounds, but I can never forget the enthusiasm he manifested when he said:

"I pointed the bow of the little craft to the southward with her wings spread, mainsail abeam and jib abreast the opposite bow. She speeded on her way to new sealing grounds until she brought us in sight of land not laid down on my chart. I cruised for several days in order to satisfy myself it was not an island. I ran into several bays without meeting with any seal, and headed northward, drifting along under easy canvas, laying to at night which consumed the majority of the day, most of the time the mist so dense I could not see the lookout on the forecastle.

"One night I came on deck at midnight, relieved my mate and took the watch. I struck one bell which brought a response that startled me but I soon resumed my pace, turned my thoughts homeward and applied myself to the occupation of building castles in the air till the binnacle time keeper told the first hour of the day. I struck two bells, that were answered by a human hand, though I could not credit my ears, and thought I was dreaming except for the screeching of the 'Penguins,' 'Albatross' and 'Mosher Carp.' I was sure there was no living object within leagues of the sloop. But the sound of the bells continued until the sun lifted the fog. My chief officer, who laughed at the idea of a human being close on board and said that sound was 'tricky,' called me at seven bells during his watch saying that voices were heard, and before the trencher board was laid the fog lifted, presenting to our view a Frigate on the starboard bow and a sloop of war on the lee quarter with Russian colors flying. Close alongside was a boat with an officer in full uniform who stepped into the waist of the sloop and gave me a message requesting that I would repair on board his ship. I assented, at once entered the boat laid alongside, mounted on deck, and, 'souwester' on my head, a sealskin coat and boots, I was ushered into the presence of the venerable commander who was sitting at the table in his cabin, himself and a group of officers in full dress.

"The gray headed mariner rose and took me by the hand, saying through the medium of his interpreter, 'You are welcome, young man, be seated.' He placed a chair by his side and put the following questions to me:

" 'What is your name?'

"Nathaniel B. Palmer.

" 'Where are you from?'

"Stonington, Connecticut, U.S.A.

" 'The name of your boat?'

"Hero, sir.

" 'What are you doing here?'

"On a sealing expedition.

" 'What success?'

"I gave him an account of my voyage, tonnage of sloop, number of men and general details, when he said, 'How far south have you been?' I gave him the latitude and longitude of my lowest point, and told him what I had discovered. He rose much agitated, begging that I would produce my Log Book and Chart, with which request I complied, and a boat was sent for it. In the meantime luncheon was served, many questions put concerning the seal fishing, population of my sailing port, etc. When the Log Book and Chart were laid on the table he examined them carefully without comment, then rose from his seat saying, 'What do I see and what do I hear from a boy in his teens, that he is commander of a tiny boat of the size of a launch of my frigate, has pushed his way to the pole through storm and ice and sought the point I, in command of one of the best appointed fleets at the disposal of my august master, have for three long weary anxious years sought day and night for.'

"With his hand on my head he added, 'What shall I say to my master? What will he think of me? But be that as it may, my grief is your joy. Wear your laurels with my sincere prayers for your welfare. I name the land you have discovered, in honor of yourself, noble boy, Palmers Land.' "

And to my old and loved friend (Bush continued) is due the honor of this discovery though England, I am sorry to say, through one of her naval officers attempted to steal the thunder, which Admiral Austin assured Captain Palmer that he would endeavor to correct and give to him the proper credit.

The sequel:

Captain Palmer got the proper credit at home, but England never retreated from its own claim, today still calling the area "Graham Land." As later exploration has revealed, Palmer Land is actually a peninsula of the Antarctic Continent, and Palmer had not reached the South Pole. But his fame is secure, although his discovery was perhaps less important than his

great contributions to the design of the famous American Clipper Ships. He followed the New England pattern of long-life, living until 1877.

WILLIAM CULLEN BRYANT

". . . I am married in spite of myself."

BRYANT is a famous poet, his name inseparably linked with *Thanatopsis*. He is also remembered as a famous editor of the old New York Evening Post.

His personality was marked by a sweetness of character (so ap-

propriately delineated in the bronze statue overlooking the small park behind the New York City Public Library, named in his honor), which is apparent in the following letter:

June, 1821

Dear Mother: I hasten to send you the melancholy intelligence of what has lately happened to me.

Early on the evening of the eleventh day of the present month I was at a neighboring house in this village. Several people of both sexes were assembled in one of the apartments, and three or four others, with myself, were in another. At last came in a little elderly gentleman, pale, thin, with a solemn countenance, hooked nose, and hollow eyes. It was not long before we were summoned to attend in the apartment where he and the rest of the company were gathered. We went in and took our seats; the little elderly gentleman with the hooked nose prayed, and we all stood up. When he had finished, most of us sat down. The gentleman with the hooked nose then muttered certain cabalistical expressions which I was too much frightened to remember, but I recollect that at the conclusion I was given to understand that I was married to a young lady of the name of Frances Fairchild, whom I perceived standing by my side, and I hope in the course of a few months to have the pleasure of introducing to you as your daughter-in-law, which is a matter of some interest to the poor girl, who has neither father nor mother in the world . . .

I looked only for goodness of heart, an ingenuous and affectionate disposition, a good understanding, etc., and the character of my wife is too frank and single-hearted to suffer me to fear that I may be disappointed. I do myself wrong; I did not look for these nor any other qualities, but they trapped me before I was aware, and now I am married in spite of myself.

Thus the current of destiny carries us along. None but a madman would swim against the stream, and none but a fool would exert himself to swim with it. The best way is to float quietly with the tide . . .

Your affectionate son,
William

WILLIAM WIRT

". . . the arduous steep which leads to the Temple of the Goddess . . ."

A self-educated lawyer, biographer and novelist, William Wirt received extraordinary publicity in 1807, at the age of 35, when he was chosen to prosecute Aaron Burr, on trial for treason.

As Attorney General, he started the practice of publishing his legal presentations for reference as precedents, and, in a day when law was a profession learned by selected youths in the offices of lawyers, he devised perhaps the first coordinated program for pursuing the study of law.

Fortunately, he was a fluent letter writer and we thus have a clear indication of his rules of study (not unlike the curricula in modern law schools), set forth with the same attention to correct detail that marked his letter on wifehood, written seventeen years earlier to his niece and ward.

Washington, July 22, 1822

Sir:

I regret extremely that I have to answer your very polite and obliging letter of the 3rd. inst. currente calamo–It arrived while I was absent on a professional tour–and I have returned early in time to equip myself for an expedition to the Bedford Springs in Penn. rendered necessary by the state of my health.

It is not entirely certain whether I shall myself be a resident of this place at the close of the next winter, the earliest period at which you speak of being here. I have some thought of moving to Baltimore before that time. In this uncertainty I can only say that if I should be here and your inclination hold, I shall be very willing to receive you as a student and to spirit you with my opinion in the direction of your studies.

The plan of study which I have used has depended on the time which the student proposes to devote to it. In every plan, however, Blackstone is the best introductory author as opening to the student all the original sources of his science besides giving him a clear and comprehensive view of its present state. In all studies historical, political or an other dependent for their perfection on the march of mind a synopsis like that of Blackstone is of great value. Geography, for example, is best taught by stamping, in the first place, on the mind the great outlines of the different countries and their relative position toward each other—the details are afterward, encountered with more intelligence and consequently with more enjoyment—for the student, at every step, knows, afterwards, of his whereabout with relation to the whole; and is in no danger of being bewildered or confounded by the apprehension of interminable labor or inextricable labyrinths —as it is with the law—Blackstone, therefore, thoroughly understood . . . I direct the attention of students in the next place to the great sources from which all the laws of civilized countries are derived; and take them through the following course which is enlarged or contracted in proportion to the time they have to bestow.......1. The law of nature and nations . . . 2. The Roman civil law . . . and, if time, the references in the Corpus Iuris Civilis, . . . 3. The Common Law . . . 4. The Statute Law of State Decisions of the residence & contemplated place of practice of the student. This course, particularly the latter part of it, should be combined with a regular attendance on the rules of court in some well-kept clerk's office, with the advantage of having declarations and pleadings in the office of some regular and extensive practitioner—with the study of Chitty's Pleadings . . .

I have said nothing of historical studies—belles-lettres—composition—reciting passages from poets and debating; though I deem them all essential in the preparation of an accomplished advocate. Regular days should be set for composition and the compositions should be submitted to the best critic of whom you can make a friend—You should inflame your emulation by the frequent study of Cicero's Orator and of his Brutus, above all, and imagine yourself to belong to that splendid galaxy of Roman Orators which he there displays. Quintilian's Institutes, too, should be thoroughly studied and the dialogue . . . the letters of Pliny the younger, especially those to Tacitus—with the orations of Demosthenes, Cicero . . . and Ld. Chatham—I do not mean that these should be read merely but that they should be studied and analized . . . Then exercises with a debating society under the direction of an experienced man of vigorous intellect and correct taste, accompanying your law course, will diversify your employments most agreeably and usefully and recreate and cheer you on your ascent up the arduous steep which leads to the Temple of the Goddess, you so properly worship.

I beg you to excuse this scroll, the effect of haste, and believe me with the warmest wishes for your success.

Your obed. serv.
Wm. Wirt

HENRY CLAY

". . . Gen¹ Jackson could not be elected . . ."

IN 1824, such a large number of men received electoral votes for the Presidency that none had a majority and—as the Constitution provides—selection became the responsibility of the House of Representatives.

Henry Clay, a Congressman, was one of the contenders and ran fourth. Among the leaders were John Quincy Adams and Andrew Jackson. Since he was out of the running, Clay, as a Congressman, was in a position to cast a vote for one of his rivals.

Jackson counted on the support of his fellow westerner, but Clay threw his vote and his support to Adams, a move instrumental in Jackson's defeat. Soon thereafter, he resigned to become Adams' Secretary of State, occasioning charges of collusion, which muddied the waters of many political debates in succeeding years.

In later years there came to light a letter by Clay, written to a friend already working for his election, that throws unique light on Clay's coldly political mind and helps to round out the portrait of this enigmatic man.

Wash^n. 7th Jan 24

Dr Sir

I duly received your favor of the 12th . . . from N. Orleans and hope this letter will find you arrived at Ashland. I wrote you a few days ago. Nothing new has since occurred. I am satisfied that the entire recovery and preservation of my health is in my power, if I can take the necessary exercise, and particularly on horseback—This I endeavor to do, whenever the weather admits of it.

My election to the Presidency I think is certain, if I can be made one of the three highest, from among whom the H. of R. will undoubtedly, from present appearances, have to make the selection. Mine would in that event be certain, whilst I think it equally certain that Genl Jackson could not be elected, if he should even be one of the three highest. He will probably obtain the vote of Alabama, and I think of Mississippi also. I sometimes fear that he will take Louisiana from me. If I get Ohio, Kentucky, Louisiana, Indiana, Illinois and Missouri, I think with my prospects on this side of the Mountains I shall be made one of the three highest. I do not believe that the chance of my getting New York is surpassed by that of any other Candidate. I may say that I shall certainly receive two votes, probably more, in Maryland. I have good prospects in Penns². in New Jersey and in S°. Carolina. If Crawford, Adams and I should be the three highest, it continues to be generally thought that my election in the H. of R. is secure.

Mr. Crawford's health is now better. That of your father is good.

Give my love to Anne and believe me

Affectionately Yours
H. Clay

Mr. James Erwin

HENRY WADSWORTH LONGFELLOW

". . . I will be eminent in something."

A schoolboy letter written by Longfellow, at the age of 17, might well make us grateful that he did not decide to become a dictator or other type of predator. For even at that age he was unusually determined to reach the top in whatever endeavor he should enter.

He was, fortunately, determined to become an author, and unlike millions of undergraduates who each year still nurture the same ambition, he succeeded with a vengeance.

He wanted desperately to spend a year at Cambridge, and so wrote his parents in 1826, winning his point with the following arguments:

Somehow, and yet I hardly know why, I am unwilling to study a profession. I cannot make a lawyer of any eminence, because I have not the talent for argument; I am not good enough for a minister,—and as to Physic, I utterly and absolutely detest it.

. . . I have already hinted to you what would best please me. I want to spend one year at Cambridge for the purpose of reading history, and of becoming familiar with the best authors in polite literature; whilst at the same time I can be acquiring the Italian language, without an acquaintance with which I shall be shut out from one of the most beautiful departments of letters . . . The fact is—and I will not disguise it in the least, for I think I ought not—the fact is, I most eagerly aspire after future eminence in literature; my whole soul burns most ardently for it, and every earthly thought enters in it . . . Whether Nature has given me any capacity for knowledge or not, she has at any rate given me a very strong predilection for literary pursuits, and I am almost confident in believing that, if I can ever rise in the world, it must be by the exercise of my talent in the wide field of literature . . . With such a belief I must say that I am unwilling to engage in the study of law . . . Whatever I do study ought to be engaged in with all my soul,–for I WILL BE EMINENT in something . . . Let me reside one year at Cambridge; let me study belles-lettres; and after that time it will not require a spirit of prophecy to predict with some degree of certainty what kind of a figure I could make in the literary world. If I fail there, there is still time left for the study of a profession . . .

MARQUIS DE LAFAYETTE

"The magnificent problem of liberty has been solved . . ."

IN 1777, a 20-year-old French nobleman left his then-neutral homeland in order to join the American Revolution. He became, in a single year, a commander of a division of troops and a wounded casualty of the Battle of Brandywine. When the war ended, he was one of the great heroes of the American people, a famous soldier and an emissary of the Colonies to his own government when it swung around to active support of the war.

This, in brief, was the American career of Lafayette, whose long lifetime saw him participating in two revolutions in his own country, in roles ranging from national hero to imprisoned "rebel," and whose death, in 1834, would be observed finally as the death of a hero.

He was the only citizen of a foreign country granted honorary American citizenship, for himself and his descendants, who now are known as the Chambrun family.

In 1824–25, Lafayette paid a long visit to the United States to reacquaint himself with the country to which he had given his youth. He stayed a year, visiting all of the twenty-four States. On his return to France, he wrote a letter to an unidentified general in the United States, in which he summed up his impressions.

LaGrange, January 6, 1826

Will you pardon me, my dear General, for having been so tardy in offering to you this expression of my gratitude and my affection? I have much need for the indulgence of my friends, and yet if they could realize what a mass of letters I brought back from the United States, how many I have received here as well as how many visits and what anguish I have suffered for one of my granddaughters who happily has not succumbed to her illness, they would find me not as blameworthy as I seem. I have been particularly sensible of the evidence of your esteem and your friendship, my dear General.

It was really a happy voyage on which you compliment me in such a cordial manner. The courtesies which were heaped upon me were such as to afford me continued feelings of pleasure. But I have had even greater ones, if that were possible, in beholding the twenty-four federated republics and the government of the Union raised to a degree of prosperity that surpasses by far all that my imagination, prejudiced as it was in favor of the United States, could ever have foreseen. The magnificent problem of liberty has been solved, demonstrated, and practiced in such a manner as not to leave much to be said by the defenders of the European institutions.

In a few days I am going to Paris until the beginning of Spring. I shall return here as soon as I can. Here and there we are neighbors. I am desirous of profiting from this by having the pleasure of embracing you and in the meantime I beg you to accept my appreciation, my wishes for a happy New Year, and expression of my most sincere friendship.

Lafayette

P.S. You have doubtless missed the excellent General Foy. It is a great loss for France and for his personal friends.

The sequel:

Lafayette has become a legend; a symbol of the great sacrifices made by men of ideals in the cause of the American Revolution. In 1917, when General John J. Pershing took a small staff to France as a symbol of the great armies being prepared by the United States to help win victory in World War I, he visited Lafayette's tomb, to lay a wreath and say the simple words "Lafayette, we are here."

Twenty-eight years later, in the disillusioning days of 1945, toward the end of World War II, Carl I. Wheat had a limited edition of this letter specially printed for distribution to leading Americans, because the expressed sentiments are "good and appropriate in these maelstrom days."

NATHANIEL PARKER WILLIS

*"Mrs. Trollope quite extinguished the trade in
spit-boxes . . ."*

IN 1829, a tall, handsome, slightly over-dressed dandy, fresh from Yale University (which he attended despite his Boston nativity) descended on New York with the intention of living the elegant life and finding a means to support himself in it.

Unlike his fellow New Englanders, William Cullen Bryant and James Fenimore Cooper, who wrote their versions of the glories of the new country, Nathaniel Parker Willis was a chronicler of manners and customs—a forerunner of the "society commentators" of modern journalism.

In fairness, it must be noted that what Willis set out to do, he did with outstanding success. Through the fluff of his writings there runs a solid core of human documentation of the period, written with a sharp and witty pen.

Soon after reaching New York, Willis convinced George P. Morris, owner of the *New York Mirror*, that his talents deserved a roving European assignment. From that day, his vocation was the writing of commentaries on current life, particularly the preoccupation of the "ladies" of the period with improving their manners, their homes, and society. On this subject, Willis wrote pithily in a letter from his collection entitled *Letters from Under a Bridge*.

New York

I venture to say that a young lady could scarcely be found in the United States, who would not give you on demand a complete list of our national faults and foibles, as recorded by Hall, Hamilton, Trollope and Martineau. Why, they form the common staple of conversation! Hamilton's book was scarcely dry from the press before orders were made out to an immense extent for egg-cups and silver forks. Mrs. Trollope quite extinguished the trade in spit-boxes and made fortunes for the fingerglass manufacturers; and Captain Marryat, I understand, is besieged in every city by the importers, to know upon what deficiency of table furniture he intends to be severe.

ELLEN BIGELOW

". . . which, considering . . . may be set down as a very good trip."

AN air flight from Buffalo, N.Y., to Chicago, Ill., is now little more than a commuting hop; the trip by car is an easy day's drive.

In 1835, Miss Ellen Bigelow, a woman well-equipped with health, a sense of humor and graphic powers of description, wrote to an aunt describing this trip, made in fourteen days by water (with an additional two required simply to clear the harbor at Buffalo), as "a very good trip."

For those of us who now complain about the length of winter, we add that on leaving Buffalo early in May, the flotilla of assembled ships had to wait for ice on the lake to thaw, so they could smash their way through it on departure.

Chicago, Ill., June 27, 1835

At sunrise, Saturday, May 2nd, we entered Buffalo, and to our dismay, the lake was covered as far as the eye could see with solid ice. By the advice of Mr. L., we went to the "Mansion House," where Dr. Harding left us and sallied forth to determine what could be done. He returned with the news that he had secured a passage for us on board the Brig Illinois, Captain Wagstaff, which would be the first vessel out of port, and that we must establish ourselves on board in the afternoon . . .

The Illinois is the largest vessel on the lake . . . Freight was taken to the extent of what she would bear, consequently the deck was so crowded with bags, boxes and barrels of every description, that no rest could be found even for the sole of a foot. The cabin, if possible, was more disagreeable still. We were gathered together from every quarter of the earth, men, women and children, talking, laughing, crying, screaming and scolding. Such a bedlam I am sure was never seen before. Persons applied for passage till the cabins and staterooms were completely filled, and room was then made among the freight in the hold, where about 30 people were stowed away . . . Our vessel lay at the wharf for days from the time we entered it, and a more hateful scrape I never got into . . .

Several steamboats were injured in the fruitless attempt to get through the ice. The Ohio tried it, broke both paddles and so damaged her engine that three days were required to repair it. The second effort was more successful. A channel was formed through which the vessels could pass. The steamers Thomas Jeffererson, Ohio, Gov. Marcy and Charles Townsend, brigs Illinois and Indiana, schooners Huron, Michigan and Barker immediately hoisted sail, and Friday, May 8th, with a strong northeasterly wind we left Buffalo. Our brig was a first-rate sailor. She dashed gallantly through the ice, cleared it all before her, passed every vessel, and in one hour's time was fairly upon the broad bosom of the lake. The wind continued steady and the water smooth, till Saturday morning, when it commenced blowing very severely. The sea ran high and the vessel pitched and tossed incessantly. The consequence was, of course, that we were all dreadfully seasick. Captain Wagstaff persuaded us to leave our berths and go on deck, in the hope that the air would relieve us. About a dozen others were our companions in misery, and the different positions chosen with the peculiar expression which distinguished each face would have been a grand study for a painter.

We stayed on deck till it began to storm violently, when we retreated to our berths. Dr. H. had as much as he could do to go from one patient to another, administering ether, laudanum and divers other specifics for seasickness. Towards night, the wind lulled a little and we were all flattering ourselves with the hope of rest, when about 10 o'clock to our great horror, the vessel struck a rock. Great alarm was excited, but the waves were running high and soon took us off. All betook ourselves again to our beds, and save myself, were soon soundly sleeping. A fit of foreboding would not suffer me to close my eyes. My fears were shortly realized. About 12 o'clock all were awakened by a loud shout from the cook that we were going to the bottom, and sure enough, there was little doubt of it, for one moment sufficed to convince us that we were already there. The vessel had grounded upon a rocky shoal and every wave made her quiver and shake like one with the ague. We remained there about an hour, and an hour of greater confusion and fright I never passed.

The cabin was crowded with half dressed beings of every size, sex and color. Deputations were dispatched every few minutes to ascertain the state of things, but very little comfort could be obtained from their contradictory reports.

Thus we sat in fear and trembling till the deck load was thrown overboard, when the cheerful voice of an old Irish sailor apprized us that the vessel was off. Had the brig been an old one, she must have received much injury from the strain to which she was exposed, but being entirely new, the damage sustained was only a splintering of the keel beneath her bows. The accident resulted from no want of skill in our captain, who was a most perfect master of his profession . . .

We reached Detroit Monday, and found it more of a place than I expected. We were obliged to anchor 20 miles from Detroit, as we were in the neighborhood of the flats, which could be passed only by daylight. The only channel through which a vessel could be passed was so narrow that it is requisite to point it out by stakes, and as its location varies with change of seasons, it is necessary that they should be often moved. This duty it seems was neglected by the revenue officers, and by following the channel of a former season, we were soon brought hard aground.

The schooner Michigan directly in our wake, went to windward of us, and stuck fast alongside, a circumstance at which we all rejoiced, wicked though it might be. We were less lonely in consequence of it than we should otherwise have been, and beside that our captain had laid a wager with the master of the Michigan that he would be in Chicago first, and we were all anxious he should win.

Much labor was required to heave the vessel off, by carrying out the anchor, but as all finite things have an end, it was at last accomplished.

We had hardly proceeded a mile before we were in the same scrape again, and by the time we had extricated ourselves, the wind had died away and we were obliged to anchor.

Setting sail the next day, the vessel had proceeded a few miles, when a sudden blow of wind took the sail flat aback, whirled her off her course, and we were fast aground again . . .

At the mouth of the River St. Claire, is the entrance to Lake Huron. The waters of Superior, Michigan and Huron have here their outlet, less than half a mile in width, and the current is consequently very rapid, seven and a half miles an hour. Very few vessels can pass without the aid of a steamboat unless they have a strong breeze. We had just given up all of hopes of proceeding when a steamboat hove in sight, which proved to be the General Gratiot, coming out expressly to tow us up the Rapids. We were immediately lashed to their side, and the brig Indiana, with which we were in company, mate and exact counterpart of our vessel, was lashed to the other side. A wind very opportunely sprung up to aid us on the way, and we passed Fort Gratiot with all sails set and flying colors in compliment to the troops paraded in front of the barracks. Both vessels carried an unusual quantity of canvas in proportion to their burden, and filled as it was in addition to the steamboat, we stemmed the current most bravely and were soon separated from the General Gratiot and alone upon Lake Huron . . .

We went speedily and prosperously through the Straits of Mackinaw, down Lake Michigan and anchored at Chicago Friday afternoon, May 24th, just 14 days from the time we left Buffalo, which, considering the divers perils we encountered and the delay occasioned by getting aground upon the flats, foul winds, etc., may be set down as a very good trip.

ABRAHAM LINCOLN

". . . you choose to wound my feelings . . ."

FROM the age of 31 to the age of 37, Abraham Lincoln lived in Salem, Illinois, and came close to making a record as a "dismal failure." One of the many jobs he held in that period was that of postmaster.

Even in a small town this was a demanding job, particularly in the bookkeeping, as prepayment of letter mail by means of postage stamps was not yet the practice. On the other hand, newspapers were given preferential rates in consideration of prepayment of postage on them.

In an undated letter, from the archives of the Post Office Department, Lincoln wryly discusses this aspect of his work with an apparently cautious customer.

Mr. Spears:

At your request I send to you a receipt for the postage on your paper. I am somewhat surprised at your request. I will, however, comply with it. The law requires newspaper postage to be paid in advance, and now that I have waited a full year, you choose to wound my feelings by insinuating that unless you get a receipt, I will probably make you pay again.

Respectfully signed,
Abraham Lincoln
Postmaster
Salem, Illinois

JAMES BOWIE

"I wish to know if a truce . . ."

ON February 23, 1836, there began a relatively small engagement in the war between Mexico and Texas, as forces under General Santa Anna surrounded the Alamo, an adobe fortress held by a handful of volunteers led by James Bowie. There was some confusion as to whether the engagement might not be concluded with a parley, but exchanges of gunfire upset this hope during the day.

Knowing the overwhelming odds against his small troop (grandly entitled the "Volunteers of Bejar") Bowie took a roughly torn sheet of coarse paper and wrote a note that is one of history's most poignant and brave mementos.

Commander of the
Army of Texas

With regard to have fired a cannon shot from this fortress at the time of raising a red flag over the tower, and soon thereafter I was informed that from your Army there had sounded a call for a flag of truce, which was not heard before the firing of the said shot, I wish to know if a truce actually has been asked for, for which reason I send my second Adjutant Benito Jameson, under the guarantee of a white flag, which I believe will be respected by you and your forces.

Texas,

God and
Fortress of the Alamo February 23, 1836

(sd) James Bowie
Commander of the Volunteers of Bejar

To the Commander of
the invading forces
upon Bejar.

The sequel:

No truce could be arranged. On March 6, 1836, the starved and parched little troup under Bowie, and including W. B. Travis and David Crockett, was overwhelmed by the Mexicans and massacred.

WILLIAM B. TRAVIS

"Victory or Death!"

WHILE Bowie was sending his desperate message out of the Alamo, to learn if a truce could be arranged, Lieutenant Colonel William B. Travis, acting Commander of the Fort and therefore senior to Bowie, sent out, on the same day, an appeal for help, which by its brevity and method of address, underscored the doomed outlook of the 150 men bottled up there.

Andrew Ponton, Judge
Gonzales
To Any of the Inhabitants, Texas

Commandancy of Bejar ⎱ 1836
Feb. 23rd 3'o'clock P.M. ⎰

To Andrew Ponton Judge & to the Citizens of Gonzales—

The enemy in large force is in sight—we want men and provisions—send them to us—we have 150 men & are determined to defend the Alamo to the last.

Give us assistance—

W. B. Travis
Lt. Col. Comdg.

P.S. Send an express to San Felipe with news night & day—

Travis

Two other letters by Travis emphasize the deeply human reactions of the men in the Alamo. They naturally felt great fear, knowing the odds against them, but they were determined to defend their beliefs, to die for them, if necessary.

On the day after his brief, desperate appeal, Travis wrote a more coherent letter, addressing it to "All Americans in the World."

To the People in Texas, and All Americans in the World:
Comandancy of the Alamo, Bejar, Feb. 24, 1836
Fellow-Citizens and Compatriots:
I am besieged by a thousand or more of the Mexicans, under Santa Anna. I have sustained a continual bombardment and cannonade for twenty-four hours, and have not lost a man. The enemy have demanded a surrender at discretion, otherwise the garrison is to be put to the sword, if the fort is taken. I have answered the summons with a cannon-shot, and our flag still waves proudly from our walls. I shall never surrender or retreat: then I call on you, in the name of Liberty, of Patriotism, and of everything dear to the American character, to come to our aid with all despatch. The enemy are receiving reinforcements daily, and will no doubt increase to three or four thousand in four or five days. Though this call may be neglected, I am determined to sustain myself as long as possible, and die like a soldier who never forgets what is due to his own honour and that of his country. Victory or Death!

> W. Barrett Travis
> Lieutenant Colonel, Commanding

Seven more hectic days passed; days of continuous fighting and ceaseless vigilance. Some of the Texans were sent out as couriers and thereby escaped; others came in as reinforcements. The men could eat, as Travis reported, in a postscript to the last letter that they had found "eighty or ninety bushels" of corn, and they had "got into the walls twenty or thirty head of beeves."

They were, however, outnumbered a hundred to one; all that remained to be seen was when and if Santa Anna would decide to sacrifice a part of his army to overwhelm the Alamo.

This was the situation on March 3, 1836, when Travis—undoubtedly after conferences with Bowie and David Crockett—wrote the following, more in a spirit of jubilant sacrifice than in despondency.

To the President of the Convention
Comandancy of the Alamo, Bejar, March 3, 1836.

Sir:

. . . From the 25th to the present date, the enemy have kept up a bombardment from two howitzers . . . and a heavy cannonade from two long nine-pounders, mounted on a battery on the opposite side of the river, at the distance of four hundred yards from our walls. During this period, the enemy have been busily employed in encircling us with intrenched encampments on all sides . . . we have been so fortunate as not to lose a man from any cause, and we have killed many of the enemy. The spirits of my men are still high, although they have had much to depress them. We have contended for ten days against an enemy whose numbers are variously estimated at from fifteen hundred to six thousand men, with Gen. Ramirez Sezma and Col. Bartres, the aide-de-camp of Santa Anna, at their head. A report was circulated that Santa Anna himself was with the enemy, but I think it was false. A reinforcement of about one thousand men is now entering Bexar from the west, and I think it more than probable that Santa Anna is now in town, from the rejoicing we hear . . .

I look to the colonies alone for aid; unless it arrives soon I will have to fight the enemy on his own terms . . .

The power of Santa Anna is to be met here or in the colonies; we had better meet them here, than to suffer a war of desolation to rage in our settlements. A blood-red banner waves from the church of Bexar; and in the camp above us, in token that the war is one of vengeance against rebels; they have declared us as such, and demanded that we should surrender at discretion, or that this garrison will be put to the sword. Their threats have had no influence on me or my men, but to make all fight with desperation, and that high-souled courage which characterizes the patriot, who is willing to die in defence of his country's liberty and his own honour . . .

The bearer of this will give your honourable body, a statement more in detail, should he escape through the enemy's lines. God and Texas!—Victory or Death!!

Your obedient ser't.
W. Barrett Travis
Lieut. Col. Comm.

The sequel:

For God and Texas, every man within the Alamo fought to the last breath. On the morning of March 6, 1836, the Mexican forces stormed the Alamo. Travis died on the walls, encouraging his men until a second shot, following a first wound, felled him. Crockett, the famous hunter, and Bowie, were also found among the dead.

Texas' 25,000 American settlers finally won their independence, using the phrase "Remember the Alamo" as an inspirational watchword throughout the struggle.

WASHINGTON IRVING

". . . a time when you will meet your friends at dinner."

IN 1836, William Cullen Bryant returned from abroad and received an invitation to dinner.

New York, March 3, 1836

To William Cullen Bryant.

Dear Sir: Learning with pleasure your arrival in New York, and desiring to express our high sense of your literary merits and estimable character, we beg leave to congratulate you upon your safe return, and to request that you will name a time when you will meet your friends at dinner.

Very respectfully and sincerely, your obedient servants,

Washington Irving
F. G. Halleck
A. B. Durand
G. C. Verplanck
William Dunlap
Samuel F. B. Morse
Thatcher C. Payne
Robert Sedgwick

W. T. McCoun
Henry James Anderson
H. Inman
John W. Francis
Theodore S. Fay
George D. Strong
C. Fenno Hoffman
C. W. Lawrence
Prosper M. Wetmore
George P. Morris
Henry Ogden
Edward Sanford
Morgan L. Smith
J. C. Hart
J. K. Paulding

WILLIAM CULLEN BRYANT

". . . nothing to merit such a distinction."

THERE were many men in New York who would have given a fortune to win an invitation to dinner such as the one sent to Bryant. But the gentle poet was unlike most other men as indicated by his reply to the preceding dinner invitation.

New York, April 2, 1836

Gentlemen: It is unnecessary for me to say how much the honor you have done me has increased the pleasure of my return to my native land, and how high a value I place on such a testimony of kindness from hands like yours. I cannot but feel, however, that although it might be worthily conferred upon one whose literary labors had contributed to raise the reputation of his country, yet that I, who have passed the period of my absence only in observation and study, have done nothing to merit such a distinction. This alone would be a sufficient motive for me, even were there no others which I might mention, to decline your flattering invitation.

I am, gentlemen, with greatest consideration and regard,

Your obedient servant,
William C. Bryant

RICHARD RUSH

"The English are all mad about this royal young lady . . ."

BY 1837, most Americans, and not a few Britons, shared the feeling that the recent Kings of England had abused the crown almost to the point of deposition. In that year, the girl, Victoria, became Queen of England, and the western world watched with interest.

By chance, Richard Rush was then in London, as a personal representative of the President, negotiating United States acceptance of a $500,000 bequest, left by an eccentric Englishman named John Smithson (never known to have visited the United States). This bequest provided for an American museum, later to become the Smithsonian Institution.

London was not strange to Rush. At the age of 57 he had enjoyed a rich career, including the posts of Comptroller of the Treasury Department, acting Secretary of State and American Minister to London. Later in his life, he served as Attorney General and Minister to France, and helped to initiate the Monroe Doctrine.

Rush wrote a letter to his friend, Henry Dilworth, then Solicitor of the Treasury Department, relating the impact of the new Queen on English life and including some confidential thoughts about the Bank of the United States.

London November 11.1837

My dear sir:

Having put up the Court Journal for Mrs. Rush today I cannot refrain from doing the same for Mrs. Gilpin, and beg you to hand to her with my kind compliments and remembrances. It contains an account of Cinderella's visit to the City day before yesterday and the grand entertainment she had at Guildhall. I did not see the spectacle, but Ben did, that is the procession and pageant through the streets, he having a scintilla of claim, ex officio, to be there; and our friend the minister kindly took him in his carriage. The English are all mad about this royal young lady, and their very madness is perhaps insensibly infusing new life into their monarchy. Tens of thousands, and amongst them public men, grave-minded and almost half republican, who were getting a little ashamed to be talking of the "king their master" of late years, have no objection to calling a blooming young queen mistress, but on the contrary vie with one another in shouting it out, devotion to sex drowning every other feeling, or serving as a cover for this.

It was remarked by a foreign historian that the joy of the English at the return of Charles II was like a dog wagging his tail at the return of his master. This instinct in Englishmen towards their kings and queens, which had begun to abate somewhat under the dawnings of popular ascendancy since the passing of the reform bill, seems to have burst out afresh and is overflowing on all sides. O'Connell joins the chorus; he ventures to lead it. John Bull and the universal populace roar out their loyalty in notes that you might almost hear across the Atlantic. Do not be surprised if you find parliament dipping into the nations purse more deeply than for a century past to give brilliancy to the throne, now the magnet of all hearts by the romantic incident of so young a female sitting upon it, who anon is seen in her coach drawn not by white mice, but eight true horses, cream-coloured and harnassed with gold, and anon at the banquet table that glitters like the sun. How far the cause of reform will keep pace with this regenerated devotion to the throne among all classes in England, lies hidden in the future. Will this little fairy Queen, who now dazzles all eyes, come to such an end as Maria Antoinette? God forbid. Or will the people grow as submissive to her as to Elizabeth, and she, grown in years, and spoiled by power and pomp and adulation, come at last to rule as imperiously? The latter is scarcely to be looked in modern times, and the fate of Maria Antoinette seems an extreme case not likely to be re-enacted. Happy could there be a middle course for England under this new and virgin reign, like that which France called out for in 1830—a monarchy surrounded by republican institutions. But will this come to pass? The experiment will be an anxious one, and the result is uncertain. Nous verrons, nous verrons, as Mr. Randolph was fond of saying when I knew him here. The principle of popular reform and this enthusiasm for the throne and its magnificence, it must be confessed, do not mingle very well together. They are, in fact, antagonist principles, like our administration and the bank. One or the other must be driven out. We shall see which before long, perhaps at the approaching session of parliament.

And now of the bank, for which, chiefly, I take up the pen to you on this occasion. It is a subject far more important to us than a little English queen's visit to the local Mayor of London. The stationary embassy which this ambitious and encroaching corporation has now fairly established to represent its will and carry out its intentions in this great capital of the commercial world, in my humble opinion deserves notice. Our government having failed at the late special session of congress to carry the subtreasury plan in the house of Representatives, I dare mention to predict that the embassy in question is destined to give it much trouble in the future contests to be waged in congress, and out of it, between the rival powers of popular sovereignty and the sovereignty of banks. It will become a centre round which the great means which the bank of the United States has heretofore possessed here, will rally and act with increased effect. The bank will gain new confidence and strength with the English commercial public by the permanent presence in London of a well informed, well-endowed, envoy, known and domiciliated here, whose duty it will be to make the most on all occasions of the bank cause, not only in his own person but through the many who will gather round him and be ready and eager to serve him. The measure will give fresh encouragement to all the plans and hopes of the bank. Such a mission cannot fail to hold out patronage and welcome, not, it may be, by any proclamation in words but by what every body will understand as well, to all the element of hostility in this quarter to our government as now administered . . .

I have brought myself to believe that there are steps by which much of this injurious influence, for injurious I think it has been, might be counteracted, and that they are within the power of our government. I would add within its duty, if self-justice and self-protection be duties. You cannot, it is true, write a nation down in these ways, or circumvent it to its ruin; but you may go far towards impairing or even oversetting administrations, if the hostile agents be not watched and counteracted. I may on a future occasion state my further ideas should they seem to you worth following up and I be kept here long enough by the trust I have in hand, which however I must hope, and most anxiously, may not prove the case, my constant efforts being to make a speedy finish of it . . .

I do not write for print, of course, even should any thing I have said be worth it which I do not suppose. Your letter that Ben brought me has already drawn too much upon you in reply I fear; but well knowing the interruptions of official men in Washington, I have made you large returns for that valuable letter, and I touch a topick in this of no slight public importance unless I deceive myself. When the day comes for us to meet again, I will tell you in what way your letter proved specially valuable at the moment that it happened to reach me. I flatter myself that it was not useless in its operation on our public affairs.

With renewed compliments to Mrs. Gilpin with the Court Journal, I beg you my dear sir, to believe me with the most friendly esteem

Yours very sincerely
Richard Rush

H. D. Gilpin Esq.

Christopher Columbus—with six tat-
tooed New World Indians—was given
a magnificent reception at the Court
of Barcelona in February, 1493, for
his supposed discovery of a new route
to China and India. (Bettman Archive)

Captain John Smith, when he was
leader of the Jamestown colony.
(Bettman Archive)

The young author-patriot, Thomas Jefferson, drafting the Declaration of Independence. Painting by N. C. Wyeth © by Morrell Company. (Bettman Archive)

John Hancock, famous for putting his "John Hancock" so boldly on the Declaration of Independence. Painting by J. S. Copley. (Bettman Archive)

Benjamin Franklin, who wrote the famous letter of advice recommending old women rather than young women as mistresses, painted in his serene old age by Charles Wilson Peale. (Bettman Archive)

George Washington bids farewell to General Lafayette at Mt. Vernon, in 1784. From a lithograph by C. P. Tholey. (Bettman Archive)

The famous duel between Alexander Hamilton and Aaron Burr in 1804. (Bettman Archive)

James Bowie fires his last shots before death, as Santa Anna's troops overwhelm the Alamo. (Bettman Archive)

"We have met the Enemy and they are ours," wrote Commodore Perry, reporting the outcome of his famous battle with British naval forces on Lake Erie. Painting by J. W. Jarvis. (Bettman Archive)

Mrs. James (Dolly) Madison bore the trials of being First Lady during troubled times with courage and calm good humor, as shown by her letter describing her forced evacuation of the White House in 1814. (Library of Congress)

Brigham Young at the site of the Mormon settlement in Utah—the Great Salt Lake. (Bettman Archive)

Abraham Lincoln and Stephen Douglas in one of their famous debates (Bettman Archive)

A little girl visits Abraham Lincoln at his desk. (Bettman Archive)

William Cullen Bryant in his study. From a steel engraving. (Bettman Archive)

The only portrait ever painted of Henry David Thoreau, by his sister, Sophia. (Bettman Archive)

The "Sage of Concord," Ralph Waldo Emerson. From a photograph. (Bettman Archive)

The face of Emily Dickinson reflects the same beauty and perceptiveness as her poetry. (Bettman Archive)

P. T. Barnum, promoter of Tom Thumb and the Wild Man From Borneo, super-salesman of the circus, who said "there's one born every minute." (Wide World Photo)

"Go West Young Man" was the famous advice of Horace Greeley, here shown in an 1855 daguerreotype photograph. (Wide World Photo)

Thomas A. Edison and his first Ediphone. (Underwood and Underwood)

JAMES KENT

"My passion for reading . . . is unabated."

IN 1842, James Kent wrote in a firm, clear hand to his friend, Ambrose Spencer, who lived in Lyons, N.Y.; a long, chatty letter, wherein he recounted, among other things, that he was changing his church, that he had been bled "for the first time in my life," that his wife of 57 years was well, and that his country cottage outside New York City was well stocked and ready for summer occupancy.

There is no hint, in this letter, that its author was (on the first day of that year's spring) 79 years old, long since retired from New York's highest court and from Columbia College, where he had been the first professor of law. Nor does the letter indicate his authorship of the massive *Commentaries on the American Law,* a work which has given him a place in the history of law alongside William Blackstone of England, and Joseph Story of the United States.

New York March 21.1842

My Dear Friend

Since I wrote to you this last winter I have joined the Congregation of the Rev. Mr. Pine's Episcopal Church which is in the 4th avenue not far from my house & hired a Pew. My inducements were several (1) The Bleecker Street Presbyterian Church was near a mile off & too far for convenience to Mrs. Kent & me, & besides the Church is inextricably involved in debt & the Pew which I own there will be swept away in the pending Sale of the Church, & though the Church will be bought in by leading members of it for the debt, I should have to repurchase a Pew if I took any. (2) I have long had an unconquerable Distaste to the Presbyterian mode of Preaching. That of Dr. Phillips in the Wall Street Church & that of Dr. Mason in the Bleecker Street Church was constantly on dry, hard, metaphysical & scholastic Divinity, & which never did & never could suit my taste. (3) My Hearing is quite impaired. It was considerably so before

I left the Court of Chancery. I could not hear one fiftieth part of what was said in Prayer or in the Sermon, whereas in the Episcopal Church there is the excellent Liturgy & Litany which opens before me & I can join in their Prayers & Praises, & this after all is true real worship. (4) My family are all gone over to the Episcopal Church & left my dear wife & me quite alone in the old Church. My son & his wife go to Dr. Hawke's Church. My eldest Daughter Mrs. Kane who lives with me & her Husband prefer also the Episcopal mode of worship, & my youngest Daughter is the wife of the Rev. Dr. Stone of the Episcopal Church in S. Brooklyn, where they have built him a stone church equal to any in New York except the new Trinity which is rising up. All these Influences were not to be resisted.

Since January I was for a month quite diseased owing to a cortive state of the Bowels, owing probably to too much & too indiscriminate eating. I was afflicted with a dull, constant Pain which threatened constipation & Inflammation. It lasted for a month & dreadfully annoyed me before I called in medical aid, & I was bled, (for the first time in my life) blistered & scarred by Cathartics. It reduced my strength & flesh rapidly & greatly, but I got well & am now as well as ever, only not yet quite so strong, & it has led me to be more vigilant & wary as to what & as to how much I eat. I was always temperate in Drinking, though I am no Ultruist in anything, & keep aloof from all associations of that nature, be they what they may. My Passion for reading Literature & law & Politics & everything else that is instructive and amusing is unabated. I get hold of every law Report in the US. that I can & read it & make notes to be used in the 5th Edit. of my Commentaries if ever I should issue one. I believe I told you I have a Country Cottage of about 7 or 8 acres of Ground clinging to it 20 miles west of me, & there my Son's small family (for he has but one Son) & mine live together during the Summer. I have my ice House filled & the gardner engaged & the whole establishment is delightful. I keep there (but not in town) a C____ & Horse for family use.

Excuse me from talking so much about myself. It is the Inclination & Privilege of old age to dwell on such topics. The affairs of the world recede from the attention & gradually lose their hold on our Interest & feelings, & we are very apt to admire the past & condemn the present. However that may be, Politics do not now deeply interest me & I feel quite indifferent as to Elections. My beloved wife who has lived with me 57 years is in excellent Health & Spirits & walks about Town daily & almost daily visits the Brooklyn daughter who has two fine Boys. I have in the whole 4 grand Children. It is most pleasant to chat with an old Friend & my respect, Esteem & attachment to you are solid & several. Very-very few of my old Friends & contemporaries are left. My Friend Sylvannus Miller has been this winter breaking down in Health & my wife's Companion, the widow of General Bailey is in wretched Health. Indeed one half of my old acquaintance seem to be as poor in Property as in Health. I have great reason to be thankful to Divine Providence for the guardian Care & Blessings which have been thrown around me & my family.

> Adieu my dear sir
> & believe me   affecy yours
> JAMES KENT

Hon. Ambrose Spencer

The sequel:

While the aged jurist remarked on his difficulty in hearing, his vitality was such that he lived another five years after the writing of this delightful letter.

HENRY D. THOREAU

"The richest gifts . . . are the least marketable."

ONE day, in 1843, Thoreau sat down and wrote a letter to Ralph Waldo Emerson, who, although only 34 years old, was already a literary giant among giants. Thoreau had known Emerson for four years.

The years were yet to come in which Thoreau would retire to a hermit-like existence just to sit and think, at Walden Pond, on Emerson's own property. Still further in the future were his written works, and the many volumes of his diary.

This letter of Thoreau's is unique in that it asks nothing. It does not seek to force an idea on the recipient. It does not explain; it is simply a letter about the joy of living, as seen through the open eyes of an open mind.

Henry D. Thoreau to Ralph Waldo Emerson

February 12, 1843

Dear Friend,—As the packet still tarries, I will send you some thoughts, which I have lately relearned, as the latest public and private news.

How mean are our relations to one another! Let us pause till they are nobler. A little silence, a little rest, is good. It would be sufficient employment only to cultivate true ones.

The richest gifts we can bestow are the least marketable. We hate the kindness which we understand. A noble person confers no such gift as his whole confidence: none so exalts the giver and the receiver; it produces the truest gratitude. Perhaps it is only essential to friendship that some vital trust should have been reposed by the one in the other. I feel addressed and probed even to the remote parts of my being when one nobly shows, even in trivial things, an implicit faith in me. When such divine commodities are so near and cheap, how strange that it should have to be each day's discovery! A threat or a curse may be forgotten, but this mild trust translates me. I am no more of this earth; it acts dynamically; it changes my very substance. I cannot do what before I did. I cannot be what before I was. Other chains may be broken, but in the darkest night, in the remotest place, I trail this thread. Then things cannot happen. What if God were to confide in us for a moment! Should we not then be gods?

How subtle a thing is this confidence! Nothing sensible passes between; never any consequences are to be apprehended should it be misplaced. Yet something has transpired. A new behavior springs; the ship carries new ballast in her hold. A sufficiently great and generous trust could never be abused. It should be cause to lay down one's life,—which would not be to lose it. Can there be any mistake up there? Don't the gods know where to invest their wealth? Such confidence, too, would be reciprocal. When one confides greatly in you, he will feel the roots of an equal trust fastening themselves in him. When such trust has been received or reposed, we dare not speak, hardly to see each other; our voices sound harsh and untrustworthy. We are as instruments which the Powers have dealt with. Through what straits would we not carry this little burden of a magnanimous trust! Yet no harm could possibly come, but simply faithlessness. Not a feather, not a straw, is intrusted; that packet is empty. It is only committed to us, and, as it were, all things are committed to us.

The kindness I have longest remembered has been of this sort,– the sort unsaid; so far behind the speaker's lips that almost it already lay in my heart. It did not have far to go to be communicated. The gods cannot misunderstand, man cannot explain. We communicate like the burrows of foxes, in silence and darkness, under ground. We are undermined by faith and love. How much more full is Nature where we think the empty space is than where we place the solids!–full of fluid influences. Should we ever communicate but by these? The spirit abhors a vacuum more than Nature. There is a tide which pierces the pores of the air. These aerial rivers, let us not pollute their currents. What meadows do they course through? How many fine mails there are which traverse their routes! He is privileged who gets his letter franked by them.

I believe these things.

Henry D. Thoreau

The sequel:

In the world of literature today, Thoreau is rapidly becoming somewhat like the Declaration of Independence; everyone knows about him, but few read, and even fewer study, the intense depths of meaning in his child-of-nature expressions.

In 1854, he published *Walden*, seven years after his two-year retreat on the shores of that period. He died in 1862, aged 45.

WILLIAM STRICKLAND

"In this City of Magnificent Distances . . ."

WILLIAM STRICKLAND's reputation is equally divided between the heights he reached as the foremost architect of his period and the depths of his punning form of humor, which he cultivated throughout a long life.

Formally, he has the ponderous reputation of being America's second great professional architect, following in the footsteps of Benjamin Latrobe, under whom he studied and with whom he shares the credit for introducing the classic revival theme into American architecture. In 1836, he cooperated in founding, and became the first president of, the American Institute of Architecture.

By that year, his forty-fourth, he had completed the Bank of the United States (now the historical monument known as the Old Customhouse) in Philadelphia, originally designed by Latrobe before the latter died of yellow fever in New Orleans; had restored Independence Hall in 1828, and designed and built the Philadelphia Merchants' Exchange.

In 1844, Strickland went to Washington, in an unsuccessful effort to obtain the commission to build new headquarters for the Army and Navy. On that visit, he wrote a letter to John Struthers, a Philadelphia stone cutter, commenting acidly on Washington and coining a phrase that has lived ever since: changing Thomas Jefferson's description of Washington as a planned "City of Magnificent Vistas," to the more realistic "City of Magnificent Distances."

Fuller Hotel
Washington, Jan 11/44

Dear John,

I have been in Washington now nearly a week and have just entered into the threshold of my business—In this City of Magnificent Distances you can't find a man without a mile, and as Paddy would say, and then he is sure to be out.—Congress do not sit till 12 oClock everyday, and the Members do not dine till 6 or 7 oClock.—

President making is the order of the day and frolicking that of the night. The motto is every man for himself, and God for us all. —All the holes of office are stopped, in other words, John, there are a great many more pigs than teats. Tyler is between two stools and you know the rest.—But we Tyler men are to turn to Clay as sure as fate.

The Treasury is M.T. and the Committee of Ways and Means are hard at work to find out the way to create the almighty dollar. —I think that there is a chance of getting an appropriation for the War and Navy buildings, but this will not be until the close of the session, and yet it is necessary to talk, and coax and wheedle them into doing what is right and proper—Col. Abert is my friend here, and so is the Secʸ at War, and I can depend upon them I think in any emergency with reference to those buildings.

When Robt Tyler comes to town he has promised to fix up some office for me ad interim.—Tyson is also friendly, but here there is no such thing as getting an office, without cutting off some man's head, and that you know, John is a bloody business—

I have paid a visit to your friend Brown, who arrived here from Scotland last October.—He looks as fat as a whale, but complains of having nothing to do; but I believe John, he is pretty well off in this "worlds gear"—I do not think he has any influence with any of the members of Congress, the most of which are new hands. However he looks like a good fellow and he is disposed to befriend me.—He sends his best respects to you, and made many enquiries about your health and business—

Farewell! and believe me to be

Yours always truly,
W. Strickland

My respects to Mrs. Struthers, William and all the family.   W.S.

W. B. WADE

"Monterey is a beautiful city . . ."

THE invasion of Mexico, in 1846, certified the permanence of Texas as a part of the Union, constituted the first invasion of a foreign country by United States forces, and—as a not inconsiderable sideline—took into foreign regions a swashbuckling group of young Americans.

For a century thereafter, the American picture of Mexico was derived largely from their letters home. As letters were still important records of great events, the best of them contained much beside battle accounts.

There were the generals, and older men, who wrote thousands of letters home from this campaign, many available in other collections. There were the youths, seeing the jaunt as an adventure, whose excitement struggled inwardly with their homesickness.

From among the latter, comes this letter written by W. B. Wade, to his sister in Mississippi. His view was not as broad as that of men who wrote from command posts, but he saw men die and he killed men, and still he had time to talk of the beauty of Monterey.

Minimum editing has been done, to insert a few obviously implied punctuation marks, and to break the epistle into modern paragraphs, details with which the young writer had no concern.

Monterey   September 28th 1846

Dear Sister

Once again;

Either by the interposition of Providence; by chance; or by the general good luck which has usually attended me, I am permitted to write to you again from the Theatre of War; and that too, just after the only battle has been fought; which, (I think) will take place, during the present War, between the combined forces of Mexico, arrayed against the American Army. I wrote to you from Seralvo, about ten days ago, and it was the general impression then, that the Mexican Army would meet us, and fight us, in the passes of the mountains between that place and this; but we were disapointed.

We reached here on Saturday morning. Gen. Taylor and his staff rode out of camp towards the City of Monterey about 4 miles off and was making some few observations about the City when he was fired upon from one of the forts, and a few 18 pound shots came whistling about his ears, which was the only approach we made towards a fight on that day. As the next day was Sunday we concluded not to commence operations but only went down to mark out the position of some of our batteries, had a few more shots fired at us, and returned. But on Monday Morning the Ball opened up in all its richness, and splendor and a grand and magnificent scene it was too.

About sunrise our Regiment formed, and took up the line of March towards Monterey, went about 3 miles and took our position just behind one of our batteries; when the Commander of the battery went to Col. Davis and told him that he had better make his men lie down, as the Mexicans had been throwing shot at his Mortar all the morning and that they fell just about where we were then standing. We had scarcely been ordered down by Col. Davis and got our position, when 6.13.18 pound shot grape and cannister whistled over our heads as thick as hailstones; and they kept it up for about an hour at the expiration of which time we were ordered up and to load quickly; to go down about a quarter of a mile further to make an attack upon a fort which had twice before, that morning, been attacked by the Regulars, and they had been repulsed and forced to fall back both times. But I suppose Old Jack thought if any body could rout them it was the Mississippians; so we went down under a most [sic] fire of Cannon balls Grape shots and Cannister kept up by four batteries all playing upon us at the same time; until we got within two hundred yards of the fort when the musketry opened upon us and I do not think that I ever saw hail fall faster than did the musket balls and grape fall around and amongst us.

Amidst all this we kept up a fire upon the fort; but it began to get too hot for us and we had either to charge the Fort and rout them or fall back as the regulars had done before us. Col. McClung seeing this ordered us to charge upon the Fort and led the charge, calling upon Tombigby Boys to follow him; and nobly did they respond to the call with shout that echoed through City, and that tolled the death knell of many a Mexican soldier did they rush upon the Fort, and cause every one within it to fly with the utmost terror and confusion—Col. McClung not satisfied with having taken the first fort with Col. Davis ordered the charge upon the second and as we approached it you might have seen the Mexicans running in every direction like sheep just out of a pen and it was really fun for us to pick them off with our rifles as they ran. We charged upon the second fort and took it and were about to charge upon the 3rd, when in going out of the 2nd advancing upon the 3rd fort Col. McClung was shot down.

We however followed Col. Davis in the charge upon the 3rd Fort and would have taken it had we not been ordered back by the Gen. commanding us to fall back. In the Charge upon the 1st fort McClung was the first man in the fort, Patterson was the 2nd and I think that Dr. Gregory was the 3rd. I would have been about the 3rd or 4th myself but I carried both a rifle and a sword and in crossing the ditch my sword dropped out of the scabbard and I was delayed in getting it.

We fought the whole of Monday round about the forts picking off the Mexicans with our rifles as they would show their heads and at night we returned to the camp. In the first days fight we had no men killed; but several wounded of which number were W. H. Bell wounded in the arm, D. B. Lewis in the arm, E. B. Lewis shot through the head but not yet dead, C. Martins leg broke, Stuart shot through the arm, McNorris struck in the Breast by a spent cannon ball and Longstreet slightly wounded in the head. These compose the number wounded on the first day.

On Tuesday the 2nd day, there was no engagement with small arms by Volunters. We were ordered to go to town and take possession of the Fort which we had taken the preceding day. The Regiment marched down under a very heavy fine rain. The other forts not yet taken remained there during the day and night, they firing at us all the while. Gen Worth had an engagement on this day at the other end of town and took one other fortification from them called the Bishops Castle. On the 3rd day early in the morning the Regiment was ordered out to attack a fort which was up in town. We marched gallantly up to the attack, Patterson had command of the Company today, our Capt. being sick. I was very sick myself but was determined the company should incur no danger which I did not share so I went along. They commenced firing upon us with musketry within two hundred yards of the Fort and kept it up until we got under cover of the houses between the fort and the centre of the City. After getting in there we scattered about and had a fine time of it shooting the Mexicans as they dodged trying to get from the fort into the City, we remained in there all day took dinner with the ladies who were exceedingly polite to us (more from form than love though). They brought us oranges and made lemonade and we fared finely.

Late in the evening we were ordered to retire which we did very reluctantly. In this last day's fight we had no men wounded but two killed. Tyree from Aberdeen and Inedeco from Columbus. The next day they surrendered and are to march out of town during the next week so I think the war is closed and I wish to come home as soon as possible.

If Mr. Black is still at our house and has any connection with the paper give him a list of the killed and wounded in our company and request him to publish it. The loss of the Regiment was between 60 and 75 killed and wounded. Col. McClung was very seriously wounded but will recover. One man in our company E. B. Lewis I think will hardly recover. All the rest of the Company well, Patterson sends his respects and desires me to say to you that he has been very busy or he would have written to you. We remain here during the Armistice which lasts 8 weeks. Write soon and pay the postage of your letter or it will not come further than Mattamoros.

Give my love to Ma, and Mat and all the folks. Tell them I expect that we will be disbanded in a few weeks. Monterey is a beautiful City surrounded by Mountains. I will give you a description of it in the next letter I write. Send me any paper that gives a description of the battle. Be sure to write.

W. B. Wade

JAMES FENIMORE COOPER

"Novelties are puissant in this country . . ."

IN 1846, the average life span was much shorter than it is today, a fact reflected in a letter written by Cooper, in what he considered his declining years—he was then 57 years old.

The author, whose works including *The Last of the Mohicans* are still popular, felt he had lost both his genius and his following. He was tired and plagued by litigation. He expressed these feelings in a reply to an admirer, who suggested that he write a new novel, with a southern background.

My time is nearly done. At 57 the world is not apt to believe that a man can write fiction, and I have already long known that the country is tired of me. Novelties are puissant in this country, and new names take the names of old ones so rapidly that one scarcely learns to distinguish who are in favor before a successor is pointed out. My clients, such as they are, are in Europe, and long have been, and there is no great use in going out of my way to awaken a feeling in this country that has long gone out.

The sequel:

Cooper lived until 1851, remembered by many friends as delightful company and an active, extraordinary writer until his death.

EMILY DICKINSON

". . . comfort and happiness in everything . . ."

FOR some unexplained reason—perhaps public reading tastes—there is a vast literature dealing with schools and colleges for boys, but virtually none covering the same range for girls and women, certainly nothing to compare with the "Tom Brown" books, etc.

Yet a century and more ago, there were flourishing schools for young women, albeit they were called mostly "female seminaries." One was Mount Holyoke College, founded in 1840 at South Hadley, Massachusetts.

Seven years after it was founded —and already so successful that it could hold to high standards with an enrollment of 300 girls—a teenager named Emily Dickinson enrolled for a year of study.

Not yet matured into the career that made her one of this country's ranking poets, she had already developed perceptive gifts, making one of her letters home a delightful and human document of school days in 1847.

Mt. Holyoke Seminary
Nov. 6, 1847

My Dear Abiah,

I am really at Mt. Holyoke Seminary and this is to be my home for a long year. Your affectionate letter was joyfully received and I wish that this might make you as happy as your's did me. It has been nearly six weeks since I left home and is a longer time, than I was ever away from home before now. I was very homesick for a few days and it seemed to me I could not live here. But I am now contented and quite happy, if I can be happy when absent from my dear home and friends . . .

As you desire it, I will give you a full account of myself since I first left the paternal roof. I came to S. Hadley six weeks ago next Thursday. I was much fatigued with the ride and had a severe cold besides, which prevented me from commencing my examinations until the next day, when I began. I finished them in three days and found them about what I had anticipated, though the old scholars say, they are more strict than they have ever been before. As you can easily imagine, I was much delighted to finish without failures and I came to the conclusion then, that I should not be at all homesick, but the reactions left me as homesick a girl as it is not usual to see. I am now quite contented and am very much occupied now in reviewing the Junior studies, as I wish to enter the middle class. The school is very large, and though quite a number have left, on account of finding the examinations more difficult than anticipated, yet there are nearly 300 now. Perhaps you know that Miss Lyon is raising her standard of scholarship a good deal, on account of the number of applicants this year and on account of that she makes the examinations more severe than usual. You cannot imagine how trying they are, because if we cannot go through them all in a specified time, we are sent home. I cannot be too thankful that I got through as soon as I did and I am sure that I never would endure the suspense which I endured during those days again for all the treasures of the world . . .

I will tell you my order of time for the day, as you were so kind as to give me your's. At 6 o'clock, we all rise. We breakfast at 7. Our study hours begin at 8. At 9 we all meet in Seminary Hall for devotions. At 10¼ I recite a review of Ancient History in connection with which we read Goldsmith and Grimshaw. At 11 I recite a lesson in "Pope's Essay on Man" which is merely transposition. At 12 I practise Calisthenics and at 12¼ read until dinner which is at 12½. After dinner from 1½ until 2 I sing in Seminary Hall. From 2¾ until 3¾ I practise upon the Piano. At 3¾ I go to Section, where we give in all our accounts for the day, including absence–Tardiness Communications–Breaking Silent Study hours–Receiving Company in our rooms and ten thousand other things which I will not take time or place to mention. At 4½ we go into Seminary Hall and receive advice from Miss Lyon in the form of a lecture. We have supper at 6 and silent study hours from then until the retiring bell, which rings at 8¾ but the tardy bell does not ring until 9¾, so that we don't often obey the first warning to retire.

Unless we have a good and reasonable excuse for failure upon any of the items that I mentioned above, they are recorded and a black <u>mark</u> stands against our names. As you can easily imagine, we do not like very well to get "exceptions" as they are called scientifically here. My domestic work is not difficult and consists in carrying the knives from the 1st tier of tables at morning and noon, and at night washing and wiping the same quantity of knives.

I am quite well and hope to be able to spend the year here free from sickness. You have probably heard many reports of the food here and if so I can tell you, that I have yet seen nothing corresponding to my ideas on that point, from what I have heard. Everything is wholesome and abundant and much nicer than I should imagine could be provided for almost 300 girls. We have also a great variety upon our tables and frequent changes. One thing is certain and that is, that Miss Lyon and all the teachers, seem to consult our comfort and happiness in everything they do and you know that is pleasant. When I left home I did not think I should find a companion or a dear friend in all the multitude. I expected to find rough and uncultivated manners, and to be sure I have found some of that stamp, but on the whole, there is an ease and grace and a desire to make one another happy, which delights and at the same time surprises me very much . . .

EDGAR ALLAN POE

". . . I . . . underwent all the agonies of her death."

IN his 39th year, Edgar Allan Poe wrote a letter to a younger admirer whom he had never met, with either the evident or unconscious purpose of leaving some rationale for the hell-on-earth out of which had flowed his poetic genius. His correspondent was George Eveleth, a medical student who had been one of the first to write to Poe in appreciation of his work.

Poe's embittered theme was that the debauchery that had marked his recent years had been the result of his troubles, primarily his wife's ill health and his financial problems, to say nothing of the pitfalls in his life exemplified by hard-bargaining publishers and unappreciative critics.

His letter dealt with his maturity following a hard youth marked by orphanage, expulsion from the University of Virginia and court martial at West Point, due (for he was a brilliant student) to his drinking, gambling and other overpowering habits.

At the age of 24 he had married his cousin, Virginia Clemm, who was then only 13. It was not an elopment, but a marriage shepherded by Virginia's mother, who thereafter devoted her life to caring for this "family."

When Poe wrote to Eveleth, mingling explanations with descriptions of high hopes and Quixotic plans, Virginia had been dead a year and Poe had yet a year to live.

New York–Jan. 4, 1848.

My Dear Sir–Your last, dated July 26, ends with–"Write will you not?" I have been living ever since in a constant state of intention to write, and finally concluded not to write at all until I could say something definite about The Stylus and other matters.

You perceive that I now send you a Prospectus–but before I speak further on this topic, let me succinctly reply to various points in your letter.

1–"Hawthorne" is out—how do you like it?

2–"The Rationale of Verse" was found to come down too heavily (as I forewarned you it did) upon some of poor Colton's personal friends in Frongpondium—the "pundits," you know; so I gave him "a song" for it & took it back. The song was "Ulalume a Ballad" published in the December number of the Am. Rev. I enclose it as copied by the Home Journal (Willis's paper) with the editor's remarks—please let me know how you like "Ulalume."

As for the "Rat. of Verse" I sold it to Graham at a round advance on Colton's price, and in Graham's hands it is still—but not to remain even there; for I mean to get it back, revise or rewrite it (since "Evangeline" has been published) and deliver it as a lecture when I go South & West on my Magazine expedition.

3–I have been "so still" on account of preparation for the magazine campaign–also have been working at my book—nevertheless I have written some trifles not yet published—some which have been.

4–My health is better—best. I have never been so well.

5–I do not well see how I could have otherwise replied to English. You must know him, (English) before you can well estimate my reply. He is so thorough a "blatherskite" that to have replied to him with dignity would have been the extreme of the ludicrous. The only true plan—not to have replied to him at all—was precluded on account of the nature of some of his accusations—forgery for instance. To such charges, even from the Autocrat of all Asses—a man is compelled to answer. There he had me. Answer him I must. But how?

Believe me there exists no such dilemma as that in which a gentleman is placed when he is forced to reply to a blackguard. If he had any genius then is the time for its display. I confess to you that I rather like that reply of mine in a literary sense—and so do a great many of my friends. It fully answered its purpose beyond a doubt—would to Heaven every work of art did as much!

You err in supposing me to have been "peevish" when I wrote the reply:—the peevishness was all "put on" as a part of my argument—of my plan:—so was the "indignation" with which I wound up. How could I be either peevish or indignant about a matter so well adapted to further my purposes? Were I able to afford so expensive a luxury as personal and especially as refutable abuse, I would willingly pay any man $2000 per annum, to hammer away at me all the year round. I suppose you know that I sued the Mirror & got a verdict. English eloped.

5–The "common friend" referred to is Mrs. Frances S. Osgood, the poetess.

6–I agree with you only in part as regards Miss Fuller. She has some general but no particular, critical powers. She belongs to a school of criticism—the Göthean, aesthetic, eulogistic. The creed of this school is that, in criticising an author you must imitate him, ape him, out-Herod Herod. She is grossly dishonest. She abuses Lowell, for example, (the best of our poets, perhaps) on account of a personal quarrel with him. She has omitted all mention of me for the same reason—although, a short time before the issue of her book, she praised me highly in the Tribune. I enclose you her criticism that you may judge for yourself. She praised "Witchcraft" because Mathews (who toadies her) wrote it. In a word, she is an ill-tempered and very inconsistent old maid—avoid her.

7–Nothing was omitted in "Marie Roget" but what I omitted myself: all that is mystification. The story was originally published in Snowden's "Lady's Companion." The "naval officer" who committed the murder (or rather the accidental death arising from an attempt at abortion) confessed it; and the whole matter is now well understood—but, for the sake of relatives, this is a topic on which I must not speak further.

8–"The Gold Bug" was originally sent to Graham; but he not liking it, I got him to take some critical papers instead, and sent it to The Dollar Newspaper which had offered $100 for the best story. It obtained the premium, and made a great noise.

9–The "necessities" were pecuniary ones. I referred to a sneer at my poverty on the part of the Mirror.

10–You say–"Can you hint to me what was the terrible evil which caused the irregularities so profoundly lamented?" Yes; I can do more than hint. This "evil" was the greatest which can befall a man. Six years ago, a wife, whom I loved as no man ever loved before, ruptured a blood-vessel in singing. Her life was despaired of. I took leave of her forever & underwent all the agonies of her death. She recovered partially and I again hoped.

At the end of a year the vessel broke again—I went through precisely the same scene. Again in about a year afterward. Then again—again—again & even once again at varying intervals.

Each time I felt all the agonies of her death—and at each accession of the disorder I loved her more dearly & clung to her life with more desperate pertinacity. But I am constitutionally sensitive —nervous in a very unusual degree. I became insane, with long intervals of horrible sanity. During these fits of absolute unconsciousness I drank, God only knows how often or how much.

As a matter of course, my enemies referred the insanity to the drink rather than the drink to the insanity. I had indeed, nearly abandoned all hope of a permanent cure when I found one in the death of my wife. This I can & do endure as becomes a man—it was the horrible never-ending oscillation between hope & despair which I could not longer have endured, without total loss of reason. In the death of what was my life, then, I receive a new, but —oh God! how melancholy an existence!

And now, having replied to all your queries let me refer to The Stylus. I am resolved to be my own publisher. To be controlled is to be ruined. My ambition is great. If I succeed, I put myself (within 2 years) in possession of a fortune & infinitely more. My plan is to go through the South & West & endeavour to interest my friends so as to commence with a list of at least 500 subscribers. With this list I can take the matter into my own hands. There are some few of my friends who have sufficient confidence in me to advance their subscriptions—but at all events succeed I will. Can you or will you help me? I have room to say no more.

Truly yours—

E. A. Poe

MATTHEW F. WARD

". . . her face is a very pleasing one."

TWELVE years after Victoria became Queen of England and nine years after her marriage to Prince Albert, she was seen and described by an American, Matthew F. Ward, a forerunner of the modern news correspondent in his attempt to give factual word pictures rather than the super-glossy adulatory type of letters that had been popular a decade earlier.

Traveling for his health in Europe in 1849, he wrote a series of "letters" for the Louisville (Ky.) Journal, of which No. 66 was posted from London. He found the queen somewhat less beautiful than he had imagined ("love and porter have done their work") but her face "a very pleasing one"; Albert "apple-cheeked," and the Queen's movements about London very closely guarded in contrast to the idolatry in which the English generally were supposed to hold her.

London, 1849

After dodging about the Park, watching at corners, and hunting the opera house for the last two weeks, I have at last been gratified by a sight of Her Majesty the Queen. By the by, tis somewhat singular that we democratic Americans should all feel such intense curiosity to get a peep at royal personages. Our institutions ought to convince us that they are no better or more remarkable than ourselves; but every man does not practise his own preaching, and I believe the earliest desire of almost all Americans, upon arriving in London, is to see the Queen.

I was surprised to discover that this curiosity should so generally extend to the Londoners themselves, with whom one would imagine that the Queen had long since ceased to be a "novelty." But although an effort is made to keep her movements as secret as possible, it is generally discovered when she intends visiting any place of amusement, by the unusual number of policemen, stationed along the streets through which she must pass . . .

Love and porter have done their work upon the person of the Queen, as they must do upon all that is feminine in England—and the women as they advance in years and matrimony, grow thin or stout as the effects of the one or the other predominate. The singular regular features of the Queen have become rather sharp, her neck looks scrawny, and a malt liquor flash pervades her whole countenance. And yet, though she has lost that plumpness of person and beauty of feature that she once possessed, her face is a very pleasing one . . .

The royal consort sat by her side—one of the best looking dumpling-faced fellows one could meet anywhere . . .

And then—and—but I can't go on; really I think no man earns his money more dearly than the Prince, and that his various and important services justly enable him to the gratitude of the country.

M.

OLIVER WENDELL HOLMES

". . . an argument of great weight . . ."

THE "Autocrat of the Breakfast Table," poet, lecturer and (as we often forget) noted doctor and author of medical books, became both famous and rich before he died at the age of 85 in 1894. But when he was in his early forties and the father of a large family, he shared with most authors the great need of, and consequent respect for, money.

Circa 1851, Holmes wrote a

rhapsodic note to the publisher, James Thomas Fields, occasioned by the offer of $100 for a new poem. It may have been "Astraea."

Fields, already an established publisher of books, a few years later took over the editorship of The Atlantic Monthly, which was named by Holmes, and their editor-author relationship successfully continued.

But at the time of this note (not precisely dated) $100 was worth the turning of a metaphorical handspring.

$100.00

My Dear Sir,–The above is an argument of great weight to all those who, like the late John Rogers, are surrounded by a numerous family.

I will incubate this golden egg two days, and present you with the resulting chicken upon the third.

Yours very truly,
O. W. Holmes.

P.S. You will perceive that the last sentence is figurative, and implies that I shall watch and fast over your proposition for forty-eight hours. But I couldn't on any account be so sneaky as to get up and recite poor old "Hanover" over again. Oh, no! If anything, it must be of the "paullo majora."

"Silvae sint consule dignae." Let us have a brand-new poem or none.

Yours as on the preceding page.

DAME SHIRLEY

"Gold mining is nature's great lottery scheme."

SOON after the discovery of gold in California, an eastern physician, Dr. Clappe, migrated to the west and went with his wife into the Sierras. There he combined the practice of medicine with mining for gold, on his own account and with various partners.

The objective eye of history certainly would have passed over both the practice and the prospecting of Dr. Clappe, but for the fortuitous circumstance that his wife wrote one of the most informative and graphic records of the gold rush.

Signing her letters as "Dame Shirley," she brought to life the chance-taking, the triumphs and the heartbreak of the gold seekers, with such success that her writings were republished as recently as 1922 by Thomas C. Russell, under the title "The Shirley Letters."

Her complete, formal name was Louise Amelia Knapp Smith Clappe, which is clearly an excellent reason for writing under the nom-de-plume "Dame Shirley."

From our Log Cabin
Indian Bar, April 10, 1852.

Having got our gold mines discovered, and claimed, I will try to give you a faint idea of how they work them. Here, in the mountains, the labor of excavation is extremely difficult, on account of the immense rocks which form a large portion of the soil. Of course no man can work out a claim alone. For that reason, and also for the same that makes partnerships desirable, they congregate in companies of four or six, generally designating themselves by the name of the place from whence the majority of the members have emigrated; as, for example, the Illinois, Bunker Hill, Bay State, etc., companies. In many places the surface soil, or in mining phrase, the top dirt, pays when worked in a Long-Tom. This machine (I have never been able to discover the derivation of its name) is a trough, generally about twenty feet in length and eight inches in depth, formed of wood, with the exception of six feet at one end, called the "riddle" (query, why "riddle?"), which is made of sheet-iron perforated with holes about the size of a large marble. Underneath this colander-like portion of the long-tom, is placed another trough, about ten feet long, the sides six inches, perhaps, in height, which, divided through the middle by a slender slat, is called the riffle-box.

It takes several persons to manage properly a long-tom. Three or four men station themselves with spades at the head of the machine, while at the foot of it stands an individual armed "wid de shovel an' de hoe." The spadesmen throw in large quantities of the precious dirt, which is washed down to the riddle by a stream of water leading into the long-tom through wooden gutters or sluices. When the soil reaches the riddle, it is kept constantly in motion by the man with the hoe. Of course, by this means, all the dirt and gold escapes through the perforations into the riffle-box below, one compartment of which is placed just beyond the riddle. Most of the dirt washes over the sides of the riffle-box, but the gold, being so astonishingly heavy, remains safely at the bottom of it. When the machine gets too full of stones to be worked easily, the man whose business it is to attend to them throws them out with his shovel, looking carefully among them as he does so for any pieces of gold which may have been too large to pass through the holes of the riddle. I am sorry to say that he generally loses his labor. At night they pan out the gold, which has been collected in the riffle-box during the day.

Many of the miners decline washing the top dirt at all, but try to reach as quickly as possible the bed-rock, where are found the richest deposits of gold. The river is supposed to have formerly flowed over this bed-rock, in the crevices of which it left, as it passed away, the largest portions of the so eagerly sought for ore. The group of mountains amidst which we are living is a spur of the Sierra Nevada, and the bed-rock, which in this vicinity is of slate, is said to run through the entire range, lying, in distance varying from a few feet to eighty or ninety, beneath the surface of the soil. On Indian Bar the bed-rock falls in almost perpendicular benches, while at Rich Bar the friction of the river has formed it into large, deep basins, in which the gold, instead of being found, as you would naturally suppose, in the bottom of it, lies, for the most part, just below the rim . . .

When a company wish to reach the bed-rock as quickly as possible, they sink a shaft (which is nothing more nor less than digging a well) until they "strike it." They then commence drifting coyote holes, as they call them, in search of crevices, which, as I told you before, often pay immensely. These coyote holes sometimes extend hundreds of feet into the side of the hill. Of course they are obliged to use lights in working them. They generally proceed until the air is so impure as to extinguish the lights, when they return to the entrance of the excavation and commence another, perhaps close to it. When they think that a coyote hole has been faithfully worked, they clean it up, which is done by scraping the surface of the bed-rock with a knife, lest by chance they have overlooked a crevice, and they are often richly rewarded for this precaution.

Now I must tell you how those having claims on the hills procure the water for washing them. The expense of raising it in any way from the river is too enormous to be thought of for a moment. In most cases it is brought from ravines in the mountains. A company, to which a friend of ours belongs, has dug a ditch about a foot in width and depth, and more than three miles in length, which is fed in this way. I wish that you could see this ditch. I never beheld a natural streamlet more exquisitely beautiful. It undulates over the mossy roots and the gray old rocks like a capricious snake, singing all the time a low song with the "liquidest murmur," and one might almost fancy it the airy and coquettish Undine herself. When it reaches the top of the hill, the sparkling thing is divided into five or six branches, each one of which supplies one, two, or three long-toms. There is an extra one, called the waste-ditch, leading to the river, into which the water is shut off at night and on Sundays. This race (another and peculiar name for it) has already cost the company more than five thousand dollars. They sell the water to others at the following rates: Those that have the first use of it pay ten per cent upon all the gold that they take out. As the water runs off from their machine, (it now goes by the elegant name of "tailings"), it is taken by a company lower down, and as it is not worth so much as when it was clear, the latter pay but seven per cent. If any others wish the tailings, now still less valuable than at first, they pay four per cent on all the gold which they take out, be it much or little. The water companies are constantly in trouble, and the arbitrations on that subject are very frequent.

I think I gave you a vague idea of fluming in a former letter . . .

As to the rockers, so often mentioned in story and song, I have not spoken of them since I commenced this letter. The truth is, that I have seldom seen them used, though hundreds are lying ownerless along the banks of the river. I suppose that other machines are better adapted to mining operations in the mountains.

Gold mining is Nature's great lottery scheme. A man may work in a claim for many months, and be poorer at the end of the time than when he commenced, or he may take out thousands in a few hours. It is a mere matter of chance. A friend of ours, a young Spanish surgeon from Guatemala, a person of intelligence and education, told us that after working a claim for six months he had taken out but six ounces.

RALPH WALDO EMERSON

"I greet you at the beginning of a great career . . ."

FROM Concord, Massachusetts, where his reputation as sage and poet had made his home the center of a world-wide intellectual universe, 52-year-old Ralph Waldo Emerson, wrote a short letter to an unknown younger man named Walt Whitman, then 36, who had sent Emerson a copy of a new volume of poems entitled *Leaves of Grass*.

Masstts.	1855
Concord	21 July

Dear Sir,

I am not blind to the worth of the wonderful gift of "Leaves of Grass." I find it the most extraordinary piece of wit & wisdom that America has yet contributed. I am very happy in reading it, as great power makes me happy. It meets the demand I am always making of what seemed the sterile and stingy nature, as if too much handiwork or too much symbolic in the temperament were making our western wits fat & mean. I give you joy of your free and brave thought. I have great joy in it. I find incomparable things said incomparably well, as they must be. I find the courage of treatment, which so delights me, and which large perception only can inspire. I greet you at the beginning of a great career, which yet must have had a long foreground somewhere for such a start. I rubbed my eyes a little to see if the sunbeams were no illusion; but the solid sense of the book is a great certainty. It has the best merits, namely of fortifying and encouraging.

I did not know until I, last night, saw the book advertised in a newspaper, that I could trust the name as real and available for a post office. I wish to see my benefactor, and have felt much like shirking my tasks, and visiting New York, to pay you my respects.

R. W. Emerson

Mr. Walt Whitman

The sequel:

Emerson sent this letter to Whitman in care of the latter's publishers, Fowler & Wells, at 38 Broadway, New York.

It is a significant commentary that Ralph Waldo Emerson, immensely successful socially and financially, as well as intellectually, linked his praise to Whitman's name and yet, because of the boldness of his poems, Whitman was socially ostracized; forced to eke out a living as a copy clerk in a government department in Washington, in a job kindly obtained for him through the patronage of friends.

ROGER BROOKE TANEY

"The opinion must be left to speak for itself."

TWO days after the inauguration of President Buchanan, in 1857, the Supreme Court of the United States handed down a decision that, as much as any single action, inflamed abolitionist sentiment in the North and headed the nation inevitably toward the Civil War. The decision concerned the Dred Scott case, and the view of the Supreme Court was written personally by the Chief Justice of the United States, Mr. Taney, himself a Southerner born and bred in Maryland, a slave state and—most remarkable—a jurist then in his eightieth year.

The decision in this case was a crucial test of the power of the Supreme Court, over which Justice Taney had presided since 1836. It ruled the Missouri Compromise of 1820 to be unconstitutional. Specifically, Dred Scott, a born slave, had escaped from Missouri to Minnesota and the court held that mere escape did not grant Scott the rights of citizenship, or, specifically, the right to sue in a Federal Court.

The decision, handed down early in March, caused a national uproar, much of which centered on the "slavery background" of Justice Taney. A few months later, in August, the Reverend Samuel Nott, a Congregationalist minister at Wareham, Mass., wrote a review of the case, which he submitted to Justice Taney for review. In his reply, the jurist set forth, in confidence, his own views on slavery, as well as demonstrating the extraordinary clarity of his mind.

Fauquier, White Sulphur Springs, Virginia
August 19th, 1857.

Sir,—I received some time ago your letter, and pamphlet on "Slavery, and the Remedy," which you have been kind enough to send me. They were received when I was much out of health, and about to leave home for the summer. And it was not in my power to give the pamphlet an attentive perusal until within a few days past. I have read it with great pleasure. The just, impartial, and fraternal spirit in which it is written entitles it to a respectful consideration, in the South as well as the North. And if any thing can allay the unhappy excitement which is daily producing so much evil to the African as well as the white race, it is the discussion of the subject in the temper in which you have treated it. For you have looked into it and considered it in all its bearings, in the spirit of a statesman as well as a philanthropist. I am glad to find that it has been so well received as to reach the fifth edition.

Every intelligent person whose life has been passed in a slaveholding State, and who has carefully observed the character and capacity of the African race, will see that a general and sudden emancipation would be absolute ruin to the negroes, as well as to the white population. In Maryland and Virginia every facility has been given to emancipation where the freed person was of an age and condition of health that would enable him to provide for himself by his own labor. And before the present excitement was gotten up, the freed negro was permitted to remain in the State, and to follow any occupation of honest labor and industry that he might himself prefer. And in this state of the law manumissions were frequent and numerous. They sprang from the kindness and sympathy of the master for the negro, or from scruples of conscience; and were often made without sufficiently considering his capacity and fitness for freedom. And in the greater number of cases that have come under my observation, freedom has been a serious misfortune to the manumitted slave; and he has most commonly brought upon himself privations and sufferings which he would not have been called on to endure in a state of slavery. In many cases, however, it has undoubtedly promoted his happiness. But all experience proves that the relative position of the two races, when placed in contact with each other, must necessarily become such as you describe. Nor is it felt as a painful degradation by the black race. On the contrary, upon referring to the last census, you will find that more free negroes remain in Maryland than in any one of the Northern States, notwithstanding the disabiliites and stricter police to which they are subjected. And there is a still greater number in Virginia. I speak from memory, without having the census before me. But I think I am not mistaken in the fact.

It is difficult for any one who has not lived in a slaveholding State to comprehend the relations which practically exist between the slaves and their masters. They are in general kind on both sides, unless the slave is tampered with by ill-disposed persons; and his life is usually cheerful and contented, and free from any distressing wants or anxieties. He is well taken care of in infancy, in sickness, and in old age. There are indeed exceptions,—painful exceptions. But this will always be the case, where power combined with bad passions or a mercenary spirit is on one side, and weakness on the other. It frequently happens when both parties are of the same race, although the weaker and dependent one may not be legally a slave.

Unquestionably it is the duty of every master to watch over the religious and moral culture of his slaves, and to give them every comfort and privilege that is not incompatible with the continued existence of the relations between them. And so far as my knowledge extends, this duty is faithfully performed by the great body of hereditary slaveholders in Maryland and Virginia. I speak of these States only, because with respect to them I have personal knowledge of the subject. But I have no reason to suppose it is otherwise in States farther south. And I know it has been the desire of the statesmen of Maryland to secure to the slave by law every protection from maltreatment by the master that can with safety be given, and without impairing that degree of authority which is essential to the interest and well-being of both. But this question is a very delicate one, and must at all times be approached with the utmost caution. The safe and true line must always depend upon existing circumstances, and they must be thoroughly inquired into and understood before there can be any safe or useful legislation in a State.

The pains which have unhappily been taken for some years past to produce discontent and ill-feeling in the subject race, has rendered any movement in that direction still more difficult. For it has naturally made the master more sensitive and jealous of any new restriction upon the power he has heretofore exercised, and which he has been accustomed to think essential to the maintenance of his authority as master. And he also feels that any step in that direction at the present time might injuriously affect the minds of the slaves. They are for the most part weak, credulous, and easily misled by stronger minds. And if in the present state of things additional restrictions were placed on the authority of the master, or new privileges granted to them, they would probably be told that they were wrung from the master by their Northern friends; and be taught to regard them as the first step to a speedy and universal emancipation, placing them on a perfect equality with the white race. It is easy to foresee what would be the sad result of such an impression upon the minds of this weak and credulous race.

Your review of the decision in the case of Dred Scott is a fair one, and states truly the opinion of the Court. It will, I hope, correct some of the misrepresentations which have so industriously been made; and made too, I fear, by many who must have known better. But I do not mean to publish any vindication of the opinion; or of my own consistency, or the consistency of the Court. For it would not become the Supreme Court, or any member of it, to go outside of the appropriate sphere of judicial proceedings; and engage in a controversy with any one who may choose from any motive to misrepresent its opinion. The opinion must be left to speak for itself. And it is for that reason that I hope you will pardon me for requesting that you will not permit this letter to be published in the newspapers or otherwise. Not that I am not perfectly ready on all proper occasions to say publicly every thing I have said in this letter. But in the judicial position I have the honor to occupy, I ought not to appear as a volunteer in any political discussion; and still less would it become me out of Court and off the bench to discuss a question which has been there determined. And I have written to you (although a stranger) thus freely from the personal respect with which the perusal of your pamphlet has inspired me. I am not a slaveholder. More than thirty years ago I manumitted every slave I ever owned, except two, who were too old, when they became my property, to provide for themselves. These two I supported in comfort as long as they lived. And I am glad to say that none of those whom I manumitted disappointed my expectations, but have shown by their conduct that they were worthy of freedom; and know how to use it.

> With great respect, I am, sir,
>> Your ob't serv't,
>>> R. B. Taney.

The Revd Samuel Nott,
> Wareham, Mass.

The sequel:

Chief Justice Taney lived for seven more years and, although gradually growing more feeble, retained his position as head of the Supreme Court. He died in 1864.

BRIGHAM YOUNG

". . . retire forthwith from the Territory . . ."

IN 1857, four years before the Civil War, the United States found itself at war with one of its own Territories—the Mormon settlement of Utah, founded a decade earlier—over the avowed practice of polygamy by Brigham Young's followers and the harassment of settlers bound for California by Mormons, who believed that their land and way of life were threatened.

In 1857, President Buchanan took the extreme step of sending a small army under General Albert S. Johnston to put down the "Mormon rebellion." Brigham Young, as officially appointed Governor of the Territory, mustered his own forces, named D. H. Wells as "general" of his army, harassed John-ston's supply trains, and finally "ordered" him to get out.

Nothing like this occurred later, in the Civil War, where Secession in the case of each state was an action undertaken solemnly by State Governments. Young had acted as a Federal official holding his Commission from the same President who sent troops against him. His letter was rigid, correct and—perhaps in retrospect—one of the superb bluffs of modern history.

Governors Office, Utah Territory
Great Salt Lake City, Sept. 29, 1857.

To the Officer, Commanding
the forces now invading Utah Territory.

Sir,   By reference to the Act of Congress passed Sept. 9 1850 organizing the Territory of Utah published in a Copy of the Laws of Utah, herewith forwarded pp. 146 &7, you will find the following:

Sec. 2.   And be it further enacted that the Executive power and authority in and over said Territory of Utah shall be vested in a Governor, who shall hold his Office for four years and until his Successor shall be appointed and qualified unless sooner removed by the President of the United States. The Governor shall reside within said Territory, shall be Commander in Chief of the Militia thereof etc etc.

I am still the Governor and Superintendent of Indian Affairs for the Territory, no Successor having been appointed and qualified as provided by Law, nor have I been removed by the President of the United States. By virtue of the Authority thus vested in me, I have issued and forwarded you a Copy of my Proclamation, forbidding the entrance of Armed forces into this Territory. This you have disregarded. I now further direct, that you retire forthwith from the Territory, by the same route you entered. Should you deem this impracticable and prefer to remain until Spring in the vicinity of your present encampment Blacks Fork or Green

R. you can do so in peace and unmolested, on conditions that you deposit your arms and ammunition with Lewis Robison, Quarter Master General of the Territory, and leave in the Spring, as soon as the condition of the roads will permit you to march. And should you fall short of provisions, they can be furnished you, upon making the proper applications therefor. Genl. D. H. Wells will forward this and receive any communication you may have to make.

Very Respectfully

The sequel:

The action was, of course, foredoomed. Young was removed as Governor and the "war" was ended without serious bloodshed. Yet it was Young himself, fighting for what he conceived to be right principles, whose statesmanship has been credited by later historians with averting the tragedy that otherwise might have occurred.

In time, polygamy was outlawed in Utah, the Territory became a State, and Young, who lived another twenty contentious years, became a hero of one of the oddest chapters in the development of the United States.

ABRAHAM LINCOLN

". . . an engagement for you and myself to divide time . . ."

IN 1960, the two leading candidates for the Presidency of the United States, Vice President Richard M. Nixon and Senator John F. Kennedy, faced each other in a series of debates before television cameras.

This was a logical development using modern techniques and growing out of honored historic precedent. A famous example of this precedent started 102 years earlier, in the then-new State of Illinois, when Abraham Lincoln challenged the silver-tongued Senator Stephen A. Douglas to open debate, in their campaign for the latter's Senate seat.

From his headquarters in Chicago, in July, Lincoln wrote a typically brief letter.

Chicago, Ill., July 24, 1858

Hon. S. A. Douglas
   My Dear Sir,
   Will it be agreeable to you to make an engagement for you and myself to divide time, and address the same audiences during the present canvass? Mr. Judd, who will hand this to you, is authorized to receive your answer; and if agreeable to you to inquire into the terms of such an arrangement.

Your obet. Servant
A. Lincoln

The sequel:

A reply and two subsequent letters set the stage for the notable Lincoln-Douglas debates, prior to that year's election. These speeches also set the tone for subsequent intense debates over the slavery issue. Lincoln lost that Senatorial election but, as he probably hoped, his appearance on the same platform with the nationally known Douglas increased his stature and started him on the course that led to his nomination for the Presidency two years later. Parenthetically, after Senator Kennedy's victory in 1960, more than a few Republicans criticized the losing Nixon for having acceded to the television debate suggestion on the grounds that he thus helped to give the Massachusetts Senator as wide a national "image" as the Vice President enjoyed.

JOHN BROWN

"Be faithful until death."

IT is a brave historian who will describe without many qualifications John Brown, the militant abolitionist, either as a martyr to his beliefs or as a murderer who took the law into his own hands.

At the age of 59, faithfully followed by a whole squad of his own sons and a few others, making a total of twenty-one persons, he crossed the Potomac River near Charlestown, Va. (now West Virginia) on the night of October 16, 1859, and seized an arsenal at

Harper's Ferry. His seizure—following on other forays in the Middle West in which men had died—was the signal for an uprising by citizens in a war to abolish slavery. But no uprising followed.

Instead, the Government at Washington sent out a company of Marines to put down the "rebellion." Commanding the troops was a dignified, gray-bearded officer, a former Superintendent of West Point Academy, by the name of Colonel Robert E. Lee.

Had Brown surrendered to Lee, political expediency might have dictated a mild jail sentence or perhaps even acquittal. But he and his force resisted. Five of Lee's Marines were killed and ten of Brown's men. Inevitably, Brown was tried for insurrection and on Nov. 2, 1859, he was condemned to die on the gallows, a sentence he received with a brief and eloquent retort that "I feel no consciousness of guilt."

On Nov. 30, while final preparations were being made to execute this sentence, he wrote a letter to his family.

Charlestown, Prison, Jefferson Co., Va.
30th Nov 1859

My Dearly Beloved Wife, Sons: & Daughters, Everyone

As I now begin what is probably the last letter I shall ever write to any of you; I conclude to write you all at the same time . . . I am waiting the hour of my public murder with great composure of mind, & cheerfulness: feeling the strongest assurance that in no other possible way could I be used to so much advance the cause of God; & of humanity: & that nothing that either I or all my family have sacrificed or suffered: will be lost.

The reflection that a wise & merciful, as well as just & holy God: rules not only the affairs of this world; but of all worlds; is a rock to set our feet upon; under all circumstances: even those more severely trying ones: into which our own follies; & rongs have placed us. I have now no doubt but that our seeming disaster: will ultimately result in the most glorious success. So my dear shattered & broken family be of good cheer; & believe & trust in God; "with all your heart & with all your soul;" for "he doeth All things well." Do not feel ashamed on my account; nor for one moment despair of the cause; or grow weary of well doing. I bless God; I never felt stronger confidence in the certain and near approach of a bright Morning; & a glorious day; than I have felt; do now feel; since my confinement here.

I am endeavoring to "return" like a "poor Prodigal" as I am, to my Father: against whom I have always sined: in the hope; that he may kindly, & forgivingly "meet me: though a verry great way off." Oh my dear Wife & Children would "to God you could know how I have been travelling in birth for you" all: that no one of you "may fail of the grace of God, through Jesus Christ:" that no one of you may be blind to the truth: & glorious "light of his word," in which Life; & Immortality; are brought to light.

I beseech you every one to make the bible your dayly & nightly study; with a childlike honest, candid, teachable spirit: out of love and respect for your husband; & Father: & I beseech the God of my Fathers; to open all your eyes to a discovery of the truth. You cannot imagine how much you may soon need the consolations of the Christian religion.

Circumstances like my own; for more than a month past; convince me beyond all doubt: of our great need: of something more to rest our hopes on; than merely our own vague theories framed up, while our prejudices are excited; or our vanity worked up to its highest pitch.

Oh do not trust your eternal all uppon the boisterous Ocean, without even a Helm; or Compass to aid you in steering. I do not ask any of you; to throw away your reason: I only ask you, to make a candid & sober use of your reason: My dear younger children will you listen to the last poor admonition of one who can only love you? Oh be determined at once to give you whole hearts to God; & let nothing shake; or alter; that resolution. You need have no fear of regreting it.

Do not be vain; and thoughtless: but sober minded. And let me entreat you all to love the whole remnant of our once great family: "with a pure heart fervently." Try to build again: your broken walls: & to make the utmost of every stone that is left. Nothing can so tend to make life a blessing as the consciousness that you love: & are beloved: & "love ye the stranger" still. It is ground of the utmost comfort to my mind: to know that so many of you as have had the opportunity; have given full proof of your fidelity to the great family of man.

Be faithful until death. From the exercise of habitual love to man: it cannot be very hard: to learn to love his maker. I must yet insert a reason for my firm belief in the Divine inspiration of the Bible: notwithstanding I am (perhaps naturally) skeptical: (certainly not, credulous.) I wish you all to consider it most thoroughly; when you read the blessed book; & see whether you can not discover such evidence yourselves. It is the purity of heart, feeling, or motive: as well as word, & action which is everywhere insisted on; that distinguish it from all other teachings; that commends it to my conscience; whether my heart be "willing, & obedient" or not. The inducements that it holds out; are another reason of my conviction of its truth: genuineness: that I cannot here omit; in this my last argument for the Bible.

Eternal life; is that my soul is "panting after" this moment. I mention this; as reason for endeavoring to leave a valuable copy of the Bible to be carefully preserved in remembrance of me: to so many of my posterity; instead of some other things of equal cost.

I beseech you all to live in habitual contentment with verry moderate circumstances: & gains, of worldly store: & most earnestly to teach this: to your children; & Childrens Children; after you: by example: as well; as precept. Be determined to know by experience as soon as may be: whether bible instruction is of Divine origin or not; which says; "Owe no man anything but to love one another." John Rogers wrote to his children, "Abhor the arrant whore of Rome." John Brown writes to his children to abhor with undiing hatred, also: that "sum of al vilainies;" Slavery.

Remember that "he that is slow to anger is better than the mighty: and he that ruleth his spirit; than he that taketh a city." Remember also: that "they that be wise shall shine; and they that turn many to righteousness: as the stars forever; & ever." And now dearly beloved Farewell, to God & the word of his grace I comme(n)d you all.

Your Affectionate Husband & Father
John Brown

The sequel:

At dawn two days after writing this letter John Brown was hanged. Colonel Lee returned to more routine peacetime duties in the blue uniform he wore for two more years until, facing his own desperate choice between loyalty to the Union or to his native State of Virginia, he turned his back forever on Washington to lead the armies of the Confederacy.

FRANK HALL

"I expect to make this country my home . . ."

ON January 2, 1917, the Colorado papers reported the death of an 82-year-old man, who had been mining editor of the Denver Post in his latter years and who as his obituary stated "remained at work almost to the day of his death."

The veteran was Frank Hall, who had gone to Colorado to make a quick fortune—to remain not more than five years—but who remained to become a pioneer editor of the Territory, stretching his short stay to a length of fifty-seven years. In those years, he also found time to act as Secretary of the Territory, under appointment from President Grant; to write a famous history of Colorado and, in general, to become one of the state's legendary figures.

All of which supplies the background interest for a letter written to his mother and brother, in 1861, by a 26-year-old gold prospector, born in Poughkeepsie, N.Y., more recently an emigrant to the west from Syracuse, N.Y.

In this brief report, showing the natural reportorial capabilities of a born newspaperman, Hall graphically described frontier life, frontier justice, and the hopes and dreams that animated the practical pioneers, as well as the boomers of the days of the "golden west."

Spanish Bar, Colorado Tty.
May 6th 1861

Dear Brother,

Your letter came fuly to hand a few days since & you may be assured that I was pleased to hear from you. I have but little news to offer in reply but will endeavor to entertain you with the small stock I have on hand at present. I have just finished a long letter to Mother, and I shall send this with hers tomorrow Evening by the Express to James Ville & Mother will forward it to you. Your life on the Ocean must have been rather interesting although I should judge very monotonous at times. The perils of the "great deep" are perhaps one source of interest that relieves the otherwise unvaried sameness of a sailors life, & I think that no adventure is so completely charming as when there's a spice of danger in it. For many years and particularly in early youth, my nature was shrinking & timid, always avoiding danger or its proximity, but experience has taught me the folly of this, & such scenes as try mens souls have become not only familiar but inviting. We see all kinds of people here and are necessarily brought in Contact with many strange & desperate Characters. One of these made his appearance in our midst a short time ago with a drove of stolen cattle. The owner being here at the time, caused the Gents arrest. He was tried by jury I being one of the number & his guilt fully proven was sentenced to the Whipping Post, & fifty lashes on his bare back. He afterward–the same week I believe, went to Golden City & stole something & they whipped him there, & a few days subsequent we heard of his stabbing a man on the Cache Le Poudre River for which he was hung. It was a young man apparently about 25 yrs of age. Mighty rapid career of crime wasn't it. The principal modes of dealing with such chaps is to shave one half their head, whip them like the devil with orders to leave the District within one half hour & never be seen there again on penalty of instant death. Sometimes they swear vengeance, but at such times permission is given to the bystanders to shoot the prisoner on sight if ever found within the limits of the District. We have been compelled to act with severity in order to protect our rights & our property, & the slightest offense against our laws is visited with its meed of punishment.

I hope to return next fall and then I can decide whether it will be best for you to return with me the following spring. My partner has just returned from a prospecting tour accross the Snowy Range, & reported the snow from 5 to 20 feet deep on a level. He propected several gulches which were found to be very rich. In the same vicinity (Georgia Gulch) many owners of Claims made from $40,000 to $50,000 last season. We have Claims over there which are deemed very rich, but the snow is too deep to work them before the first of June. He will start again just as soon as we can hear from our agents whom he left there to keep us posted, regarding the weather, & movements of the Miners. I shall probably remain here & attend to our interest in this section & for the purpose of fitting out "pack trains" for Georgia Gulch & Vicinity. I should like very much to have you come to the country should it be advisable, which I shall probably know how things look before I return. If my partner secures a large interest over the Range I shall have more business than I can possibly attend to & want you to help me. The section he has visited is decidedly a Gulch Mining Country, while our wealth in this vicinity consists of Quartz Leads, & these require Capital to work them profitably. Gulch Mining turns our money "from the word go" and plenty of it. I expect to make this country my home for the next five years unless I should be so fortunate as to make a "big strike" before that time. I feel confident that time, Faith & Energy will give me all I want of this worlds goods & I'm bound to stick to it like grim death . . .

For information of the boys in Syracuse I am obliged to you and hope you will write often & keep me well posted about them & their doings. I shall write to George Colton soon & congratulate him upon the happy Marriage he is about entering into. I guess that you & I are bound to live and die old bachelors or in other words Single Blessedness. Well who cares, responsibility will sit so much more lightly upon our shoulders. Now Al please write me often & I will reciprocate promptly & also write to Mother often She thinks so much of letters from us. I write her regularly every Month & I shall continue to do so while I remain here. Give my regards to any & all of My Old friends of Syracuse whenever you may see or write them & Oblige your

Aff Brother
Frank Hall

ROBERT E. LEE

"We require no extraneous aid, if true to ourselves."

ON Christmas Day in 1861, less than a year after he had sacrificed his home, fortune and a brilliant U.S. Army career to lead the Army of Virginia in the Civil War, a lonely soldier sat down to write his thoughts, his convictions, his doubts and some practical family suggestions to his wife.

In this letter, General Lee gives us insight into his character and ideas, whether we consider them right or wrong in retrospect, that can serve as the cornerstone for a completely new study of him.

The letter is printed with footnotes supplied by Louis H. Manarin, Associate Editor of the Robert E. Lee Papers, under assignment to collate the heretofore unpublished writings by General Lee in the custodianship of the Virginia Civil War Commission.

Coosawhatchie, South Carolina
25 Dec 61

I cannot let this day of greatful rejoicing pass, dear Mary, without some communion with you. I am thankful for the many among the past that I have passed with you, & the remembrance of them fills me with pleasure. For those on which we have been separated we must not repine. If it will make us more resigned & better prepared for what is in store for us, we should rejoice. Now we must be content with the many blessings we receive. If we can only become sensible of our transgressions, so as to be fully penitent & forgiven, that this heavy punishment under which we labour may with justice be removed from us & the whole nation, what a gracious consummation of all that we have endured it will be! I hope you had a pleasant visit to Richmond. So you do not like my invitation to Fayetteville?[1] I thought I gave you the choice of

---

[1] In several earlier letters to his wife, General Lee urged her to move away from the theater of war. He suggested she move to some isolated place in south-central Virginia or central North Carolina. She remained in Virginia, however, and in 1864, she set up a permanent residence in Richmond.

Richmond too, as well as Charleston & Savannah, but for the threatening movements of the enemy. Well it shows the perverseness of human nature. To reject those agreeable cities that were accessible & select a decrepit & deserted village because inaccessible. If you were to see the place, I think you would leave it too. I am here but little myself. The days I am not away, I visit some point exposed to the enemy & after our dinner at early candle light, am engaged in writing till 11 or 12 at night. But this place is too exposed to attack for the residence of a person as hard to move as you are. You would be captured while you were waiting "a moment." As to our old home, if not destroyed, it will be difficult ever to be recognized.[2] Even if the enemy had wished to preserve it, it would almost have been impossible. With the number of troops encamped around it, the change of officers, &¢., the want of fuel, shelter, &¢., & all the dire necessities of war, it is vain to think of its being in a habitable condition. I fear too books, furniture, & the relics of Mount Vernon will be gone. It is better to make up our minds to a general loss. They cannot take away the remembrances of the spot, & the memories of those that to us rendered it sacred. That will remain to us as long as life will last, & that we can preserve. In the absence of a home, I wish I could purchase Stratford.[3] That is the only other place that I could go to, now accessible to us, that would inspire me with feelings of pleasure & local love. You & the girls could remain there in quiet. It is a poor place, but we could make enough cornbread & bacon for our support, & the girls could weave us clothes. I wonder if it is for sale & at how much. Ask Fitzhugh[4] to try & find out when he gets to Fredericksburg. You must not build your hopes on peace on account of the United States going into a war with England.[5] She will be very loath to do that, notwith-

2 Lee is referring to Arlington, which is now known as the Lee-Custis Mansion, Arlington National Cemetery. The house was evacuated by Mrs. ᵀee early in the war and occupied by Union forces prior to the battle of First Manassas. It was in Union hands throughout the war and the dead from both sides were buried on the grounds. The entire estate was taken over by the Federal Government and designated as a national cemetery.

3 Stratford, ancestral home of the Lees, and General Lee's birthplace, is located in Westmoreland County, Virginia.

4 William Henry Fitzhugh Lee, son of R. E. Lee.

5 Lee is referring to the Trent Affair which involved the seizure of two Confederate officials from an English ship by a Northern vessel.

standing the bluster of the Northern papers. Her rulers are not entirely mad, & if they find England is in earnest, & that war or a restitution of their captives must be the consequence, they will adopt the latter. We must make up our minds to fight our battles & win our independence alone. No one will help us. We require no extraneous aid, if true to ourselves. But we must be patient. It is not a light achievement & cannot be accomplished at once. I am very glad to hear of poor Anne. Her miseries are increased by the war too. I am also glad to hear of the kind sympathies & aid of Elianor Rodgers & Edmund. I had not heard of poor little Geary's sickness & do not know to what you allude when speaking of "Parke's affliction." We must expect Mrs. Bonaparte & our other put by friends to be opposed to us. They wish to save their demis(e). It is necessary to them to preserve their good dinners. It will not last. I have received your letter enclosing Charlotte's &¢. I cannot write to her (to)night. I wrote a few days since, giving you all the news, & have now therefore nothing to relate. The enemy is still quiet & increasing in strength. We grow in size slowly but are working hard. I have had a day of labour instead of rest & have written at intervals to some of the children. I hope they are with you & enclose my letters. Give much love to F(itzhugh), C(ustis), A(nnie), A(gnes), little Rob & all.[6]

Affecty & truly yours

R. E. LEE

P.S. I recollect having seen that a Mr. Butler was killed in Kentucky, whom I supposed was Edward. I hoped it was not true as I have seen nothing of Lewis. It is that to which you doubtless allude in speaking of Parke &¢. All must suffer.

R. E. L.

[6] Five of General Lee's children. Mary and Mildred are not mentioned.

LETTER FROM THE MONITOR

"... 3 or 4 such as this could whip the world."

ON March 9, 1862, two naval vessels fought to a draw off Hampton Roads, Virginia, in a contest as dramatic and electrifying to human imagination of that day as would later be the launching of the first space ships.

In almost simultaneous development, unknown to each other, the contending sides in the Civil War had both developed experimental and crude types of "iron clad" warships. The South built the Merrimac (officially spelled the Merrimack), whose high sides were protected from cannon balls by steel rails. This terrifying monster appeared in Hampton Road, on March 7, and attacked three powerful Northern blockading warships. The Cumberland was sunk by her guns and the Congress and Minnesota put out of action, without damage to the Merrimac. In the ensuing panic, the public in the North envisaged such ships bombarding every seaport city and destroying shipping at will.

However, the Union Navy was ready to unveil its own secret weapon, the Monitor, a low-lying specially designed ship constructed by John Erickson—steel clad and carrying two heavy guns. The ships fought to a draw, but in the space of a few hours delivered a death blow to all the wooden navies of the world.

Aboard the Monitor was a young and literate seaman, whose last name is unknown, who after the battle sat down and wrote a letter to his father, a priceless record from one who was there.

Battle was fought Sunday, March 9, '62
at Hampton Roads, Va. 8 to 12 a.m.

My Dear Father:

We had a very unpleasant passage out. The first night went off well. The next day it blew hard from nw. From the Capes of Delaware to Smith Island we had heavy seas. They rolled over her (the Monitor) several feet deep. The water ran down around the tower bottom and wheel house. The sea broke into the blower pipes and caused a great deal of trouble and into the smoke funnels and caused the gas to escape into the fire room. The engineers and fireman on duty were brought out almost lifeless and we had for some time no control of the ship. All that night no one slept much . . . About 2 a.m. the wheel ropes got off the wheel and we were broadside to seas rolling over & over in all kinds of ways.

In the morning we got in with the land: we were very glad. Off Cape Henry we got a pilot. He told us that at 2 p.m. the Merrimac came down from Norfolk and steamed to Newport News. She sunk the Cumberland frigate by running her ram into her and then taking raking positions and killed 120 men at the guns. They fought till she went over on her port side by lying with her mastheads out of water. The rest of the crew and officers saved themselves the best way they could or were taken prisoners.

The Congress frigate fought for some time until she (was) struck through the deck (which) set her on fire. We saw her burning when we came in. By and by she blew up. We got to Hampton about 8 p.m. of the 8th of March, Saturday. After anchoring the Captain (Lt. John L. Worden) went on board the flagship and got orders to proceed to the scene of the demolition and if he could to save the Minnesota, then aground at Newport News. So up we went and anchored close to her (the Merrimac) intending to attack her in the morning, having already exchanged some broadsides before dark. In the morning we saw the Merrimac and two wooden steamers under Sewells Point. We got under way immediately and soon after, went to quarters on a slim breakfast and but little rest.

I was down on the berth deck with the powder division and all I know is from others. The shot, shell, and grape flew by with a whizz and struck all over. We were struck 21 times by the Merrimac, (and by) 2 shots from the Minnesota. Seven shots struck the tower, 7 or 8 tore up the edge of the deck & side, one shell burst right in the portholes but hurt no one; another stuck fast in a dent it made in the tower 2½ inches deep, right on a rivet. Those that struck the sides dented & bent the iron plates but not so much as to hinder us from immediate action. One shot took a corner of the pilot house like you would rough a piece of bread in spreading it. Another, fired about 20 yards from the fore part of the house, cracked the iron bar and the dust from the projectile flew into the eyes of the Captain. He had to go out of the house and his face was covered with blood and smoke. After the action closed we sent him on shore and he went up to Washington to get the best medical aid and see the President.

The Quarter Master, Peter Williams, the Asst. Secy of the Navy says he will give a Master Mate's rate for his reward. Pete saw more of her (the Merrimac) than any one else. He saw right into the bore of the gun. . . . Pete says, "Captain, that is for us," and rip! she came. After that we fired but few shots. After an action of about 4 hours we made her run with the after ports down in the water as though she was badly injured, the men running out of the ports into the boats and two wooden (ships) towing her. We gave the wooden boats a shot and made the timber fly. They went off to Norfolk.

We put two shots one after the other into one place on her (the Merrimac's) water line, another just above; 2 shots passed through her roof, several glanced off, and one went through her quarter. We struck her prow or ram and sent the splinters about. The iron flew lively from her very often. She flew a Black Flag with a white cross. Her flag staff we blew a piece off; the flag with one shot was cut half away. We made a hole in her roof that a man stood straight up in when she passed by the point after action.

Thousands of soldiers, men of war people, and shore folks were looking at us, and some of the best glasses in the country were in use. We fought over 4 miles of ground and steamed around and around her, keeping at close quarters. We could steam faster than she. We can make about 6 knots, she not so much. We fired away at the Merrimac for some time before she took notice of us. Our Captain says, "Hold your fire; I will put you alongside directly," so after our first fire rip she came right into us and our 175 lbs. of shot went right through her. Just think of them at but a few feet and theirs not going through our tower. We were very close (in) all the action. Twice we touched and the shot and shell did everlastingly fly around the decks. They tried to put rifle bullets into the holes in the ports and sights but did not.

Our Captain was as cool as a man playing a game of chess. He passed the word to keep cool and not lose a shot. One man was knocked down by the head of a bolt but was all right in a few hours. The other Master was in the tower and had his knee against the side of the tower and a shell struck the tower on the outside at the same time. He was knocked down by it but was soon about again. The concussions caused a little uneasiness in the ears of the men in the tower, but not much. I was in charge down below with the powder division attending to shot, &¢. The time passed very quick away and everyone was in the best humor until our Captain was wounded, and then our pilot house was thought to be unsafe so we did not follow up the Merrimac. If it had not been for that we might have sunk her outright.

We returned to save the Minnesota. In the night she got off and returned to Hampton Roads. In the morning we steamed to Hampton Roads and as we passed the ships we were cheered by everyone, the men of our ship returning it. The soldiers and people of the forts also, and every one of the guard and passing boats. The feeling everywhere was of the most excitable enthusiasm & gratitude. We have been up & down the harbor and to Newport News and hundreds of officers, soldiers & seamen have been aboard and gave us their account of what they saw and how they feel about it.

Our orders are to keep on the defensive for awhile and to look out for the Merrimac. The batteries around Sewell's Point we can see and today the Sawyer Jim on the Rip Raps were firing shell right onto the point, the shells bursting about but I don't know with what effect yet.

We have had changes in officers. Another Captain has come. His name is Jeffers, a man they say is a good fighter. He says he will carry us as well as our other Captain.

I am well and hope you all are. I don't know how long it will be before we have another fight. We are anxious for it. We cleared away for action yesterday noon and steamed over to the point but no vessel was there. The fort has ceased firing on our passing vessels. Today they are removing the troops away from some of the batteries. We hear that we have injured her (the fort) very much and the Captain and 2 Lieutenants are also much hurt, 17 men killed, &¢. We have papers from the North, of March

11, giving us great praise for our fight. The Captain of a French steamer has been on board and was highly pleased. He witnessed the fight. The Rinaldo, Capt. Montague of H.B.M. that took Mason & Slidell from Boston to Bermuda was on board and said his wooden ship was good for nothing alongside of us, that 3 or 4 such as this could whip the world.

I will now close. If any one of my friends wants to know what was done, just pass the letter around, for it is the longest I ever wrote or will do again.

I remain your son,
John

I will write again.

ABRAHAM LINCOLN

". . . the grief of a loss so overwhelming."

IN 1864, although the Union had all but won the Civil War, the battles were not yet ended. There was time, however, for the war-torn Lincoln to pen a note to a Mrs. Lydia Bixby, whose five sons had been killed serving with the Union army.

Executive Mansion
Washington, Nov. 21, 1864

To Mrs. Bixby, Boston, Mass.
Dear Madam:
I have been shown in the files of the War Department a statement of the Adjutant General of Massachusetts that you are the mother of five sons who have died gloriously on the field of battle. I feel how weak and fruitless must be any word of mine which should attempt to beguile you from the grief of a loss so overwhelming. But I anont refrain from tending you the consolation that may be found in the thanks of the republic they died to save. I pray that our Heavenly Father may assuage the anguish

of your bereavement, and leave you only the cherished memory of the loved and lost, and the solemn pride that must be yours to have laid so costly a sacrifice upon the altar of freedom.

Yours very sincerely and respectfully,
A. Lincoln

CARL SCHURZ

"He is the people personified . . ."

CARL SCHURZ exemplifies the miracles of America as a melting pot, mingling those brilliant thinkers from Europe who for diverse causes migrated to the United States.

Already a graduate of the University of Bonn, Schurz was compelled to flee from Germany to Switzerland in 1849, at the age of 20, for revolutionary activities. In 1852 he came to the United States, settling first in Philadelphia, then Watertown, Wis., where between lecturing and writing he entered politics as a member of the newly formed Republican Party.

In 1858, Schurz was campaigning for Abraham Lincoln in the celebrated Illinois Senatorial contest between Lincoln and Stephen A. Douglas, where he formed a friendship with Lincoln that was fully reciprocated.

After Lincoln's election to the Presidency in 1860, and the beginning of the Civil War, the student-politician was made (in the political custom of the day) a Brigadier General of volunteers and later a Major General, following an interval of less than one year, in 1861, when he served as Lincoln's Minister to Spain. Oddly enough, as a politically appointed soldier, he saw more action than many professional officers, including the battles of Chancellorville, Gettysburg and Chattanooga, and, in 1865, with Sherman's army in North Carolina.

In 1864, after he had asked to be relieved in the west, he wrote a letter that was a classic in delineating the best aims of the Union and that, considering its authorship while Lincoln still lived, was prophetic indeed.

It is all the more impressive as it was sent as a private and friendly transmittal of thoughts to Theodore Petrasch, an old German friend with whom he had corresponded voluminously since his flight from Germany, and who, at Schurz's instigation, had migrated to the United States only that year.

Bethlehem (Pa.) Oct. 12, 1864

. . . I cannot share your opinion about what I ought to do or not do in the present crisis. You certainly would not have judged in this manner had you participated in the great battle which lies behind us. Perhaps you were surprised when I came out publicly for the present administration. I believe, however, that a few words on my view of things will make the matter clear to you. Every crisis in human affairs has its main question to which all side issues must unconditionally subordinate themselves. We are engaged in a war in which the existence of the nation—and that means everything—is involved. A party has arisen in this country which threatens to throw away all the results of the war, and this at a moment when by a firm adherence to the present policy the outcome can hardly be doubtful.

The government has unquestionably committed great errors. The individuals who direct the affairs of the country are doubtless not ideal statesmen, although not nearly so undistinguished as people would like to represent them; but all this is incidental. The main thing is that the policy of the government moves in the right direction—that is to say, the slaveholder will be overthrown and slavery abolished . . .

Under such conditions my choice was easily made; it was not doubtful for a moment. If Fremont and McClellan had been my bosom friends, and the members of the present government my mortal enemies, I would have come out for the latter without hesitation . . . Your opinion of the President is too deprecatory. He is indeed a man without higher education and his manners harmonize little with the European conception of the dignity of a ruler. He is an over-grown nature-child and does not understand artifices of speech and attitude. But he is a man of profound feeling, just and firm principles, and incomparable integrity. One can always rely upon his motives, and the characteristic gift of this people, a sound common sense, is developed in him to a marvelous degree . . .

I know the man from personal observation as well as anyone and better than most. I am quite familiar with the motives of his policies. I have seen him fight his way heroically through many a terrible battle and work his way with true-hearted strength through many a desperate situation. I have often criticised him severely and subsequently have not infrequently found that he was right. I also understand his weaknesses; they are the weaknesses of a great man. That he has made great mistakes in the endless complications of his office cannot be denied but can easily be explained. Other men in the same position would perhaps not have made the same mistakes, but they would have made others. Lincoln's personality, however, has in this crisis a quite peculiar significance.

Free from the aspirations of genius, he will never become dangerous to a free commonwealth. He is the people personified; that is the secret of his popularity. His government is the most representative that has ever existed in world history. I will make a prophecy which will perhaps sound strange at the moment. In fifty years, perhaps much sooner, Lincoln's name will stand written upon the honor roll of the American Republic next to that of Washington, and there it will remain for all time. The children of those who now disparage him will bless him . . .

The sequel:

To a degree, the young Schurz's ability to understand this greatness, at a time of great political debate that threatened to tear apart the Union before the Civil War was ended, explained his own greatness.

After risking his whole future in support of Lincoln, he left politics to become a newspaper correspondent and editor, in St. Louis, Missouri. There, while acting as correspondent for the *New York Tribune,* he became co-owner and editor of the German language daily *Westliche Post.* Already he was embarked on a new phase of his career, the education of fellow German immigrants as American citizens.

In 1869, Schurz was appointed Senator from Missouri. He bitterly fought both the policies of President Ulysses S. Grant and the reconstruction program forced on the South.

In his later years he was Secretary of the Interior under President Rutherford B. Hayes, and in turn supporter of the Presidential candidacies of Cleveland, McKinley and Bryan. Turning again to editing and writing in his later years, he remained active until his death in 1906.

As an interesting footnote, Schurz visited Germany in 1868, two years before Bismarck, the "Iron Chancellor," put together the German Empire under Prussian domination. Schurz was in Berlin in January. On February 3, 1868, he wrote from Wiesbaden to his friend Adolf Meyer: "He (Bismarck) sent word through our Secretary of Legation Bucher that he wanted to see me. After our first meeting, he invited me to dinner, on occasion I had him to myself for two hours, and afterwards I saw him once more. I have reason to believe that it was his idea in the beginning to attract me into the Prussian state service."

ULYSSES S. GRANT

"Delay no longer for weather, or reinforcements."

THERE are as many word pictures of General Grant as there are commentators on him, and his leadership in the later campaigns of the Civil War, a very large share of them uncomplimentary. At one time it seemed that Grant had only one trusting friend, and that was President Lincoln.

Perhaps this was because Lincoln could know things about Grant's actions as Commanding General that were otherwise known only to a small coterie of men, either jealous of Grant or wanting him to fail.

There is no place or space here for critical judgment or appraisal (if one were qualified to make it), but two unpublished short notes, which Grant wrote as orders, reveal his direct mind, his firmness and (in their handwriting) an unexpected tidiness.

Grant was at his headquarters at City Point, Virginia, in the cold, wet days of early December, 1864. Far to the westward, as travel moved, but connected by telegraph lines, was an army under General George H. Thomas, who had to move fast in order to expedite Grant's plans and win a victory, to cut off forces that otherwise would reinforce General Robert E. Lee, in the East.

Grant wrote two messages to Thomas that showed his concern and a strained patience, each in his own hand and each marked, in the upper left hand corner, with the word "cipher," thus directing that they be coded before being sent.

City Point, Va., Dec. 9th, 1864
Maj. Gen. Thomas, Nashville, Tenn.
Your dispatch of 1 p.m. today received. I have as much con-

fidence in your conducting a battle rightly as I have in any other officer. But it has seemed to me that you have been slow and I have had no explanation of affairs to convince me otherwise. Receiving your dispatch to Gen. Halleck of 2 p.m. before I did the one to me, I telegraphed to suspend the order relieving you until we should hear further. I hope most sincerely that there will be no necessity of repeating the order and that the facts will show that you have been right all the time.

U. S. Grant
Lt. Gen.

City Point, Va., Dec. 11th, 1864
Maj. Gen. Thomas, Nashville, Tenn.
If you delay attack longer the mortifying spectacle will be witnessed of a Rebel Army moving for the Ohio River and you will be forced to act, accepting such weather as you find. Let there be no further delay. Hood cannot stand even a drawn battle, so far from his supplies of ordnance stores. If he retreats and you follow him he must loose his material and much of his Army. I am in hopes of receiving a dispatch from you today announcing that you have moved. Delay no longer for weather, or reinforcements.

U. S. Grant
Lt. Gen.

The sequel:

Thus spurred, Thomas moved at last. Attacking Hood on December 15, he won a decisive victory on the second day. Lost to Lee was another force on which he had desperately counted.

GRO SVENDSEN

". . . it was raised on land that we call our own . . ."

THEY asked so little, the pioneers who packed their bundles and said final farewells to European homes, crossed the Atlantic Ocean by steerage, and trekked westward to the seemingly boundless prairies.

Some became rich and many of their descendants have become famous. Yet the later years of success accent the courage, the dreams and the satisfaction-with-so-little, that marked the beginnings.

Some of the rich legacies of the private expression of these hopes and dreams are found in the letters of Gro Svendsen, written to her family in Norway and telling of her life in Iowa.

Estherville, Emmett Co., Iowa
December 3, 1865

Previous Parents, Sisters, and Brothers:

. . . We have had a good year, a rich harvest both from the grain that we sowed as well as from the wild fruit and grain. We have plowed and fenced in three acres of new land. On this plot we raised ninety bushels of corn, twenty-four bushels of potatoes, and a plant called sugar cane or sorghum. This sugar cane is pressed and cooked into syrup or molasses. From our patch of sugar cane we got nine gallons of syrup (a gallon is equal to four potter). The man whose pressing and cooking machine we used also got nine gallons so we actually got eighteen gallons all told. We also got some fruit from our garden. It would take too long to list all of it, but I must tell you something about a fruit called "watermelon." We have an enormous quantity of them; I can't compare them to anything I ever saw in Norway. They are as big as a child's head; some are larger. They are round, and the inside is red or yellow. The melons are sweet and juicy. They are eaten just as they are taken from the field, provided they are ripe. I have cooked molasses from them, and I have also brewed juice several times. (Hops grow wild here. They are very plentiful, and we use them throughout the year.) We sometimes sell melons to wayfarers passing by. We usually get ten cents apiece for them. However, most of the melons we shared with our friends and neighbors, many of whom had walked several miles in order to get a chance to taste our watermelons and muskmelons. The latter fruit is not quite so good as the first.

Our harvest was not abundant, but since it was enough to supply our needs for the year and since it was raised on land that we call our own, I want to tell you about it.

This summer we plowed up three acres of land that we plan to sow with wheat next year. Had we known that Ole would come back, we would have plowed up more land this summer. Not knowing when he would return, we let it go with just three acres. By the time he did come home, it was too late to plow any more, so we're letting it go till next summer. So you see we haven't so many acres "under the plow" as they say . . .

This winter we are feeding twenty-one head of cattle, two pigs (a sow and a boar), two horses (a mare and a colt), and three sheep belonging to brother Ole. We also have two bulls belonging to brother Sevat Svendsen. We are paid cash for feeding these cattle. All told we have sixteen farm animals of our own, not counting the young cattle.

We have only four cows. The heifer will bear her first calf this winter, and then we shall have five cows if all goes well. We have only one sheep . . . I have sheared the sheep twice this year. The wool, which was of excellent quality, weighed all of seven pounds.

We butchered two pigs this week, one fully grown, the other eight or nine months old. We had fattened them since last September so they were quite large.

I also want to tell you that this fall we have sold butter for thirty-five dollars—not so much, but I am satisfied for the time being.

Last fall we built a stable for twelve head of cattle. We built it of timber, and right now we are building another like it, but this one is a little larger. They are built a short distance from each other so that we can have a shed between for the bulls (about like the Sansat stable). I can't compare them to the stables in Norway, but around here they are supposed to be among the best. There are many varieties of stable to be seen here. Some are built of branches and hay; others of sod or turf. I have seen a barn where the walls were built of layers of manure piled up one above the other.

Our house is very small and humble, but it's a shelter from the cold winter. I shall say no more about it. However, next spring, if we are all here and all is well, we hope to build a large and comfortable house. We shall build even though it costs a great deal of money to build houses in this country.

The spring of 1864 we bought twelve and a half acres of woodland for one hundred dollars, or eight dollars an acre. We borrowed the money from old Svend at seven percent interest with five years to pay. The trees are exceptionally fine, so if we should want to sell the land again, it would not be difficult to get twice the amount that we paid for it. There is not a great deal of woodland here, and therefore that type of land is much in demand and the prices are steadily rising.

Our woodland is six miles from home, a long way to haul wood; but the road is good. The main road is just outside our door, and it runs past the very edge of the woods. The woodland is two miles from the sawmill in the village of Estherville.

We have had very little pastoral service so far, but we soon hope to get more. A certain Pastor Torgersen has taken it upon himself to visit this congregation two or three times a year. I think we have been very fortunate this fall to have had two services. Two years ago we had thirteen Norwegian families in this congregation, and now we have thirty families and more are constantly moving in. Maybe in time we may be so many that we can have our own pastor.

I have told you in part just how we live. It's so incomplete . . .

Now I have used up all the paper, and I still have so much more to tell you. You no doubt will have to pay extra postage for this letter . . .

CHARLES W. ELIOT

". . . our struggle is a struggle of humanity
against barbarism . . ."

CHARLES W. ELIOT's long career, including forty years as President of Harvard, which he built into its great modern pattern, his writings and public addresses and his "retirement" occupation as an international leader in the struggle for higher educational standards, all seem to push far into the past the violent energies of his youth.

However, much of Eliot's future vigor pours forth in a letter written from Rome in 1865, to his mother, when word of the assassination of Abraham Lincoln reached him him there. Eliot, then 30, had gone to Rome for two years of special studies—a period that incidentally left him with near-hatred for Rome's decadence.

He lived for sixty-one more years, all of them active, and this letter indicates the pattern of morality that would guide him.

Dear Mother,—Thursday, Apr. 27th, in the morning we got the news of the assassination at Washington, the bare facts without particulars, Seward's recovery being said to be hopeless. It must have come just as suddenly to you at home. What a horrible shock it was—the loss of great battles would have been as nothing—battles and campaigns can be retrieved, but now the horrible crime of assassination for political reasons has stained indelibly the annals of the republic.

That is the horror of it to my mind—the men can be replaced, the policy of the government will probably be unchanged, the war will go on without any intermission or faltering, but the dreadful fact remains that an American President has been assassinated by an American. This is a crowning fruit of slavery to our eyes, but to the world and history it is a legitimate fruit of American institutions, such as they have actually been since the Republic was founded. First, civil war, and now, political assassination. Oh, are we copying Rome?

We have been proud of the security of our public servants without guards or any sort of protection against the people—we have said that assassination might be a possible crime for French or Italian or Mexican republicans, but never for Americans. . . . In our admiration of the soldierly virtues of Lee and his army, we felt like embracing our enemies and welcoming them back to Peace and Country. But here is the most dastardly crime thrown across the path of conciliation. It is the last proof that our struggle is a struggle of humanity against barbarism, but how shall we redeem or get rid of the barbarians?

I am no worshipper of men—even now, I don't like to hear Lincoln's name put too near Washington's, but his character seems to me a rough and ungraceful but truly noble growth of republican institutions. He grew to his work, which was holy and it hallowed him. You can count on your fingers the names which History will rank with his. It is the glory and strength of our institutions that we do not depend on any one man or any men for security or for the working vigor of our government. If the assassins thought that the government would be thrown into confusion by their work, they will be disappointed—Lincoln's death will consecrate his policy in the eyes of the people and men will be found to carry it out. He did not lead the people—he rather followed the wisest and best thought of the people, and his successors will do likewise . . .

WILLIAM HENRY JACKSON

"Great times I had with that six yoke of cattle . . ."

A few years after Matthew Brady made his momentous pictorial record of the Civil War, another photographer became famous for his pictures of the vast stretches of the west, photographs that formed the basis of many of the great mural paintings of the Rocky Mountains. This man, who "pioneered" photography in our west, was William Henry Jackson.

Before he ever turned to photography, this gifted young artist had traveled the western territories, with a sketch book in his small knapsack and a bull whip in his hand, as a driver of the teams of twelve oxen linked in six yokes, that plodded at two miles an hour over the plains and through the mountain passes.

When he was 18, Jackson became a "bull whacker" by joining an outfit at Nebraska City, Neb., a small settlement south of Omaha, on the eastern border of Nebraska. When he got to Salt Lake City, Utah—700 miles and three months later—he wrote a letter describing his experiences to his parents, a bull whacker's view of the trip from the Missouri River to Great Salt Lake.

G. S. L. City, Oct. 30th '66

My Dear Father & Mother:

In my letter to you dated the 24th I said nothing of my trip across the plains, and promised to give full particulars in another letter. I should have done so sooner, but my paper gave out in writing that letter & I have not been able to obtain any since— until this morning. As in my first letter, I will open my diary before me & tell my story as plainly as possible from that. I cannot very well send you any sketches with this as they are all too large to mail in my letters. Before I leave here, however, I shall send them all to you. If I carry them with me much longer I may lose them all. I have lost too many already.

As I have before written, we arrived in Nebraska City early Tuesday morning, June 21, and after picking out our outfit, walked out to the corrall—some 4 miles from town. The cattle were herded on the prairie nearby & the wagons all loaded preparatory to starting. Got our dinner that day—baked bread in small iron skillets, fried bacon, & boiled coffee. Relished it very much. That day we all picked out our yokes, chains &c. At night we slept in the wagons on top of the freight—each wagon being covered with a good sheeting. The next morning I helped to yoke up. Were up long before sunrise, and drove in the cattle at once. Such a time I never saw. The "bulls" were wild, many of them had never been yoked even, and if you can imagine the time the boys had who had never had a bow in their hands. The wagons were corralled in a circle, with openings opposite each other forming a good sized yard. The 325 head that we had just crowded the corrall full with hardly a foot to spare. It was no easy task for us green hands to go into that corrall—the bulls ramming and crowding about, pick out your "wheelers" then your "leaders" "swing" & "pointers" and make no mistake. But thats not the worst of it. After half an hours chasing through the mass after a wild fellow, you corner him & manage to fasten the bow by working very carefully—some other steer, having a grudge probably against the one you are gently urging up to the wagon wheel to fasten—gives him a punch in the ribs with his horns and sends him "kiting" into the herd. You hang on manfully and are snaked around "right smart;" get into a jam probably, and have to jump on some of their backs to escape being squeezed to a jelly—then take all the kicks you get, and contrary steers who will "gee" when they should "haw" and who wont stop when told to but go jamming right on, probably into other teams—a person gets all he bargains for and a good deal more. A good many of the cattle we had to larriett, and pull them right down to a wheel & then yoke. There was some queer driving that first day out. There was only a few tongues broken, however. The first few days we made but one drive a day but afterwards always made two—getting in in the morning as soon as it was light enough to see and driving till ten when we would unyoke, cook breakfast, grease up or any other little job, and yoke up again about three & drive till sundown. Our average time after we got started was 15 miles a day. The roads over the plains are most excellent. In fact I've never seen better—broad, level, & smooth, & yet there has never been the first penny expended upon them.

Until we struck the Platte, some 40 miles this side of Kearny, the road lay over rolling prairie. Along the Platte it was very level indeed, with scarcely a single rise or descent along the whole route. Our greatest affliction was the dust—it was fearful & sometimes so thick that it was impossible to see more than a single rod. When we corralled at night we more resembled Egyptian Mummies than living beings. At Kearny I managed to post two or three letters as I have before said. We made no stop there, driving right through and going some 10 or 12 miles beyond. After this commenced my career as a veritable "Bull-Whacker." Great times I had with that 6 yoke of cattle, but before I got through I had them broken into about as good a team as there was in the whole train. Had great trouble at first in making them keep up—couldn't use my whip effectively. The whips they use on the plains are enormous things made of raw hide plaited, about 12 feet long, or more, and an inch & a half in diameter at the belly & with a stock about 18 inches or two feet in length. The "Bull Whacker" takes great pride in his proficiency with his whip. The "popper" consists of a thin strip of buckskin, & with that they will make a report equal to musket every time—and draw blood from the cattle at every stroke. It was some time before I could "pop" or whip scientifically. Driving my teams at first was hard as they required constant attention, had to be at them continually with whip & voice. The first week out many of our boys were so hoarse that they could hardly speak. For the first two or three weeks my feet troubled me a great deal. They didn't blister, but were tender and sore, and ached a good deal nights. I used to come in so tired that I would bunk right in as soon as I had eat my bread & bacon & drank my coffee. The program for one day at this time will give you some idea as to how I relished this kind of life. In the morning just as dawn breaks, and before my sleep is half out, the night watch goes around pounding on the wagons and crying "Roll out! Roll out! the bulls are coming," and as they come crowding and bellowing into the corrall I always mentally, and sometimes quite audibly d—n the bulls. But there they are & I must get up. Sometimes there is a desperate resolution to lie still & sleep and let the consequences be what they may but I think better of it & conclude I might as well get up & do as the rest do. So I stretch myself again, feel for my hat, pull my old shoes on my still aching feet; & back out the wagon half awake—shoulder a yoke and commence looking for my old "off Wheeler." It is hardly light and have some difficulty in distinguishing them all—get my last "pointer" yoked after a while—drive them around to the tongue—hitch on and am all ready to start. I am usually through before some of the rest are and as I feel a little hungry I go over to the mess wagon & secure a bit of bacon & bread, if there is any—and make an early lunch—sometimes I secure it the night before & so have a bit all ready. I feel pretty hungry however before we haul up at noon for breakfast. After corralling, the cattle are turned off to feed. Two men are detailed as herders to keep them from straying. We proceed at once to get breakfast. When we had no regular cook this was usually an affair of a good deal of talk—or in other words "blowing." Who was to get wood? who was to get water? who'll mix the bread? then the coffee & this thing and that thing. After a while it is all done & we each take a piece of bread in one hand & a cup of coffee in the other, find a shady place under some wagon & devour all with a relish. In the evening it is usually dusk before we corrall and quite dark before getting supper. We go in pretty heavy on coffee & as I usually eat quite heartily I sometimes have queer dreams—going to bed immediately afterwards as we do. My dreams run invariably upon my oxen. Almost every night I imagine them up to some impropriety & go tearing out of the wagon. Crowl usually wakes up & brings me back. One dream in particular was comical. We had a big shaggy buffalo robe to sleep on—one night I got up and commenced pulling it from under Crowl's head in a very energetic manner. He, of course, demanded my reason for such a proceeding. I replied, still asleep, "I can't get these old leaders heads around." Another time I woke him with a lively blow in the face. I thought I was at the steers.

Nothing of especial interest occurred on the trip up the Platte to the crossing at Julesburgh. We camped every day within reach of the big muddy. It resembles the Missouri very much—in some places it was two or three miles wide. It is very shallow, a person can ford it almost anywhere & it has a very swift current. Went in swimming in it about every day. Up to Julesburgh we didn't see a single red-skin with the exception of a few Omahas and Ottoes the other side of Kearney. They are great on "tobac" & begged away all they had from some of the boys. We heard a thousand and one rumors however of their hostilities & at Kearny they would not let less than 30 wagons pass & every man was required to be armed. They furnished me a Sharps Carbein & I had a Colts revolver of my own. . . .

GEORGE A. CUSTER

". . . no officer could possibly supply himself with fuel at these rates."

GENERAL Custer's record is one of distinguished military service almost from the day he was graduated from West Point, in 1861.

In the Civil War, he advanced from subaltern to Major General, and when, in 1863, he became a Brigadier General, he was the youngest general in the Union Army.

One body of opinion holds that he led a column of men to extermination at "Custer's last stand," in the vain hope of achieving a victory in the Indian Wars that would overcome the bad feeling he had incurred between himself and President Ulysses S. Grant, by criticizing the latter's Secretary of War.

Be that as it may, his death on January 25, 1876, made him a controversial martyr over whom arguments still rage.

There was another Custer, the efficient and haughty young general who deemed it part of his duty to fight for the welfare of his men. This fatherly feeling flared up in 1867 when, in the middle of one of the severe winters that sweep over the Great Plains, General Custer heard that the House had passed a bill that would require Army officers to purchase their own firewood. He reached for his writing pad and wrote, in his own hand, a graphic letter of protest to Senator Sprague, before whose committee the House bill would come.

Fort Riley Kansas
Jan. 18th 1867.

Hon. W. Sprague
    U.S.S.
My dear Sir

I learn by the public prints that a bill has been passed in the House fixing the Pay of officers of the Army. I have not seen the bill but am informed that it requires officers of the Army to purchase their fuel. This provision might be practical at eastern stations but at many of the western Posts it would be wholly impracticable, for the reason that many of our western Forts and Posts have been established at points remote from timber and fuel is only obtainable at the most exorbitant prices such as no officer could pay, for example at Forts Dodge & Lyon (both in this Dist. Kansas & Colorado) wood has to be hauled upwards of one hundred miles and costs the government by contract at wholesale, from $80 (eighty) to $100 (one hundred) dollars per cord. It is evident that no officer could possibly supply himself with fuel at these rates. And yet at many of the Western Posts which I have necessarily been located at a great distance from timber, the price of fuel is even higher than above stated. In behalf of officers of the Army located in the West I trust some provision will be made in view of the above condition of affairs, which will be just to the government and to its officers. I feel confident that a thorough understanding of this matter will decide it to the satisfaction of all concerned. There are actually Posts in the Western Country at which the entire pay of a subaltern would not procure his pay (sic).

Trusting you will give this matter your attention

I remain with
great respect
your &c
G. A. Custer
Bt. Maj. Genl.
U.S.A.

The sequel:

The bill did not become law.

HORACE GREELEY

"Keep up your hope . . ."

OF all the exhortations springing from the minds of the militant newspaper editors of the Nineteenth Century, none is better known than Horace Greeley's "Go west, young man."

What is less known is that Greeley, a canny business man as well as phrase-maker, sent a colony west, and saw it thrive and prosper, after the manner of the Seventeenth Century English who "invested" in the companies that colonized the North American continent.

Greeley traveled to the west in 1859, and presumably his dreams of colonization began then, but were interrupted by the Civil War. His views infected Nathan C. Meeker, who as agricultural editor of Greeley's paper, the New York Tribune, made a similar trip in 1869 and proposed that Greeley back him in founding a colony.

Greeley called a mass meeting, which convened at the Cooper Institute on Dec. 23, 1869, and authorized a committee to locate and buy a colony site. So infectious was the colonization fever that fifty families joined in the plan, approved a project to be located in Weld County, Colorado, and headed westward in 1870. They incorporated their settlement on May 29, 1871, under the name of Greeley, in gratitude to their sponsor.

Meeker left his job to head the colony as Greeley's deputy (and to watch over the development of Greeley's own private stake) and it was to Meeker that Greeley, writing as the landlord rather than an editor, wrote the following letter, in 1872.

NEW YORK TRIBUNE

New York, Mar. 9, 1872

Friend Meeker,

I have yours of the 4th and answer in haste.

You ought to insist on being relieved from all official duties connected with the Colony. Keep up your hope, that is your share. Throw off official labors upon others. Then you can certainly make your living. I know the paper will pay but you must stop giving credit for anything whenever the service shall <u>bene</u>   .

Now take hold in your paper and drive your <u>people</u> out upon the soil. It is a <u>crowning</u> disgrace that you should <u>not have</u> flour to sell from wheat of your own raising. Resolve that you <u>will</u> have it this year. Talk savagely as to the folly of shutting yourselves up in a village and letting your water run to waste. Insist that the water shall be let in now, and ten thousand acres irrigated before May. You can't let go the <u>real</u> helm yet, but must govern the Colony through your paper. You don't talk half enough about plowing, irrigation, crops, etc.

I want to get out to see the Colony in the Fall, but I never want to see my land till it is green with growing trees. Don't let it go by this Spring.

Yours,
Horace Greeley

N. C. Meeker, Esq.
Greeley
Colorado

The sequel:

The records do not indicate how Greeley's personal investment fared, but the colony thrived. In 1877, Greeley was made the county seat of Weld County, and so remains today.

SUSAN B. ANTHONY

"Well, I have gone and done it!!"

IN 1920, American women won the right to vote, through adoption of the Nineteenth Amendment to the Constitution, ending more than a century of agitation for this now accepted right.

If this represented a triumph for any one person, it was Susan B. Anthony, who, at her death in 1906, had devoted fifty-five years to the battle for women's rights and won a permanent place in history.

In 1872, forty-eight years before

women's votes were legalized, Miss Anthony had cast the first ballot by a woman in an American election, in Rochester, N.Y., and thereby precipitated a "criminal prosecution" of herself that went to the Supreme Court.

After the Civil War Miss Anthony, already a veteran crusader for abolition of slavery and wom-

an's suffrage, contended that if freedmen could vote, women should also have the right. On election day in 1872, she rounded up fifty friends and appeared at the polls, and that night she wrote jubilantly of the day's events, to her close friend, Elizabeth Cady Stanton.

Rochester, N.Y.
November 5, 1872

Well, I have gone and done it!!—positively voted the Republican ticket—Strait—this A.M. at 7 o'clock—& swore my vote in at that . . . All my three sisters voted—Rhoda de Garmo too— Amy Post was rejected & she will immediately bring action against the registrars . . . Not a jeer not a word—not a look—disrespectful has met a single woman . . . I hope the morning's telegrams will tell of many women all over the country trying to vote . . . I hope you voted too.

The sequel:

While the registrars at the polling place were polite, as Miss Anthony noted, the authorities perforce took a different view of this illegal infringement on men's rights. Miss Anthony was arrested and found guilty of violating the election laws. She was sentenced to pay a fine, and of course refused, since publicity was her goal. The incident spread into a national sensation, as more and more women attempted to follow Miss Anthony's

example, at subsequent elections.

Eventually, the United States Supreme Court decided against the suffrage leader, but the movement, while checked by that decision, gained, rather than lost, from the publicity.

Commenting on Miss Anthony's bold actions, an editorial in The New York Times stated: "The act of Susan B. Anthony should have a place in history."

BERNARD J. McQUAID

". . . the claims of every regularly constituted
state on the reverence and obedience of its
members . . ."

IN 1960, the United States faced and met the issue of whether a member of the Roman Catholic Church might become President of the United States. Like so many questions arising in politics, it arose out of ignorance, fear, and false beliefs.

The following is a pastoral letter written in June, 1876, in which the late and famous Bishop McQuaid of Rochester, New York, expressed both a personal and Catholic outlook on the relationship of Catholics to the countries of their residence, as a memorial to the centennial celebration of American independence.

Rochester, New York
Feast of the Sacred Heart, (June 23) 1876

Beloved Brethren of the Clergy and Faithful Children of the Laity:

One hundred years ago, the colonists of this portion of the American continent, faithful to traditions handed down from father to son, that governments are instituted for the people's welfare rather than for the pleasure of rulers, unable to bear the exactions and demands of tyranny, declared in the name of God, whom they invoked, and by virtue of the eternal laws of justice, their independence of their former rulers. Seven years of struggle, accompanied by extreme sufferings and privations, secured their recognition as Sovereign States.

In the Declaration of Independence and in the long war for its recognition, Catholics took part in proportion to their number and means. When the war seemed endless and fruitless, Catholic France came to the aid of the colonists and quickly brought it to a close.

We are now called upon to celebrate, with becoming solemnity and joyfulness, the hundreth anniversary of the day on which the American colonists declared their independence of Great Britain. In the common joy we all participate, in the general celebration we join with our fellow citizens as one people—one nation. Since the earliest settlement of these States, as European immigrants arrived, while cherishing with fond affection the land of their birth, dear to their heart through many tender recollections, they sank old nationalities to take on the new. The country of their adoption became henceforth their only country, as it was their only home. Their children could know no other. Our entire population is one of immigrants of recent or of older date. He is a thoughtless or a foolish man, who designates as foreigners and aliens those who, breaking away from old ties and political claims and duties, settled for life in this new country, making here a permanent home for themselves and their children. It is a slur cast on his own ancestors a generation or two back. An early check to the flow of immigration would have left our country in the possession of the original inhabitants, and the country would have remained the wild, uncultivated waste and forest their untutored hearts loved so much.

There is then one nationality here. It is the nationality of the American people made up of citizens born on the soil, and of citizens recently arrived from other countries, but in whose souls burn a love of republican institutions and a desire to contribute to the growth, the development, the success of our common country.

The dangers from which the earlier settlers were exempt are now crowding upon us. Fortunately, time has strengthened the principles and the spirit of rule by the people, so that the strain now put on republican institutions does not prove too great. It will never prove too great as long as the people remember that all government is from God, and, whether it be by the people or by kings, it must be honestly and manfully obeyed. It will never be too great as long as the majority, the ruling power in a republic, bear in mind that the rights of the minority are not to be trifled with, and that it is as easy and unjustifiable for a number of people to become tyrannical and oppressive, as it is for the centralized power of the monarchy to act for its own pleasure and gain, regardless of the dictates of right and reason.

A population ashamed to work—large numbers of young men brought up in idleness in a country that has no place for drones—professional office-seekers with education enough to be mischievous when not employed—frightful increase of the buying and selling of votes—speculation and bartering of official patronage and influence among the highest officials of the government—abounding immorality among the people—disregard of the indissolubility of the marriage tie—neglect of the wholesome discipline in the family, and the consequent ill-directed training of children, tell us that the essential conditions of self-government are growing weak and passing away.

Thoughtful people who love this government and wish for stability and permanence of its institutions cannot throw off anxiety with regard to its future. Overconfidence in ourselves and much vainglory in the achievements of the past may lead us to claim all the merit of our virtues and work and forget that God, Who has given us the country and an opportunity to rule without despotic power under social and material advantages rarely found.

Arrived at a period in our history calling for at least a moment's consideration of one hundred year's work, growth, and astounding prosperity, it is our duty as Christians to turn to God in humility and gratitude. His merciful hand can be seen in all that has been accomplished. We work and strive, but under His watchful care. He has given us this country. He has given us these homes. He has given us free scope for selfgovernment under peculiar advantages. The example of government by the people has been felt in the European countries, so that empires and kings now seek counsel, and to some extent, control from the chosen representatives of the people. The least we can do in the midst of joyous demonstrations of patriotism, on this memorable anniversary of the Declaration of Independence, is to assemble in our churches and pour forth heartfelt thanks to God for all His mercies bestowed with so bountiful a hand on our country, and pray most earnestly for a continuance of His blessings and protection.

Wherefore on the morning of the Fourth of July, the Holy Mass will be celebrated in every church of the diocese having a resident pastor, and in all the churches in which a High Mass can be sung, it will be the Mass of the Holy Trinity, with Gloria and Credo, and the prayer "pro gratiarum actione sub unica conclusione." In churches in which only a Low Mass can be said, it will be the Mass of the day with the prayer "pro gratiarum."

It will be advisable for pastors on that day, or on some convenient Sunday, to instruct their parishioners in the duties and responsibilities of good citizenship, the claims of every regularly constituted state on the reverence and obedience of its members and the principles underlying the right of command and the law to obey, well satisfied that no patriotism will avail to maintain justice and uphold the weak that is not based on God's law.

The peace of our Lord Jesus Christ be with you, and His arm guard and prosper our beloved country.

JANE ADDAMS

". . . be sincere and don't fuss."

IN a seventy-five-year life span, Jane Addams carved out a career in serving others that culminated, in 1931, four years before her death, in her receiving the Nobel Peace Prize, jointly with Nicholas Murray Butler.

A lifelong spinster, Miss Addams found her vocation by founding, in Chicago, Hull House, a "settlement" based on an English pattern. She went on from this start to develop many methods for assisting foreign-born Americans to adjust to their new environment. In this work her life-long collaborator was Ellen Gates Starr, a classmate at Rockford College, from which both were graduated in 1881, eight years prior to the establishment of Hull House.

There are many clues to the great future development of the Addams mind and her intensely serious nature, in a letter she wrote to Ellen Starr in the summer holiday between their sophomore and junior college years.

August, 1879

What do you understand by being saved? I don't know, of course, whether I have the right idea or not, but what I call it is this—that a people or a nation are saved just as soon as they comprehend their God; almost every nation has a beautiful divinity to start with, and if they would only keep right to that they would be all right, but they don't; they keep getting farther away and lowering their ideal until at last they are lost. Comprehending your deity and being in harmony with his plan is to be saved. . . . I am far enough away now from this. Christ doesn't help me in the least. Sometimes I can work myself into admission of his life and occasionally I can catch something of his philosophy, but he doesn't bring me any nearer to the Deity. I feel a little as I do when I hear very fine music that I am incapable of understanding. This is the nearest that I get to it. I am not so much unsettled as resettled, so often, but my creed is low, be sincere and don't fuss.

WILLIAM TECUMSEH SHERMAN

". . . it is the Law of Natural Change . . ."

GENERAL SHERMAN's reputation remains today in a tug of war between scornfully opposed opinions. Many military authorities say he was the North's greatest general in the War Between the States. Many Southerners still consider him the most detestable of invaders. Yet his recorded story is one of paradoxes, boiling within that supreme paradox, the statesman-soldier.

Who recalls that when the South did collapse, he offered his own direct opponents terms so generous that they were repudiated by Washington, and toned down to the scale of those Grant offered Lee, which are popularly considered the height of generosity? And who but a few students know of Sherman's vast responsibilities directing orderly military protection and military administration of the great western territories, as post-Civil War commander in the west and as commanding general of the Army?

Inevitably, he faced decisions on the Indian question, decisions that provoked bitter controversy. In a letter to Robert Clarke, Sherman set forth views that are equally timely today, on a broader scale, and that reveal evidences of Sherman's character seen by few living persons.

Headquarters Army of the United States

Washington, D.C., Feb 29 1880

Robert Clarke Esq–
  Publisher, Cincinnati, O.
My Dear Sir,

The volume you were kind enough to send me was duly received, as also your letter always welcome. When I gave it to my ADC Genl Roe to attend to that part referring to maps or reports, and thus not having the letter itself by me, may have neglected it too long.

There is no reason why Mr. Manypenny and I should differ on an agreed case of facts—on the Indian question or any other. Two hundred years ago the good people of England were shocked at the inhumanity of our honored ancestors toward the Aborigines in Virginia and in Massachusetts. These ancestors are now to us heroes and martyrs in song and story but then were called fugitives from justice & oppression. Where are the Indians of Virginia and Massachusetts now?

No less than a hundred years ago the Ottawas, Delawares, Shawanees and Creeks possessed Ohio, Kentucky, Tennessee & Alabama, but little rivulets of Emigrants from the Atlantic Seaboard passed the Alleghenies. Conflicts of interest and of arms followed—and then the people of Virginia & Massachusetts were shocked at the barbarity of our fathers toward the Noble Warriors of the then (?) Forest. Where are these Indians now?

Within your memory and mine the Dahcotas, Sacs & Foxes, Pawnees and Comanches milled on the Great Plains from the Falls of St. Anthony to the Rio Grande—happy in the undisputed possession of countless ponies and innumerable buffalo, elk, bear

& deer. The great wave of Civilization pressed on and where are these now?

Who is to judge whether the world is better off for Minnesota, Iowa, Nebraska and Kansas with their five millions of self-supporting people, contributing over a hundred millions of bushels of wheat for the needy all over the earth, with their Colleges, schools, churches, roads and farms, than when the land was an Indian Paradise?

The Emigrants then as now were represented as the off scourings of civilization, as thieves & murderers, as lawless banditti—

And now the. . . . Great. . . . has reached the Rocky Mountains and the Pacific Ocean and we hear of the barbarity of the "pioneer." I read this morning in one of the Journals of the day that the settlers of Colorado are the scum of the earth, murdering Indians out of pure deviltry and when they can find no red victims to their hellish instincts they disguise themselves as Indians and kill white men. This was said of Ohio & Kentucky less than a hundred years ago, but I have been in Colorado—in Montana and in Idaho—and have no hesitation in saying that the Emigrants of today are of the same bold adventurous class as has displaced the Shawnees in Ohio, the Sacs & Foxes in Illinois & Iowa, the Dahcotas in Minnesota and the Pawnees in Nebraska. Two such races of man as ours and the Indian can not live side by side in peace. They must amalgamate or the stronger will displace the other, peaceably if possible, forcibly if it must. Mexico is an example of amalgamation and ours of displacement.

Volumes have been written on this subject, the best known are Smith, Lord Dartmouth, Lafayette, Sir George Simpson, Bishop Whipple and Mr. Manypenny, have all had their hearing & experiments but the process begun in Massachusetts, Pennsylvania and Virginia remains in operation today, and it needs no prophet to foretell the end. No government on earth has expended so much money, so much charity, so much forbearance in this great problem as has the Govt of the U.S. and if the Christian policy has failed it has not been for want of effort but because the problem is insoluble—unless the Indian will change his nature & habits, select his spot of earth, and become as a white man he is doomed. It is not because the white man is cruel, inhuman and grasping but because it is the Law of Natural Change & development—the wrong began at Plymouth Rock and will end in the Rocky Mountains.

Yrs truly,

W. T. Sherman

The sequel:

Sherman was right. The "laws of nature" he cited proved inexorable, at least in this case. Until his death in 1890, he spent much time defending them.

As for his personal reputation, he was finally awarded, by Act of Congress (posthumously along with Grant and Sheridan), the "tombstone rank" of General of the Army. Yet to most schoolboys he is still the Sherman who marched destructively "from Atlanta to the sea."

SAMUEL L. CLEMENS

". . . criticize a piece of literature . . . to an enemy"

THE deep and genuine humor of Samuel Clemens, so much a part of his writing, glowed as well through an infinite variety of anecdotes from his personal life.

Among these, was his invention of the "form letter," to cope with the countless aspiring authors who sent him manuscripts for his comment (as happens to most well-known writers).

The problem that beset Mark Twain the author, and Samuel L. Clemens the man, was how to reply without offending, how to check this nuisance without courting public criticism. The following letter is a typical Twain solution to this problem.

"Dear Sir or Madam.—Experience has not taught me very much, still it has taught me that it is not wise to criticize a piece of literature, except to an <u>enemy</u> of the person who wrote it;

then if you praise it the enemy admires you for your honest manliness, and if you dispraise it he admires you for your sound judgment.

Yours truly,

S. L. C.

P. T. BARNUM

". . . remove existing embarrassments . . ."

P. T. BARNUM, the circus king, was noted alike for his showmanship and for his gall; neither has been exceeded in modern times. He could perpetrate the most outrageous plans and come off with no more severe defeat than a chuckle from the public.

A Barnum classic was his proposal to the aged and distressed Ulysses S. Grant, requesting that Grant add to the sideshow of the "Greatest Show on Earth," his collections of medals and mementoes, to be shown alongside Tom Thumb, the white elephant and other famous Barnum exhibits.

Undoubtedly, Barnum saw no denigration in the offer. Where there was profit in showmanship, Barnum had no scruples considering the cash reward to both Grant and himself sufficient justification.

In 1884, as all the world knew, Grant had suffered bankrupting losses through a bank failure. He owed W. H. Vanderbilt $250,000. Friends generously offered to help, but he resolutely stuck to his honor, although he had no apparent means of repayment. To Vanderbilt, whose assistance had been obtained by the pledge of all property owned by General and Mrs. Grant, the loan was half a token of friendship and half a whip to hold over Grant and such influential friends as he had.

In this atmosphere, Barnum wrote this letter.

New York, January 12, 1885

To General U. S. Grant, twice President of the United States, etc: Honored Sir: the whole world honors and respects you. All are anxious that you should live happy and free from care. While they admire your manliness in declining the large sum recently tendered you by friends, they still desire to see you achieve financial independence in an honorable manner. Of the unique and valuable trophies with which you have been honored, we all have read, and all have a laudable desire to see these evidences of love and respect bestowed upon you by monarchs, princes and people throughout the globe.

While you would confer a great and enduring favor on your fellowmen and women by permitting them to see these trophies you could also remove existing embarrassments in a most satisfactory and honorable manner. I will give you one hundred thousand dollars cash, besides a proportion of the profits, if I may be permitted to exhibit these relics to a grateful and appreciative public, and I will give satisfactory bonds of half a million dollars for their safekeeping and return.

These precious trophies of which all your friends are so proud, would be placed before the eyes of your millions of admirers in a manner and style at once pleasing to yourself and satisfactory to the best elements of the entire community. Remembering that the mementoes of Washington, Napoleon, Frederick the Great and many other distinguished men have given immense pleasure to millions who have been permitted to see them, I trust you will in the honorable manner proposed, gratify the public and thus inculcate the lesson of honesty, perseverance and true patriotism so admirably illustrated in your career.

I have the honor to be truly your friend and admirer,

P. T. Barnum

The sequel:

Grant refused the offer, even after it was repeated with further argument by Barnum. Grant found assistance in another and unexpected direction, a lucrative offer for his Memoirs. In addition, Mark Twain (Samuel Clemens) volunteered his help in this literary effort.

Grant died six months later, in July, 1885.

WILLIAM RANDOLPH HEARST

". . . I am convinced that I could run a newspaper successfully."

ONE evening in 1885, a young man then studying in Washington, D.C., sat down and wrote a letter to his father, George Hearst, one of California's wealthy citizens, who among other properties—and principally for prestige—owned a small newspaper in San Francisco, called the Examiner.

Young William Hearst had ideas. The ideas required capital and he figured that his father had the money. Therefore, with a modesty that perhaps at the time was genuine, and with an ambition he coated with an attempt at humor, he asked for a chance to take over the Examiner.

Had his father replied in the negative, it would have been just another fruitless proposition to a father from a son, but few adults are unaware of the results of the favorable decision, written in reply to this letter.

1885 Washington

Dear Father:

I have just finished and dispatched a letter to the Editor of the Examiner in which I recommended Eugene Lent to his favorable notice, and commented on the illustrations, if you may call them such, which have lately disfigured the paper. I really believe that the Examiner has furnished what is thus far the crowning absurdity of illustrated Journalism, in illustrating an article on the chicken show by means of the identical Democratic roosters used during the late campaign. In my letter to the editor, however, I did not refer to this for fear of offending him, but I did tell him that in my opinion the cuts that have recently appeared in the paper bore an unquestionable resemblance to the Cuticura Soap advertisements; and I am really inclined to believe that our editor has illustrated many of his articles from his stock on hand of cuts representing gentlemen before and after using the efficacious remedy.

In case my remarks should have no effect and he should continue in his career of desolation, let me beg of you to remonstrate with him and thus prevent him from giving the finishing stroke to our miserable little sheet.

I have begun to have a strange fondness for our little paper—a tenderness like unto that which a mother feels for a puny or deformed offspring, and I should hate to see it die now after it had battled so long and so nobly for existence; in fact, to tell the truth, I am possessed of the weakness, which at some time or other of their lives, pervades most men; I am convinced that I could run a newspaper successfully.

Now if you should make over to me the Examiner—with enough money to carry out my schemes—I'll tell you what I would do!

In the first place I would change the general appearance of the paper and make seven wide columns where we now have nine narrow ones, then I would have the type spaced more, and these two changes would give the pages a much cleaner and neater appearance.

Secondly, it would be well to make the paper as far as possible original, to clip only when absolutely necessary and to imitate only some such leading journal as the New York World which is undoubtedly the best paper of that class to which the Examiner belongs—that class which appeals to the people and which depends for its success upon enterprise, energy and a certain startling originality and not up on the wisdom of its political opinions or the lofty style of its editorials: and to accomplish this we must have–as the World has–active, intelligent and energetic young men; we must have men who come out West in the hopeful buoyancy of youth for the purpose of making their fortunes and not a worthless scum that has been carried there by the eddies of repeated failures.

Thirdly, we must advertise the paper from Oregon to New Mexico and must also increase our number of advertisements if we have to lower our rates to do it, thus we can put on the first page that our circulation is such and our advertisements so and so and constantly increasing.

And now having spoken of the three great essential points let us turn to details. The illustrations are a detail, though a very important one. Illustrations embellish a page; illustrations attract the eye and stimulate the imagination of the masses and materially aid the comprehension of an unaccustomed reader and thus are of particular importance to that class of people which the Examiner claims to address. Such illustrations, however, as have heretofore appeared in the paper, nauseate rather than stimulate the imagination and certainly do anything but embellish a page.

Another detail of questionable importance is that we actually or apparently establish some connection between ourselves and the New York World, and obtain a certain prestige in bearing some relation to that paper. We might contract to have important telegrams forwarded or something of that sort, but understand that the principal advantage we are to derive is from the attention such a connection would excite and from the advertisement we could make of it. Whether the World would consent to such an arrangement for any reasonable sum is very doubtful, for its net profit is over one thousand dollars a day and four years ago it belonged to Jay Gould and was losing money rapidly.

And now to close with a suggestion of great consequence, namely, that all these changes be made not by degrees but at once so that the improvement will be very marked and noticeable and will attract universal attention and comment . . .

Your affectionate son,
W. R. Hearst

The sequel:

Ten years later, in 1895, with the Examiner a sensational success, and further bolstered by an inheritance of seven million dollars, William Randolph Hearst moved eastward. Now he was not asking for a chance, but determined to precipitate a war for great stakes in the age of "yellow journalism."

He purchased the *New York Evening Journal* and set out to battle the *World* in particular, albeit he had taken it formerly as his model. In fact, both papers prospered through public interest in the conflict. Hearst's newspapers, and other publications, grew into perhaps the greatest publishing chain proprietary in the United States, prior to the Depression. His financial empire weathered all storms. He bought art works, built his estate at San Simeon, Calif., a baronial castle, and failed only in his political ambitions. Although he briefly held a seat in the House of Representatives, his hopes to be Governor of New York, or Senator, went unfulfilled. He died in 1951.

GROVER CLEVELAND

"I am to be married . . ."

FROM the White House archives comes a letter, written in 1886, that is the only one of its kind and quite possibly the last of its nature ever to be written.

Eleven years earlier, in 1875, Oscar Folsom, President Cleveland's close friend and law partner in former unofficial years, had died, and in his will named Cleveland as the guardian of his 11-year-old daughter, Frances. As the girl grew up, she lived with her mother and kept in close and affectionate touch with "Uncle Cleve." On her graduation from Wells College in 1885, "Uncle Cleve" sent her, from the White House conservatory, the largest bouquet received by a member of her class. He invited the now-grown and attractive young woman to visit the White House with her mother in the fall, for the first formal reception of the 1885 season.

During that visit, Cleveland proposed marriage, and simultaneously urged that Frances go abroad with her mother for a year and think over her answer. He was 48 and she, 21; he was President of the United States, and Frances Folsom did not know even one matron in Washington. In much less than a year, she said "yes."

The wedding was set for Memorial Day, May 30th, and, on returning from Europe, the bride-to-be and her mother were met in New York by Thomas P. Lamont, a member of the President's Cabinet.

But what to do about the announcement? Under Washington protocol, then and now, the President out-ranked everyone else, including the bride's mother. Also, under no circumstances could there be a delay separating announcement of the wedding and the act itself.

So, on the afternoon of May 29, President Cleveland sat at his desk and wrote, with his own hand, identical notes to members of the Cabinet and a few close friends, and sent them out for delivery by a White House messenger.

Washington, D.C., May 29, 1866

Dear   :

I am to be married on Wednesday evening at seven o'clock at the White House to Miss Folsom. It will be a very quiet affair and I will be extremely gratified at your attendance on this occasion.

Sincerely yours
Grover Cleveland

The sequel:

The wedding was quiet, but attempts to have a private honeymoon were frustrated by sightseers, first at the "cottage" the President had purchased at Tennellytown, on the outskirts of Washington, and afterward at Deer Park, Maryland. The marriage was successful, and the new White House mistress soon made friends in Washington "society." So great was her prestige, that her mere disapproval of the then-fashionable bustle put it out of style within a year.

JAMES CARDINAL GIBBONS

". . . prudence suggests that absurdities and fallacies be allowed to perish by themselves . . ."

IN the ever-changing and amazing vortex of public debate over ideas, the voice of Henry George, urging his single-tax theory became a religious issue with such dramatic overtones that it reached the higher levels of Rome, prompting Cardinal Gibbons to write a letter that framed a landmark in the relationship between the Catholic Church and the American public.

The Rev. Edward McGlynn, 50-year-old pastor of St. Stephen's Church—a "powerful orator with a great following"—openly espoused Henry George's ideas. His superior, Archbishop Michael A. Corrigan, ordered him to desist from participation in this political debate, but he refused. The controversy prompted a number of prominent Catholic laymen to recommend that Henry George's works be placed on the Index and thus be officially condemned by the Holy See.

At that point, Cardinal Gibbons,

then the ranking American Catholic churchman, was visiting in Rome. He suggested moderation, "in dealing with so practicable a people as the Americans," and wrote a letter to Cardinal Simeoni, Prefect of Propaganda.

This letter, printed in French in the Archives of the Archdiocese of Baltimore, is carried here in translation, with footnotes, as prepared by the Right Reverend John Tracy Ellis, Secretary of the American Catholic Historical Association.

Rome, February 27, 1887

Your Eminence:

I have already had the honor of presenting to your Eminence my views on the social questions which agitate America, especially with regard to their bearing on the association of the Knights of Labor. But recently another form of social debate has developed relating to the doctrines of Mr. Henry George, an American author identified with the working classes. And since my arrival in Rome I have heard the idea discussed that the writings of Henry George should be put on the Index.[1] After having fully thought over the subject I believe it my duty to submit to your Eminence the reasons which seem to me to demonstrate that a formal condemnation of the works of Henry George would be neither opportune nor useful.

1. Henry George is in no way the originator of the theory which he advocates concerning the right of ownership in land. In his principal book, "Progress and Poverty," he cites precisely the teachings of Herbert Spencer and John Stuart Mill, two of England's chief authors. And in the English periodical work, Contemporary Review, of November 1886, a distinguished Professor quotes them more fully to prove, as he says, that Mr. George is only a plagiarist of these celebrated authors.[2] Now it seems to me that the world will judge it a bit singular if the Holy See attacks the work of a humble American artisan instead of attacking his great masters. And if there are some who, therefore, think that it is the duty of the Holy See to pronounce judgment on Spencer and Mill, perhaps it would be prudent first to take

[1] Up to 1887, George's principal works were *Progress and Poverty* (1879), *Social Problems* (1883), and *Protection or Free Trade* (1886).

[2] H. Sidgwick, *Economic Socialism* (Contemporary Review, L, November, 1886), p. 629.

counsel with their Eminences Cardinals Manning and Newman on the opportuneness of such action.[3]

2. It is well to remark that the theory of Henry George differs from that which is ordinarily called Communism and Socialism. Because as Father Valentine Steccanella shows very well in his work on Communism, published by the Propaganda Press in 1882,[4] this implies "the abolition of private property and the collectivization of all goods in the hands of the State." Now anyone who has read the books of Henry George ought to recognize that he neither teaches this nor does he at all wish it. On the contrary, he maintains the absolute ownership of all the fruits of human energy and industry, even when they amount to great riches acquired either by labor or heredity. It is only with regard to land itself that he would wish to limit the ownership of individuals by an extension of the supremum dominium of the state; and on this point he has expressly stated that he would in no way dispossess the actual owners; but he would desire simply that our system of taxation be changed in such a way that only the land would provide taxes and not the fruits of human industry. One can see, therefore, that in the practical form in which the controversy presents itself to the American public it is simply a question of the government's power over individual ownership of land. And on that there is this to be noted:

a) Anyone who studies properly the question of the relations of the State to the right of ownership of land, as it is treated by Father Steccanella and by other Catholic writers, or as it is regulated by the laws of taxation and the care of the poor in some countries, and especially in England, cannot help but understand that it is a very complex question, very much subject to the diverse circumstances of time and place, and not yet ready to be resolved by a decisive judgment.

b) The question is already before the American public as a

---

[3] "Perhaps the only ecclesiast who knew George personally was Cardinal Manning, who, in the previous year (1885), had discussed with him his proposals to alleviate the world as written in his book, *Progress and Poverty*" (Shane Leslie, *Henry Edward Manning. His Life and Labours* (London, 1921), p. 353.

[4] Valentino Steccanella, S.J., *Del communismo esame critico filosofico e politico* (Rome, 1882).

political issue, and in so practical an arena it will soon find its end;[5]

c) As Mr. George himself realizes, it is only the legislative power of the country which could bring about such a disposition of affairs; and it is quite certain that neither a Congress nor a legislature will ever be found that would vote for such a profound change in social relations, nor a President who would approve it.

d) In a country such as ours, which is by no means a country of doctrinaires and visionaries, speculative theory will not be dangerous, nor will it live long after its practical application will have been rejected; one may, therefore, in all certainty, let it die by itself.

3. Certain recent events in our country have occasioned a profound and widespread popular excitement having an intimate relation to this question.[6] Therefore, your Eminence understands better than I how necessary it is for us to have care not only to speak the truth, but also to choose well the time and the circumstances to say it, so that our action may produce salutary and not fatal results. It seems evident, therefore, that even if there is certainly a need for condemnation, now is not the time to speak out.

4. Finally, it would be prudent to apply here the principle of morality which counsels one not to pronounce a sentence the consequences of which will probably be adverse rather than favorable to the good end proposed. Now I am sure that such would be the result of a condemnation of the works of Mr. George. It would give them a popular importance that they would not ever otherwise have, and would excite an appetite of curiosity that would make them sell by the thousands of copies, and would thus extend immensely the influences that the condemnation sought to restrain and prevent.

Once again, in dealing with so practicable a people as the

[5] Gibbons was referring to George's unsuccessful effort to be elected Mayor of New York City, in the fall elections of 1886, when he was defeated by Abram S. Hewitt.

[6] Here the cardinal was alluding to the removal of Father Edward McGlynn from the pastorate of St. Stephen's Church, New York, by Archbishop Corrigan on January 14, 1887, and the storm that this action stirred up among McGlynn's many followers. For the role of McGlynn in the single-tax movement of Henry George, cf. John Tracy Ellis, *The Life of James Cardinal Gibbons, Archbishop of Baltimore, 1834–1921* (Milwaukee, 1952), I, pp. 547–594.

Americans, in whose genius bizarre and impractical ideas quickly find their grave, it seems to me that prudence suggests that absurdities and fallacies be allowed to perish by themselves, and not run the risk of giving them an importance, a life and an artificial force by the intervention of the tribunals of the Church.

J. Card. Gibbons
Archbishop of Baltimore

The sequel:

Cardinal Gibbons' letter postponed—but did not prevent—the banning of Henry George's works, as advocated by the Rev. McGlynn. Exactly two years later, in February of 1889, the Holy Office handed down its decision, but ruled that in view of the controversial nature of the subject the condemnation need not be published.

In the meantime, the deposed Rev. McGlynn had been excommunicated by the Holy See.

GEE KUNG TONG

Letter of agreement hiring a killer

IN the last quarter of the nineteenth century, there came into being in the United States the infamous Chinese tongs, organized for every sort of purpose from legitimate trade to gang control of prostitution and gambling. Some tongs later developed into respected trade associations, but the combination of greed with which Chinese immigrants preyed on their own people and a low moral structure, carried the early tong organizations to a point comparable in organization, if not in profits, with the bootleg gangs organized, by Americans, in the 1920s.

The tongs hired their thugs, sometimes called "highbinders," as members of disciplined forces in which killing was a means of protecting, or doing, business, and in which a breach of discipline by a soldier, such as a killing on his own, was not countenanced.

When the United States Industrial Commission investigated the highbinder tongs operating in San Francisco in 1901, it turned up one specific letter to a "soldier," written some years before and graphically illustrating their criminal ethics.

To Lum Hip, Salaried Soldier:

It has been said that to plan schemes and devise methods and to hold the seal is the work of the literary class, while to oppose foes, fight battles, and plant firm government is the work of the military. Now this tong appoints salaried soldiers to be ready to protect its members and assist others.

This is our object. All, therefore, who undertake the military service of this tong must obey orders, and without orders they must not dare to act. If any of our brothers are suddenly molested it will be necessary for you to act with resolute will. You will always work in the interest of the tong, and never make your office a means of private revenge. When orders are given you shall advance gallantly to your assigned task. . . .

If, in the discharge of your duty, you are slain, we will undertake to pay $500 sympathy money to your friends. If you are wounded, a doctor will be engaged to heal your wounds, and if you are laid up for any length of time, you will receive $10 a month. If you are maimed for life, and incapacitated for work, $250 will be paid to you, and a subscription taken to defray all costs of your journey home to China. Furthermore, when you exert your strength to kill or wound enemies of this tong, and in so doing are arrested and imprisoned, $100 per year will be collected for every year in jail.

Dated this 13th day of the 5th month of the 14th year of Kwong Su.

THOMAS A. EDISON

". . . my first mailing phonogram."

IN the spring of 1888, Thomas Alva Edison awaited two great events, the arrival of a baby and perfection of his dictating machine, which grew out of his invention of the music-playing phonograph.

Both were on his mind when he was visited by a Colonel Gouraud, his English commercial representative, who sailed for home with the expectation of receiving a letter or cablegram about one or the other, or both, soon after arrival.

What he did get, was the first recorded voice letter ever sent by Edison.

In my laboratory in Orange, N.J.
June 16, 1888, 3 o'clock A.M.

Friend Gouraud:

This is my first mailing phonogram. It will go to you in the regular U.S. Mail via North German Lloyd Eider. I send you by Mr. Hamilton a new phonograph, the first one of the new model which has just left my hands.

It has been put together very hurriedly and is not finished, as you will see. I have sent you a quantity of experimental phonogram blanks, and music by every mail leaving here . . .

Mrs. Edison and the baby (Madelaine) are doing very well. The baby's articulation is quite loud enough but a trifle indistinct, it can be improved but is not bad for a first experiment.

With kind regards,

Yours,
Edison

The sequel:

The invention of the "phonogram" came ten years after Edison's first patented model of the phonograph. Altogether he held 1,300 patents on his life's work. His business acumen was always sharp, and when he introduced the dictating device—taking recording out of complicated studies and making it available to any office—he specified that he wanted it sold "for business purposes only."

MARY BAKER EDDY

". . . the right intuition which guides you safely home."

THE great religious revivals of the nineteenth century produced no more dramatic and enduring development than the work of Mary Baker Eddy, discoverer of Christian Science and founder of the Christian Science Church. A cultured student and inspiring personality, whose work is a force in today's world, Mrs. Eddy first copyrighted her writings in 1875, from which date the church's growth began.

Only fifteen years later, the new church had become so widespread that it had branches throughout the United States and the British Isles. On April 2, 1892, Mrs. Eddy wrote to First Church of Christ, Scientist, Denver, a letter which is today considered a significant reflection of her thinking, in the 72nd year of her life.

Beloved Pastor and Brethren—"As in water face answereth to face," and in love continents clasp hands, so the oneness of God includes also his presence with those whose hearts unite in the purposes of goodness. Of this we may be sure: that thoughts winged with peace and love breathe a silent benediction over all the earth, cooperate with the divine power, and brood unconsciously o'er the work of His hand.

I, as a corporeal person, am not in your midst: I, as a dictator, arbiter, or ruler, am not present; but I, as a mother whose heart pulsates with every throb of theirs for the welfare of her children, am present and rejoice with them that rejoice.

May meekness, mercy, and love dwell forever in the hearts of those who worship in this tabernacle; then will they receive the heritage that God has prepared for His people,—made ready for the pure in affection, the meek in spirit, the worshipper in truth, follower in good.

Thus founded upon the rock of Christ, when storm and tempest beat against this sure foundation, you, safely sheltered in the strong tower of hope, faith and Love, are God's nestlings; and He will hide you in His feathers till the storm has passed. Into His haven of Soul there enters no element of earth to cast out angels, to silence the right intuition which guides you safely home.

Exercise more faith in God and His spiritual means and methods, than in man and his material ways and means, of establishing the Cause of Christian Science. If right yourself, God will confirm His inheritance. "Be not weary in well doing." Truth is restful and Love is triumphant.

When God went forth before His people, they were fed with manna; they marched through the wilderness; they passed through the Red Sea, untouched by the billows. At His command, the rock became a fountain; and the land of promise, green isles of refreshment. In the words of the Psalmist, when "the Lord gave the word: great was the company of those that published it."

God is good to Israel,—washed in the waters of Meribah, cleansed of the flesh,—good to His Israel encompassed not with pride, hatred, self-will, and self-justification; wherein violence covereth men as a garment, and as captives they are enchained.

Christian Scientists bring forth the fruits of Spirit, not flesh; and God giveth this "new name" to no man who honors Him not by positive proof of trustworthiness. May you be able to say, "I have not cleansed my heart in vain."

Sir Edwin Arnold, to whom I presented a copy of my first edition of "Science and Health with Key to the Scriptures," writes:—

> Peace on earth and Good-will!
> Souls that are gentle and still
> Hear the first music of this
> Far-off, infinite, Bliss!

So may the God of peace be and abide with this church.

Affectionately yours,
Mary Baker Eddy

The sequel:

Mrs. Eddy's leadership of her growing church continued until her passing in 1910, and her ideas are perpetuated through the Board of Directors of the Mother Church, The First Church of Christ, Scientist, in Boston, Massachusetts.

FRANCIS PHARCELLUS CHURCH

"Yes, Virginia, there is a Santa Claus."

ONE day a little girl, 8 years old, troubled by doubts aroused by the comments of her friends, sat down and wrote a letter to The New York Sun, a New York newspaper. She asked a question, and the inspired answer, printed as an open letter from Francis Pharcellus Church, settled this question once and for all (or at least for the immediate future).

New York, Sept. 21, 1897.

We take pleasure in answering at once and thus prominently the communication below, expressing at the same time our great gratification that its faithful author is numbered among the friends of The Sun:

"Dear Editor:

I am 8 years old.
Some of my little friends say there is no Santa Claus.
Papa says, 'If you see it in The Sun it's so.'
Please tell me the truth, is there a Santa Claus?

Virginia O'Hanlon,
115 West 95th Street"

Virginia, your little friends are wrong. They have been affected by the skepticism of a skeptical age. They do not believe except they see. They think that nothing can be which is not comprehensible by their little minds. All minds, Virginia, whether they be men's or children's, are little. In this great universe of ours man is a mere insect, an ant, in his intellect, as compared with the boundless world about him, as measured by the intelligence capable of grasping the whole of truth and knowledge.

Yes, Virginia, there is a Santa Claus. He exists as certainly as love and generosity and devotion exist, and you know that they abound and give to your life its highest beauty and joy. Alas! how dreary would be the world if there were no Santa Claus! It would be as dreary as if there were no Virginias. There would be no childlike faith then, no poetry, no romance to make tolerable this existence. We should have no enjoyment, except in sense and sight. The eternal light with which childhood fills the world would be extinguished.

Not believe in Santa Claus! You might as well not believe in fairies! You might get your papa to hire men to watch in all the chimneys on Christmas eve to catch Santa Claus, but even if they did not see Santa Claus coming down, what would that prove? Nobody sees Santa Claus, but that is no sign that there is no Santa Claus. The most real things in the world are those that neither children nor men see. Did you ever see fairies dancing on the lawn? Of course not, but that's no proof that they are not there. Nobody can conceive or imagine all the wonders there are unseen and unseeable in the world.

You tear apart the baby's rattle and see what makes the noise inside, but there is a veil covering the unseen world which not the strongest men that ever lived, could tear apart. Only faith, fancy, poetry, love, romance, can push aside that curtain and view and picture the supernal beauty and glory beyond. Is it all real? Ah, Virginia, in all this world there is nothing else real and abiding.

No Santa Claus! Thank God he lives, and he lives forever. A thousand years from now, Virginia, nay, ten times ten thousand years from now, he will continue to make glad the heart of childhood.

SAMUEL GOMPERS

". . . indemnity . . . will not be tolerated . . ."

FROM 1886 until his death in 1924 (with the exception of one year) Samuel Gompers was the president of the American Federation of Labor, which he helped to found. In that role, the immigrant English cigar maker, born in London in 1850, became one of America's most respected union leaders, despite his hard-hitting conduct of labor's fight for rights in the power struggles of the late nineteenth and early twentieth centuries.

Gompers actually led two fights, one on behalf of his union and the other against more radical organizations, such as the Knights of Labor, and ideas that would compromise the clear-cut stand he pictured for labor. Basically, he believed in limiting labor struggles to the issues of shorter hours, higher wages and better working conditions; he condemned political action by labor as an organized party force, and he also fought hard against proposals to pay off or buy off unions from the role he saw for them. It was this latter fight that prompted an historic, though brief, letter Gompers wrote, circa 1905.

After a hard-fought strike at the Armour and Company packing plant in Chicago, a James A. Cable sent Gompers a message suggesting that the unions wished to demand an indemnity, aside from their working contract, of $50,000.

Gompers stand, unpopular with fellow union leaders at the time, was stated uncompromisingly in his reply to Cable.

. . .

Now as to the other matter, that is the demand made by the unions from the company for an indemnity of $50,000 to be divided between the unions, this, let me say, should not be encouraged by the Central . . . . . . , nor will it be tolerated by the American Federation of Labor, and should be abandoned by the unions. Such a position is not only unjust, but it cannot be defended before the honest sentiment of a right thinking people of our country and will in the end, even if acceded to, rise up and haunt the unions and the general labor movement bringing disgrace upon our cause and injury to our progress. The only indemnity which organized labor seeks for any wrongs inflicted upon us and upon our members is in the shape of higher wages, shorter hours, and better conditions of labor.

THEODORE ROOSEVELT

". . . dealing with these peace envoys . . ."

THEODORE ROOSEVELT was something less than the most patient of men, but he controlled himself under circumstances that would have sorely tried the most phlegmatic temperament, when he undertook the greatest diplomatic task of his career: negotiation of peace between Japan and Russia after their brief war early in the twentieth century, in the course of which Japan obliterated Russia's presumably mighty fleet.

The conference was held in the Summer of 1905, at points ranging from Portsmouth, N.H., to Oyster Bay, Long Island, the President's home, and including ceremonial visits aboard the luxury yacht Mayflower, which served as the Presidential yacht for 30 years after the Spanish-American War.

The whole conference would have been labeled a comic opera, were not the stakes involved so great. It spread over the world, in fact, and included diplomatic dabbling between the Russian Czar (Nicky) and the German Kaiser (Willy). At the conference itself, the representatives of the contending powers exchanged the most cordial formalities on social occasions and then haggled like rug dealers at the conference table.

The American President kept his patience and brought about diplomatic accord, but one evening he pencilled a private note to his good friend, Jules Jusserand, the French Ambassador, in which he bared his feelings.

August 21, 1905

Dealing with senators is at times excellent training for the temper, but upon my word dealing with these peace envoys has been an even tougher job. To be polite and sympathetic and patient in explaining for the hundredth time something perfectly

obvious, when. . . . I really want to give utterance to whoops
of rage and jump up and knock their heads together—well, all
I can hope is that self repression will ultimately be good for my
character.

ANDREW CARNEGIE

*"Booker Washington is to rank with the few
immortals . . ."*

BOOKER T. WASHINGTON was given a luncheon under the auspices of the Anti-Slavery and Aborigines Protection Society in London. Andrew Carnegie was one of the distinguished guests invited. Not being able to attend, he wrote the following letter to John H. Harris, secretary of the Anti-Slavery and Aborigines Protection Society.

Skibo Castle
Dornech
Sutherland
Sept. 19th, 1910

Dear Mr. Harris:

I regret exceedingly to miss any opportunity of doing honor
to one of the greatest men living, Booker Washington. Taking
into account his start in life, born a slave, and now the acknowledged leader of his people, I do not know a parallel to the ascent
he has made. He has marched steadily upward to undisputed
leadership, carrying with this the confidence and approval of the
white race, and winning the warm friendship of its foremost
members—a double triumph.

Booker Washington is to rank with the few immortals as one
who has not only shown his people the promised land, but is
teaching them to prove themselves worthy of it,—a Joshua and
Moses combined.

Very truly yours,
(signed) Andrew Carnegie

MAXWELL PERKINS

". . . material things in life are only valuable as means . . ."

FOR thirty years, "Max" Perkins filled a special niche in modern literature as editor, guide and critic for a brilliant generation of American writers. His realm was the publishing house of Charles Scribner's Sons, where he entered the editorial department in 1914, after several years in the advertising department of the same firm.

During his transition period, while he was convalescing from an appendectomy, he wrote a letter to his boyhood friend and former fellow undergraduate at Harvard University, Van Wyck Brooks. Brooks had sent along a manu-script of a new book, for Perkins to pass on to the editorial department, which he soon would join. The book appeared later under the now famous title, *America's Coming of Age,* published by B. W. Huebsch.

In writing to Brooks about its rejection by William Carey Brownell, then senior editor at Scribners, Perkins not only gave his author friend some good advice but dramatically revealed the depth and breadth of his thinking and gave some hint of the capabilities that would bring him such fame as an editor, in his maturity.

Muhlenburg Hospital, May 20th

Dear Van Wyck:

Thanks for your letter, which came the night before my operation, a matter so simple and comfortable as to call for no comment here and now. I had already—after reading but a few pages of it—given your manuscript to the Editorial Department; and they had decided against it, although strongly impressed by the cleverness and mental independence of the writer; and therefore put by it into an attitude of welcome toward any other thing you may send in. I gathered that the chief objection was that "you swept these fellows into the dustbin of the past with a contemptuousness of gesture which was at least pre-mature"–Mr. Brownell's words, spoken with an appreciative smile and the assertion that you were certainly a "live wire." I think this will enable you to understand their position.

I hope to be in the office for one day on June first and will then pass the manuscript on, personally, to some other publisher, Henry Holt or Stokes, I should think, and will keep in touch with them. When I go back to work, a week later, it will be in the Editorial Department, not the Advertising. Hoppin is leaving to become a partner of Duffield, and I shall fill his place, more or less.

Why don't you write something in "lighter vein" about the sort of life you are seeing in England, from an American point of view; for you are seeing an aspect of English life not often commented upon, if ever, at first hand, for Americans. And send it to Scribner's Magazine via me.

I started once to write you at length about an idea which has bothered me for months—but bothered less and less, in one way, as it became gradually more and more convincing to me and acted to give life, in general, a purpose, and the world a meaning. It ought to be set forth by one standing or sitting, not by one lying on a bed. But I will state it roughly.

Resolved:—that should man stand entirely free of the regime of competition in the widest sense, the motive forces acting upon him would be so utterly different from those that now compel him as to mould him into an entirely different creature from that which he now is. Indeed, that this change may be that new environment which evolution requires (always) to produce a higher type of being, a real superman; and so to advance life a step nearer perfection.

Now if this is true, then the terribly depressing historical theory—so hard to resist—that man is now intrinsically no better than he was four thousand years ago, may imply nothing for the future . . .

The idea depends upon one we discussed last Spring—that of an era in which the production of necessities would be so apportioned among men that an almost negligible part of a man's time would be given to this purely material work—a conception principally supported by the fact that the power of machinery is now so great as to make possible such a reduction of actual man-work. In that case, a leisure class could be based not, as in the past, on slavery only, but on machinery; and this class could include everybody.

Now all men agree that, in theory at least, the material things in life are only valuable as means, and that the true ends are the immaterial, i.e., the intellectual and spiritual things. And if such an era of leisure from material pursuits would turn men to these unmaterial pursuits we can at last read a satisfactory answer to that puzzling question which, as Rousseau showed, could be answered before at least as well by a "no" as by a "yes"—the question, "Has the progress of science done many any real good?" If it has merely made him physically more comfortable, luxurious, even more healthy, it has not improved him intrinsically. If it has made possible his emancipation from the animal demands of existence to such an extent that his powers are therefore turned into spiritual channels, it will be the cause of the most extraordinary improvement in man's estate. And, in that case, the purpose of all this otherwise futile inventing of engines, etc., is clear as daylight.

But most men will contend that this now possible emancipation from material toil would simply reduce man to sloth or libertinism, according as he was individually made. And I answer, that appears to be so because you can only regard man through a competitive atmosphere! How can you even guess how radically he would change in the utterly different non-competitive atmosphere? You can only be sure of the tendency, not the extent of the change. You can be sure that those qualities demanded for success in a competitive regime would weaken and tend to die; and that those qualities that weaken and die now would tend to grow vigorous and to gain control. The qualities of competition are selfish, brutal, beast-like qualities as compared with the softer, generous qualities whose presence in a man handicaps him under the competitive regime; and therefore the change that would take place in him would be from selfishness toward generosity, and from material aims to spiritual aims—from the endeavour to become eminent through the power of wealth and the display of possessions, to the endeavour to perfect one's self in whatever art one was by nature driven towards, were it only that of sympathizing with all sorts of people, were it even that of writing epic poems.

But, you object, do you observe any such change in those few men who inherit wealth and, so, have leisure? No. Because they are virtually as much the creatures of competition as anyone. They have no other air to breathe but that of competition; and even the very great are circumscribed by the prevailing order. Consider the enormous power of merely local and temporary regimes over men, how the aristocracy was always, for ever so long, accepted as a permanent fact—a superior race to be obeyed and reverenced, so that its destruction was unthinkable. And the terror of the French on being at first without a king! Men had adjusted their whole existence to the regime of royalty, and those qualities in them that would have rebelled had lain dormant or died.

But how far greater and more all-pervasive is this regime of competition, which has always, everywhere, existed; has ever been the one great principle on which life operated among men. Can anyone doubt but that it has bred up a certain set of qualities and worked to suppress and repress any other qualities incompatible with it and disadvantageous to have under it; that it has held up for honor and respect those qualities whose presence in a man made him pre-eminent in it, and held up for contempt those characteristics—even though Christ put some of them first of all—which held man down in it, just as in periods of war certain characteristics, now distasteful, become the great and all-admirable ones.

And just as in those war eras men were from very babyhood taught to develop those war-qualities and to choke such as conflicted with them, so now it is in competition: from the moment of birth, consciously or otherwise, by parents, teachers and society, the qualities that further a man in the competitive way of life are nurtured and the others held down, rooted out, or allowed to remain rudimentary. Now what would happen if this great influence that pulls up one set of qualities and pulls down the other were removed: all the rudimentary ones—(who can say how many are not even recognized at all now)—would come to natural growth and the others would not come, as now, to unnatural growth. Then men would not run to sloth and dissipation, for the growth of these other tastes and interests—spiritual and intellectual—would make those things repulsive, or at least would furnish infinitely more enjoyable substitutes. It would be found that all men had in them—though now so often totally repressed —a love for some pursuit now often held contemptible. (Do we not largely here, now, hold contemptible all the arts—at least we did yesterday—and is it not because the love of them curbs a man in competition, partly?)

Now there is no positive evidence of what I hold. There could not be, since competition has always been the great prevailing influence. But there is the case of Athens, when the influence of competition was partially excluded. And did not the very things happen, to some extent, that I have named—did they not hate vice and love virtue and beauty? But how much more would this be so if competition were banished from the whole world and there was no slavery. What might not man then become?

If you understand this, it will be chiefly by imagination. I have not been able to say it fully or well, and now my pencil is used up entirely.

Yours as ever,

ALAN SEEGER

"And this is the supreme experience."

FOR more than forty-five years in the past, and who knows for how many years to come, millions of persons will remember the gripping title of a poem, "I Have a Rendezvous With Death." It is a haunting chord of words that sing alone, even without reading the poem or knowing much about its author.

Knowing more, one feels touched to recall that it was the self-composed prophecy of a young man who, on July 4, 1916, suddenly turned from a living and gifted young American poet into a bullet-riddled body wearing the uniform of the French Foreign Legion. Alan Seeger died twenty-one months after enlisting to fight for freedom, within weeks after Germany started World War I.

Two of the letters of Alan Seeger show, first, his philosophy that held firm from the day he enlisted, and, second, his insight into his own fate, and his concern that, should he fall in battle his last poems would live on.

The first letter was sent to his mother.

February 1, 1916

I am in hospital for the first time, not for a wound unfortunately, but for sickness. Funny I should be ill this winter when we are in the rear, whereas I passed the last from October to July in the trenches without missing a day. I usually have an attack of grippe every year in midwinter, but this time it took hold of me more seriously than ever before and the fever ran so high that I had to be evacuated. They call it *"bronchite."* I have been here two weeks and the fever still comes round regularly every evening, but diminishing now. The old trouble of not being able to breathe deep. I am getting well now but am weak. Until further notice do not address letters to regiment but to F. L. & T. Co. The reason is that after leaving here I shall have a *congé de convalescence,* after which I shall probably go to the dépôt at Lyon instead of directly back to the regiment, according to custom. Then I shall return to the regiment with the next detachment of reinforcements, but will not be assigned to the same battalion or company. This means very likely that I shall not return to the regiment for quite a while to come.

Seeing the division is not on the front, this does not displease me at all. The life in the rear in time of war has lots of drawbacks. What it gains in security it gains also in ennui. It is excessively hard, consisting of daily drills, and, three or four times a week, all day battalion or regiment manoeuvres, combined with long marches and all kinds of devices to keep the troops in shape. This is all right in good weather, but good weather in France is rare in winter. The divisions of the colonial corps which are to do big work in the spring are being put through the hardest kind of training, for modern warfare has proved such a novelty that organization and instruction has practically had to be begun anew. But all this is chiefly important for the officers and the *sous-officers.* I know my business well enough now to be able to dispense with it very easily. I shall get rest and a change of air, liberty and solitude and even the chance to write a little.

As for my book of poems, it is better not to talk of that. It is the great disappointment of my life. . . . When I was in Paris I met the whole Embassy, from the Ambassador down, and they have taken the matter in hand and may surreptitiously be able to extricate the manuscript. If it is lost it will be a terrible blow to me.

You are right in making the most of past moments of happiness. There is a common bourgeois notion which, associated with the common bourgeois ideal of a man finally making enough money to retire and live on his income, pictures the happy life as a kind of steady progression through a series of ups and downs toward a kind of plateau, the summit of which once attained, he can thereafter march along tranquilly on a level of unbroken and indestructible well-being. It is perfectly clear that such a notion is entirely illusory, in the multiple accidents to which life is susceptible, for even supposing that he has attained such a level by the realization of every other earthly ambition, he is always walking on the unstable brink of the love that he has created for himself and upon which he is dependent, the crumbling of which beneath his feet by death or abandonment would immediately plunge him into the blackest of abysses, where everything else that he has realized would mean nothing. As for myself, I look upon life as a series of ups and down, right up (or down) to the very end. The idea of being higher at the end than at the beginning was never part of my reveries. I never conceived the advent of a moment when turbulence and strife could be thought of as definitely put behind one. But I clung passionately to, and drank deep of, such moments of happiness as circumstances set before me—the importance to me was the moment that joy rescues from oblivion—and for me the measure of a happy life was simply the proportion in which the sum-total of these moments of happiness scattered indiscriminately through it, outbalancing the sum-total of the unhappy one.

I may not be back with the regiment until spring, but I shall march with it to the big attack. This summer will see the decisive campaign of the war. If we can break through, carry trenches and *fortins,* get them on the run, advance north, north, through nights red with the flame of burning villages, enter the big conquered cities and deliver a population for two years captive and oppressed, it would be the experience of a thousand years, an emotion that would more than compensate all the sacrifices I have made, something really worth risking your life for. If we don't do it this time, it will be about proven that it can't be done . . .

So Alan Seeger viewed the approaching campaign when the French would unsuccessfully attempt to throw back the invading tide, at this period still more than a year removed from mobilization of his own country for this war.

As he had anticipated, he eventually was sent back to his regiment, and the regiment sent into battle position on June 30, prompting Seeger to tell a comrade, "my dream is coming true," while adding a touch of disappointment at not being able to enjoy leave on July 4, in Paris. He wrote his last letter to a friend.

June 28, 1916

We go up to the attack tomorrow. This will probably be the biggest thing yet. We are to have the honor of marching in the first wave. No sacks, but two *musettes, toile de tente* slung over shoulder, plenty of cartridges, grenades, and *baionnette au canon.*

I will write you soon if I get through all right. If not, my only earthly care is for my poems. Add the ode I sent you and the three sonnets to my last volume and you will have *opera omnia quoe existent.*

I am glad to be going in the first wave. If you are in this thing at all it is best to be in to the limit. And this is the supreme experience.

WILLIAM E. BORAH

". . . to respect my convictions and my own views."

WHETHER liked or hated for his isolationism, William Edgar Borah was respected as the Senator from sparsely populated Idaho. In his long career, he was regarded as a man of political integrity and a student of political philosophy, even by those who sought by every means to strip him of his power.

Basic in Borah's philosophy was the thesis that a Senator, once elected, was supposed to think independently on the basis of public good, regardless of the popularity or unpopularity of his stand on any particular issue, assuming that the public electing him would always have the right to repudiate him if

he were wrong.

A test of this philosophy came relatively early in his career, when Borah, for reasons which he considered good, opposed the Constitutional Amendment to give equal suffrage to women. He was challenged on his stand by E. A. Burrell, a fellow Republican from Idaho, who wrote to Borah that he must support the cause because the majority of the Idaho population obviously favored it.

Borah's reply set forth his viewpoint in words that have been compared with thoughts on the same subject voiced earlier by Edmund Burke.

You say: "As our representative you have no moral or legal right to set up your individual views against the collective judgment of the people:" Yes, I have and then the people have the greater right to retire me.

But, Burrell, to say that because a man is a Senator he is to have no views of his own, no convictions, no conscience is to advocate a doctrine which upon reflection you will be ashamed of and which you yourself as a Senator would never accept. If I go before the people and pledge myself to certain policies I am bound to carry them out . . . but if questions arise here, as this question does, I have a right, and am honor bound, to respect my convictions and my own views, and then submit my case to the people, and if they approve they will keep me here and if they disapprove they will retire me. But now, Burrell, there is an easy way out of this. I dislike to give up my friends . . . but . . . I am prepared to give up both friends and party. I suggest, therefore, in perfect sincerity, that you go to Boise, ask S. D. Taylor to call the state central committee together, and if the committee . . . feels that my position will jeopardize the success of the party and will pass a resolution to that effect, I will tender my resignation as a candidate, and you can fill my place on the ticket . . . All I ask is that this action be taken prior to the 5th day of September so that I may adjust my own conduct in time to test this question and my position on these public matters before the people of my state.

You said in your conclusion that if I should change my attitude the people from coast to coast would applaud my action. They would denounce me in their hearts if not in words, as they should, as a miserable, cringing coward who would have their contempt, and, what is even worse for me, my own.

FRANKLIN K. LANE

"After all, what is property?"

THE sudden impact of World War I stirred men's minds to questions never before asked in this country by "responsible citizens."

One of these men was Franklin K. Lane, Secretary of the Interior in President Woodrow Wilson's Cabinet, a conservative and prosperous citizen. In a personal letter to Ambassador A. B. Houghton in London, he made some pithy observations on the slowness experienced in converting bureaucratic machinery to a crash war program, and then wrote lines that were prophetic.

. . . From now . . . you will see a steadier, surer movement of men, munitions, food, and ships. The whole country is solidly, strongly with the President. There are men in Congress bitterly against him but they do not dare to raise their voices, because he has the people so resolutely with him. The Russian overthrow has been a good thing for us in one way. It will cost us perhaps a million lives, but it will prove to us the value of law and order. We are to have our troubles, and must change our system of life in the next few years.

A great oil man was in the office the other day and told me in a plain, matter-of-fact way, what must be done to win—the sacrifices that must be made—and he ended by saying, "After all, what is property?" This is a very pregnant question. It is not being asked in Russia alone. Who has the right to anything? My answer is, not the man, necessarily, who has it, but the man who can use it to good purpose. The way to find the latter man is the difficulty.

We will have national woman suffrage, national prohibition, continuing inheritance tax, continuing income tax, national life insurance, an increasing grip upon the railroads, their finances and their operation as well as their rates. Each primary resource, such as land and coal and iron and copper and oil, we will more carefully conserve. There will be no longer the opportunity for the individual along these lines that there has been. Industry must find some way of profit-sharing or it will be nationalized. These things, however, must be regarded as incidents now; and the labor people, those with vision and in authority, are very willing to postpone the day of accounting until we know what the new order is to be like . . .

SHERWOOD ANDERSON

Of Mark Twain: *"He had proud conscious innocence."*

IN many ways Sherwood Anderson's still fresh memory (he died in 1941) calls up a comparison with the ancient Biblical prophets. His life was long and he never stopped growing; he had parables to tell and he told them in all the writing media. His observations and exhortations flowed through most channels of the written word—starting, in effect, with his book of short stories of a mid-western town *Winesburg, Ohio* at the start of his career in 1919, with many novels, short stories and other literary out-pourings following through a generation.

Among those who remarked this strain was Theodore Dreiser who wrote that Anderson "through all his days . . . appears to have been wandering here and there, looking, thinking, wondering." Yet when he wrote, his words exuded authority.

As so often occurs in great letters, we find Anderson best portraying himself when he writes with friendly understanding of others.

Such is this letter, penned to Van Wyck Brooks, in 1918 when the critic was writing *The Ordeal of Mark Twain*, and Anderson, from Chicago, wrote a series of letters attempting to help Brooks see Twain from Anderson's perspective.

Of these letters, Brooks wrote in 1941, shortly after Anderson's death:

"They are especially interesting because these were the years during which Sherwood was discovering himself and his world. He was, as he says, 'Setting out on new roads,' tasting the 'mid-America' that was his land, . . . touching it, catching its scent, listening, seeing . . ."

Chicago, May, 1918.

My dear Brooks

Your letter has stirred up a world of thought in me. It isn't Twain I'm thinking of but the profound truth of some of your own observations.

As far as Twain is concerned we have to remember the influences about him. Remember how he came into literature—the crude buffoon of the early days in the mining camps—the terrible cheap and second rate humor of much of *Innocence Abroad*. It seems to me that when he began he addressed an audience that gets a big laugh out of the braying of a jackass and without a doubt Mark often brayed at them. He knew that later. There was tenderness and subtility in Mark when he grew older.

You get the picture of him, Brooks—the river man who could write about going east and getting in with that New England crowd—the fellows from barren hills and barren towns. The best he got out of the bunch was Howells and Howells did Twain no good.

There's another point, Brooks, I can't help wishing Twain hadn't married such a good woman. There was such a universal inclination to tame the man—to save his soul as it were. Left alone I fancy Mark might have been willing to throw his soul overboard and then—ye gods what a fellow he might have been, what poetry might have come from him.

The big point is—it seems to me that this salvation of the soul business gets under everybody's skin. With artists it takes the form of being concerned with their occupation as writers. A struggle constantly goes on. Call the poet a poet and he is no longer the poet. You see what I mean.

There is a fellow like X. for example. He writes me long letters. His days are often made happy or miserable according to whether or not he is writing well.

Is it so important? What star dust we are. What does it matter?

The point is that I catch X. so often striving to say things in an unusual way. It makes me cringe. I want to beat him with my fists.

I pick on X. as an example because I love him and I know he feels deeply. He should write with a swing—weeping, praying and crying to the gods on paper instead of making sentences as he often does.

Well now you see I'm coming around. The cultural fellows got hold of Mark. They couldn't hold him. He was too big and too strong. He brushed their hands aside.

But their words got into his mind. In the effort to get out beyond that he became a pessimist.

Now, Brooks, you know a man cannot be a pessimist who lives near a brook or a cornfield. When the brook chatters or at night when the moon comes up and the wind plays in the corn a man hears the whispering of the gods.

Mark got that once—when he wrote Huck Finn. He forgot Howells and the good wife and everyone. Again he was the half savage, tender, god-worshiping, believing boy. He had proud conscious innocence.

I believe he wrote that book in a little hut on a hill on his farm. It poured out of him. I fancy that at night he come down from his hill stepping like a king—a splendid playboy, playing with rivers and men, ending on the Mississippi, on the broad river that is the great artery flowing out of the heart of the land.

Well, Brooks, I'm alone in a boat on that stream sometimes.

The rhythm and swing of it is in some of my songs that are to be published next month. It sometimes gets into some of the Winesburg things. I'll ride it some more perhaps. It depends on whether or not I can avoid taking myself serious. Whom the gods wish to destroy they first make dumb with the notion of being a writer.

Waldo is coming out to spend a month with me.

Wish I could see you sometime this summer. I'll be in the east for a month or more in June or July. Why you couldn't come to the mountains and have a few days walk with me?

Sherwood Anderson

LOUIS DEMBITZ BRANDEIS

"Betterment can come only through radical changes in systems . . ."

FROM 1916 to 1939, Justice Brandeis was a towering liberal member of the Supreme Court of the United States, alongside Justice Oliver Wendell Holmes, who was fifteen years his senior in age and fourteen years his senior on the highest bench.

The two jurists who grew old together shared the distinction of having been appointed from the same bar, that of Boston, but while Holmes ascended to the legal heights through the paths of scholarship as a lecturer and writer (as befitted his Brahmin background), Brandeis—born in Louisville, Kentucky, and a Bostonian only after graduation from Harvard Law School, fought his way to eminence through the courts.

As a defender of labor's rights,
as a defender of the public interest in notable battles against the then-entrenched public utilities, and, finally, as a Zionist leader, Brandeis is known as one of the most rounded intellects in the law.

Woodrow Wilson turned to him late in 1917 for suggestions as to means of creating an efficient war machine, in the face of confusions that marked American entry into World War I. On an evening in January, 1918, Justice Brandeis sat down in the crowded library of his Washington apartment and penned a letter to Colonel E. M. House, Wilson's confidential aide, making empirical suggestions that helped in that crucial year and set a pattern for other phases of mobilization adopted in World War II.

Stoneleigh Court,
January 9, 1918

My dear Colonel House:—

You have asked my opinion of the work of the War Department and the War Industry Board and Committees.

I consider the situation very serious—imperiling success abroad and also the ascendancy of the Democratic Party upon which we must rely for the attainment of our ideals at home. Betterment can come only through radical changes in systems:—such as

First: The War Department shall be relieved of all responsibility for the purchase, production, and transportation of munitions; the War Industry Board and Committee shall be abolished; and all their respective functions shall be concentrated in a munitions administration.

Second: The powers of the munitions administration shall be vested in a single head with full power of delegation; and the delegated power shall likewise be vested in single officials with full power of action within the sphere delimited (subject only to veto by the munitions administrator). There shall be no committees within the munitions administration except such advisory committees as the official shall himself appoint for his aid. The sphere of action of the several officials shall be limited to a size consistent with efficient action by him.

Third: The Labor Problem of the munitions administration cannot be effectively dealt with separately by that department. A labor administration should be created to deal with labor problems for all departments of the Government, and the power be vested in a single director with an advisory committee representing the several departments specifically interested.

Fourth: The War Department—dealing then only with purely military matters—should be reorganized so that for purposes of administration

    (a) In each branch of the service there be a single directing head;

    (b) In each branch of the service by limitation of power the practices and the institutions preventing immediate action be eliminated; and

(c) All branches of the service co-ordinated. Only questions of military policy should be determined by committees or councils.

Fifth: The Intelligence Service of the War Department and of the munitions administration cannot be effectively dealt with by them separately. A Central Intelligence Office should be created to deal with the problem for all departments of the Government and the power should be vested in a single director to co-ordinate and so far as possible consolidate the work of the several departments. He should have an advisory committee representing the several departments.

Sixth: The transportation requirements of the War and Munitions departments cannot be dealt with separately. A single director of shipping with an advisory committee representing the several departments of the Government should have power to allot shipping and make other provision in connection therewith, and the construction of ships should be divorced from the control of shipping.

Seventh: A small war council independent of all departments and composed of men freed from the detail of administration and of executive responsibility should be created to consider the broad questions of policy in internal and external affairs, and submit to the President the results of their deliberations. This instrument essential to the effective conduct of the war is not now provided by any, and cannot be provided, in the aggregate, by all of the several departments of the Government.

The above recommendations rest largely upon the obvious limitation of the power of any one man to deal effectively with many extensive and difficult problems. It is only by freeing Secretary Baker from many of the burdens now improperly resting upon him that the country can get the full benefit of his great ability and fine qualities.

Sincerely yours,
LDB

OLIVER WENDELL HOLMES

". . . I like a moment of leisure to sing my old
song . . ."

JUSTICE HOLMES, the "great dissenter" and a great liberal in his interpretations of the Constitution on the basis of the fundamental rights of the individual, has often been misinterpreted as a liberal, by those who think he advocated basic social change. Nothing could be farther from the truth, and it is more than coincidence that he carried on a debate over this philosophy with his junior friend and admirer, Justice Brandeis, who held to the axiom that social changes require changes in the social system itself.

In the reorganization period of the United States, immediately following World War I, these two great liberals were at the height of their mental powers and both were armed with long experience. Justice Brandeis outlined some of his own philosophy in his letter to Colonel House.

Holmes may have had those opinions in mind, but was more likely writing out of many long, private talks, when he sat down one evening and wrote a private note to Brandeis.

April 20, 1919

Let me not be put in an attitude of opposition when I don't oppose . . . I agree that wherever a great fortune produces an idler like the chap that shot Stanford White it produces an evil. But that does not seem to me more than an incident, dramatically impressive but not of the first or even great economic importance. The luxuries of the few I believe to be a drop in the bucket. The "sums withdrawn by Capital" that even such able men as Croly talk about seem to me merely the adjustments made by the most competent prophet to the anticipated equilibrium of social desires six month hence. They are not expenditures on luxuries, they are investments—intended to be the most profitable that can be got—and most profitable because they most nearly satisfy the consumer's demands. This adjustment would be as necessary under socialism as under any other system—otherwise the community gets less of what it wants. It never gets or can get as much as it wants. I believe that this man—the poor—now has substantially all there is . . . Generally speaking I agree with you in liking to see social experiments tried, but I do so without enthusiasm because I believe that it is merely shifting the place of pressure and that so long as we have free propagation Malthus is right in his general view. All of which you know, but I like a moment of leisure to sing my old song over again. I believe it to be responsive in substance, although not so perhaps in form.

Yours ever,
O.W.H.

EDWARD M. HOUSE

"Our annual falling out seems to have occurred."

EDWARD MANDELL HOUSE (whose familiar title of "colonel" was an honorary title bestowed by his native Texas) is probably the best known of President Woodrow Wilson's intimate friends and yet he never held an official position, other than temporary commissions for confidential assignments. He is one of a relatively short list of unofficial friends of Presidents, who won fame without title.

House worked to get Wilson nominated for the Presidency and then, as a man of independent means, moved to Washington, where he functioned as Presidential errand boy. In 1914, Wilson sent him to Europe in a vain effort to prevent the European war, which started that year. In 1915, he went back in a vain attempt to arrange an armistice. Wilson made him a member of the delegation to the Versailles Peace Conference, and House helped draw up the proposal for the League of Nations.

By 1919, he was a well-known figure, intimate with heads of other states. By that time, hints of differences between Wilson and himself (which were to be verified late in 1919) were being published.

From London, House felt it necessary to send a personal letter to his chief, whom he always addressed as "Dear Governor."

London
August 26, 1919

Dear Governor:

Our annual falling out seems to have occurred. The Foreign Office received a cable the other day saying that we were no longer on good terms and asking that the Prime Minister and Balfour be informed. The Press representatives also told me that they had the same news.

I am wondering where this particular story originated and why they wanted the Prime Minister and Balfour to be informed. Tyrrell said it came from one of their men in New York and not from Washington.

Affectionately yours,
E. M. House

The sequel:

Immediately on receipt of the note, House wrote later, President Wilson cabled him word which he paraphrased as, "Am deeply distressed by malicious story about break between us and thank you for the whole message about it. The best way to treat it is with silent contempt." There is no public record of the President's actual words, but there are indications that he felt that Colonel House was acting too much on his own authority.

JOHN FOSTER DULLES

". . . poor people trying their hand at peoples government."

JOHN FOSTER DULLES, who absorbed Wilson's philosophy at Versailles, wrote the following letter to his wife. It shows his vivid personal reaction to a communist revolt which was taking place in the Ruhr, when the Communists tried to seize power in Western Europe.

He formed judgments, then,

about the future of reparations which caused him to write from Dresden, one week after this letter, another letter to Norman H. Davis, predicting failure for that part of the treaty, unless Germany got economic freedom and a definite obligation to pay.

April 3, 1920

Dearest Janet:

. . .

I had been at Frankfurt as I wrote you last Sunday, working on the copper proposition, and left there on Wednesday morning by motor. It was a beautiful ride down the Main to the Rhine . . . At Coblence (sic) I figured that it might be interesting and useful to go up into the Ruhr region of which great stories are being told, so I got a letter from Noyes (the U.S. Rhineland Commissioner) introducing me to the British authorities at Coln and telling them to help me to get to the Ruhr. On getting to Coln Wednesday afternoon I found that the balance of our party would not get to Coln until Thursday evening or Saturday morning, so I decided to devote Thursday to investigating the Red coup in the Ruhr as an interesting contrast to the reactionary coup which I had witnessed at Berlin. The British authorities here said that there was no use trying to get any kind of a pass and that the best thing was merely to go as far as I could and when irrevocably stopped to come on back. Incidentally that is the system which works pretty well over here these days and with a little ingenuity and money you generally get through.

So I got another auto here and Thursday morning Hoskins and I started off. We only told the chauffeur that we were going to Dusseldorf as I don't think we could have gotten a car ostensibly to go further. At Dusseldorf everything appeared quite normal and we told our chauffeur that we thought we would go to Duisberg. This city is supposed to be the head of the Red government, and the chauffeur was very much alarmed and almost refused to proceed . . .

The first sign of anything unusual was just outside of Dusseldorf where we found a couple of workmen with rifles who were guarding the road and who stopped us. After pulling out our American passports and letters signed by Hoover, etc., we were allowed to proceed. As we approached Duisberg we were again stopped, this time by a small squad of reds who were guarding the approaches to Duisberg. They all had red bands around their arms and red cloth stuck in their hats, and carried rifles. They were not of course in uniform.

We had more difficulty there in getting through as they were rather suspicious of us. I think they suspected us of being there in the interests of the French . . .

We had to pass nearly a dozen guards, I should say, in getting into the interior of Duisberg, but our escort carried us through all right on the strength of his Red Army Commission. The Red Committee of five which was attempting to govern the region had its seat in the city hall. That was surrounded by a cleared area rather heavily guarded and with barbed wire entanglements in the streets. It was tremendously interesting to compare the situation with the same thing at Berlin two weeks before.

We got into the city hall and I never saw such bedlam in my life . . . The governing commission had shut themselves up in a room which was besieged with people who were supposed to await their turn to get in.

I soon saw that it would take us a couple of days if we waited our turn, so I got hold of an armed guard and explained to him the "importance" of our mission and he finally used his rifle to poke a way for us through the mob . . .

The sight inside was really pathetic. The supreme committee of five was there, all right . . . They were uneducated workmen . . .

. . . I don't think that I have ever seen a more interesting scene than that of these poor people trying their hand at peoples government . . .

WOODROW WILSON

*". . . the qualities of heart and breadth of
mind . . ."*

IN the history of politics many men irreconcilably opposed on public questions, still have had the capacity to appreciate each other as human beings.

It is unlikely that the United States has ever seen men more bitterly opposed over the question of American involvement in international commitments than the late President Woodrow Wilson and Senator William Edgar Borah. In their public differences, their mutual descriptions were vituperative, yet Wilson once said, "There is one irreconcilable I can respect."

2340 S Street, N.W.

Wilson left the Presidency in 1920, an invalid who had failed to win Senate confirmation of his own plans for the League of Nations. Two years later, the Woodrow Wilson Foundation planned a dinner in his honor and invited Senator Borah to attend.

Senator Borah's reply, as reported by the press, smothered old enmities with revelation of his own high regard for Wilson, and prompted the ill and tired former President to send him a note of appreciation.

Woodrow Wilson
Washington D C
16th February 1922

My dear Senator Borah:

I had the pleasure of reading in this morning's paper the message you sent to the Woodrow Wilson Foundation in New York, in declining their invitation to dinner, and I take the liberty of writing to express my admiration of the qualities of heart and breadth of mind of which that message gives such interesting evidence.

Allow me to subscribe myself, with sincere respect;

Your friend,
Woodrow Wilson

Honorable William E. Borah,
Washington, D.C.

WILL ROGERS

"I will go and see if London Bridge is falling down."

IN an era slightly less pompous than the nineteenth century and perhaps a little less frightened than the mid-twentieth, Will Rogers succeeded at the impossible career of a professional comedian commenting sagely, humorously and eruditely on current events.

When he turned from the stage (as star of the Ziegfeld Follies) to the typewriter, he assayed (with tacit White House approval) the task of traveling abroad as a Presidential "unofficial ambassador" and writing "confidential" reports to the President, then Calvin Coolidge, himself a notable example of the dead-pan school of humor.

The reports were about as "confidential" as a current television broadcast, being printed first in a popular magazine and afterwards in book form.

A typical report was written by Rogers in 1925, from London, while Britain was in the grip of a general strike. In reading it, younger readers should be told that its author was not entirely fictionalizing, as every name he dropped was that of a friend who held him in high regard.

London, May 13th

My Dear President:

Say, I told them about you over here. During all this calm and no excitement, everybody asked me, "How would you Americans take this if it were happening over there?"

So I just told them: "We would have all been cuckoo and crazy and shooting and rioting, and everybody up in the air—all but one man. He would have been just like your House of Lords. He might every few days ask, 'Is the strike over yet?' But he would have been the sole individual that would not have turned a hair."

Then all would ask, "Who is this remarkable man that you speak of?"

I remarked, "Calvin Coolidge."

I wish you had been there. It was just your kind of stuff. Oh, yes, I met Houghten, our Ambassador at a Dinner Party at Mrs.

Astor's. Sat next to him. I will write you later and in more confidential terms just how he is making out over here. Don't think there is a need for a change of men here now. If Kellogg should decide to get out, I think this fellow would be the man to put in there. You know, we have always used this court of St. James's as a kind of springboard to dive from into the Secretary of Stateship, and from there to oblivion. I am watching him, and believe I can get Borah to O.K. him when the time comes.

I will go and see if London Bridge is falling down. I have heard somewhere that it was.

Yours as ever,
W.R.

P.S. Watch the farmers. They are tricky.

BARTOLOMEO VANZETTI

". . . I have committed no robbery and no murder . . ."

THERE is great disagreement over what is the truth behind the dual execution of two Italian immigrants in 1927: the culmination of "the Sacco-Vanzetti case."

Shortly after midnight on August 22, 1927, these two men were led to execution in the electric chair at the Massachusetts State Prison, where the eloquent Vanzetti shouted, "Long live anarchy!" in the same breath with which he bade farewell to his wife.

What had these men done? Technically, they were executed for alleged perpetration of a dual murder and robbery on April 15, 1920, when assailants attacked two shoe-factory employees. Yet as the years wore on, in a period of considerable tension over "radicals," these men seemed to be more on trial for what later was called subversive action: Vanzetti the visionary fish peddler, and Sacco the more reticent shoemaker. Their deaths intensified rather than settled what became an international debate over their case, on which volumes have been written.

It was spurred by the question "Does a condemned man write a lie in his last letter?" For Vanzetti wrote such a letter, simple and eloquent, addressing it to Dante Sacco, the young son of his co-defendant.

August 21, 1927

MY DEAR DANTE:

I still hope, and we will fight until the last moment, to revindicate our right to live and to be free, but all the forces of the State and of the money and reaction are deadly against us because we are libertarians or anarchists.

I write little of this because you are now and yet too young to understand these things and other things of which I would like to reason with you.

But, if you do well, you will grow and understand your father's and my case and your father's and my principles, for which we will soon be put to death.

I tell you now that all that I know of your father, he is not a criminal, but one of the bravest men I ever knew. Some day you will understand what I am about to tell you. That your father has sacrificed everything dear and sacred to the human heart and soul for his fate in liberty and justice for all. That day you will be proud of your father, and if you come brave enough, you will take his place in the struggle between tyranny and liberty and you will vindicate his (our) names and our blood.

If we have to die now, you shall know, when you will be able to understand this tragedy in its fullest, how good and brave your father has been with you, your father and I, during these eight years of struggle, sorrow, passion, anguish and agony.

Even from now you shall be good, brave with your mother, with Ines, and with Susie—brave, good Susie—and do all you can to console and help them.

I would like you to also remember me as a comrade and friend to your father, your mother and Ines, Susie and you, and I assure you that neither have I been a criminal, that I have committed no robbery and no murder, but only fought modestly to abolish crimes from among mankind and for the liberty of all.

Remember Dante, each one who will say otherwise of your father and I, is a liar, insulting innocent dead men who have been brave in their life. Remember and know also, Dante, that if your father and I would have been cowards and hypocrits and rinnegetors of our faith, we would not have been put to death. They would not even have convicted a leprous dog; not even executed a deadly poisoned scorpion on such evidence as that they framed against us. They would have given a new trial to a matricide and abitual felon on the evidence we presented for a new trial.

Remember, Dante, remember always these things; we are not criminals; they convicted us on a frame-up; they denied us a new trial; and if we will be executed after seven years, four months and seventeen days of unspeakable tortures and wrong, it is for what I have already told you; because we were for the poor and against the explitation and oppression of the man by the man.

The documents of our case, which you and other ones will collect and preserve, will prove to you that your father, your mother, Ines, my family and I have been sacrificed by and to a State Reason of the American Plutocratic reaction.

The day will come when you will understand the atrocious cause of the above written words, in all its fullness. Then you will honor us.

Now Dante, be brave and good always. I embrace you.

P.S. I left the copy of An American Bible to your mother now, for she will like to read it, and she will give it to you when you will be bigger and able to understand it. Keep it for remembrance. It will also testify to you how good and generous Mrs. Gertrude Winslow has been with us all. Good-bye Dante.

Bartolomeo

F. SCOTT FITZGERALD

". . . I never believe much in happiness."

IN the generation of writers following World War I, Francis Scott Key Fitzgerald became carelessly known as the novelist whose works portrayed the "flapper era." This they did, but his best work, *The Great Gatsby,* showed a promise of far deeper and broader talents that might easily have flowered, had not illness interrupted his career and caused his premature death, in 1940, at the age of 44 years.

Samuel Gompers, cofounder and first President of the American Federation of Labor, photographed in 1909. (Underwood & Underwood)

Mary Baker Eddy, founder of Christian Science. (Underwood and Underwood)

Mark Twain in his favorite writing position. (Underwood and Underwood)

President Theodore Roosevelt, who acted as mediator in the peace negotiations between Russia and Japan in 1905. (Underwood and Underwood)

Justice Oliver Wendell Holmes, Jr., toward the end of his long career. (Underwood and Underwood)

James Cardinal Gibbons, the Archbishop of Baltimore who counseled the church against placing Henry George's works on the Index of Forbidden Books. (Wide World Photo)

F. Scott Fitzgerald, who immortalized the nineteen-twenties as the "Jazz Age," seen here with his wife, Zelda, and his daughter, Scotty, in their Paris apartment (1925). (Wide World Photo)

Nicola Sacco and Bartolomeo Vanzetti, whose murder trial became a *cause célèbre* of the nineteen-twenties and is still recalled with much debate. (Wide World Photo)

John and Elaine Barrymore at a Hollywood film premiere in 1937. (Wide World Photo)

Louis Brandeis, Associate Justice of the Supreme Court from 1916 to 1939, as he appeared on his eighty-second birthday. (Wide World Photo)

Thomas Wolfe's first published novel, *Look Homeward, Angel,* brought him immediate recognition and sparked a sharp reaction from his home town (scene of the novel) that baffled and hurt Wolfe. (Underwood and Underwood)

The whimsical humor of Ogden Nash, so vital a part of his poems, is apparent in his expressive face. (Wide World Photo)

Sherwood Anderson, in a contemplative study by Alfred Stieglitz. (By Permission, *An American Place*)

Edna St. Vincent Millay had remarkable insight, as illustrated by her evaluation of her own plays in a letter to her publisher. (Nation Wide News Service)

Franklin Delano Roosevelt signing a history-making document, the declaration of war against Japan, December 8, 1941. (Underwood and Underwood)

Robert Frost, the great American poet, at sixty-nine, when he was teaching at Dartmouth. (Wide World Photo)

John F. Kennedy, youngest President of the United States, shows that today, as always, letters are being written by great Americans that reflect the personal emotions of the writers, as well as the currents of the times. (Wide World Photo)

THOMAS JEFFERSON

[signature: Th. Jefferson]

ALEXANDER HAMILTON

[signature: A Hamilton]

HORACE GREELEY

[signature: Horace Greeley]

JOHN HANCOCK

[signature: John Hancock]

RICHARD RUSH

[signature: Richard Rush]

WILLIAM WIRT

[signature: Wm Wirt]

HENRY CLAY

[signature: H. Clay]

MARY BAKER EDDY

[signature: Mary B. G. Eddy]

JOHN F. KENNEDY

[signature: John F. Kennedy]

When Arthur Mizener wrote a biography of Fitzgerald eleven years later, he observed that nothing appeared to have been real to the novelist "until he had written about it." And Fitzgerald wrote about many things in forms other than his novels, notably the surviving letters to his daughter, Frances—his "Dear Pie."

Therefore, when he wrote to "Pie" one day in 1933, he possibly wrote more than humorous but serious fatherly admonitions; quite possibly the then 37-year-old author, with his greatest successes behind him and a novel in his typewriter (*Tender is the Night*) that would be criticized as failing to live up to his promise, he was searching for realities that he already felt were eluding him.

August 8, 1933
La Paix, Rodgers' Forge,
Towson, Maryland

Dear Pie:

I feel very strongly about you doing duty. Would you give me a little more documentation about your reading in French? I am glad you are happy—but I never believe much in happiness. I never believe in misery either. Those are things you see on the stage or the screen or the printed page, they never really happen to you in life.

All I believe in in life is the rewards for virtue (according to your talents) and the punishments for not fulfilling your duties, which are doubly costly. If there is such a volume in the camp library, will you ask Mrs. Tyson to let you look up a sonnet of Shakespeare's in which the line occurs Lilies that fester smell far worse than weeds.

Have had no thoughts today, life seems composed of getting up a Saturday Evening Post story. I think of you, and always pleasantly; but if you call me "Pappy" again I am going to take the White Cat out and beat his bottom hard, six times for every time you are impertinent. Do you react to that?

I will arrange the camp bill.

Half-wit, I will conclude. Things to worry about:

Worry about courage
Worry about cleanliness
Worry about efficiency
Worry about horsemanship . . .

Things not to worry about:

Don't worry about popular opinion

Don't worry about dolls

Don't worry about the past

Don't worry about the future

Don't worry about growing up

Don't worry about anybody getting ahead of you

Don't worry about triumph

Don't worry about failure unless it comes through your own
fault

Don't worry about mosquitoes

Don't worry about flies

Don't worry about insects in general

Don't worry about parents

Don't worry about boys

Don't worry about disappointments

Don't worry about pleasures

Don't worry about satisfactions

Things to think about:

What am I really aiming at?

How good am I really in comparison to my contemporaries
in regard to:

(a) Scholarship

(b) Do I really understand about people and am I able
to get along with them?

(c) Am I trying to make my body a useful instrument or am I neglecting it?

With dearest love,

THOMAS WOLFE

". . . something of the bitterness and intolerance
and hot temper of youth . . ."

IN 1929, a young man, then in his thirtieth year, suddenly burst on the literary scene with a big novel that sparked controversy, confusing to its author, from that date until his untimely death in 1938. The author was Thomas Wolfe, a physically big man with a prodigious memory, whose writings poured out of his store of recollections.

Necessarily, such writing is associated with the scenes and individuals of its environment. In this case, the environment was Asheville, North Carolina, Wolfe's birthplace. In fact, the controversy reportedly has long outlived the author, although it diminishes as his works, in print or play form, continue to grow.

The first of the only two books of Wolfe's published in his lifetime was *Look Homeward Angel*, published in October, 1929. Asheville seethed from the start, so noticeably that, on October 28, Wolfe sent a night letter of 159 words to Mrs. R. H. Wheaton, expressing his distress but cautioning, "say nothing."

WESTERN UNION

CFB606 159NL—New York NY 28   1929 Oct 28 PM 10 45
Mrs. R.H. Wheaton
96 Kimberly Avenue
Asheville, NC

Thanks for wonderful letter great figures in novel are Eliza Helen Gant and Ben everyone here thinks they are grand people no book should be read as gossip nor judged on isolated passages when the book and leading characters are judged as a whole they are seen to be fine people read New York Times Review for last Sunday also Herald Tribune for next Sunday or week after will send you other reviews no matter what Asheville thinks now they will understand in time that I tried to write moving honest book about great people that is the way the world outside Asheville is taking it Tell mama this and say I am writing in day or so if you doubt what I say read over chapters on Bens death and burial scenes that follow then ask if anyone dares say these are not great people book selling fast looks like success but say nothing You are great person love

Tom

Almost six years later, Wolfe was still amazed at the strong reaction to *Look Homeward Angel,* an unusual feeling indeed for a world-famous author.

He returned to New York after a four-month absence in Europe, to find a letter from one James G. Strikeleather Jr., of Asheville, recalling his past feelings; perhaps it disturbed him all the more as his second book, *Of Time and the River,* was about to be published that year.

His reply, hand-typed with the usual cross-outs and other corrections typical of the modern writer who composes on a typewriter, needs no further explanation.

New York City
July 8, 1935

Dear Mr. Strikeleather:

I got home from Europe just a few days ago and found your letter in the great stock of mail which has accumulated during the four months I was away. This explains my delay in writing you.

I want to thank you for the spirit of friendship and kindness which prompted you to write me as you did and to assure you that I am sincerely grateful for your letter. I should also like to tell you that I know I have made mistakes in the past, that I have said and written some things which I now regret, but I should like you to believe that a great many of these things were due to the inexperience, the intemperance, and the oversensitivity of youth rather than to a desire to hurt and wound people that I have known all my life. May I not tell you also that I have in my heart not one atom of bitterness or resentment towards the town and the people from which I came and which, I think, I shall always be proud and happy to acknowledge as my own. Mr. Strikeleather, may I give you one little illustration of what I think may have happened between myself and the people in Asheville? Have you ever tried to pass a man in the street and the moment you stepped to the right to go around him he would also step the same way, when you step to the left, he would follow you, and so the thing would continue until it became funny and you both stood still and looked at each other and yet all the time all you were trying to do was to be friendly to each other and to give the other fellow a free passage? Or, better still, have you ever met some one that you knew you liked and you were pretty sure he felt the same way about you and yet, figuratively speaking, you "got off on the wrong foot" with each other? Now I think that something of this sort may have happened between Asheville and myself. When I wrote "Look Homeward Angel" several years ago, I can honestly assure you I had no notion that the book would arouse the kind of comment and response and cause the kind of misunderstanding in my home town that it did do. I should like you to believe that I, myself, was just about the most surprised person in the world when I finally understood the kind of effect my book was having in Asheville. I cannot go back to "Look Homeward Angel" nor do I know exactly what I said there or what the total content of the book may be. The reason for this is pretty simple, and yet it is awfully hard to explain. It is hard to explain because the thing that makes a man write a book and the thing that makes him read a book are two such different things that it is really like the North Pole pointing toward the South. If this sounds too involved and complicated, all I mean to say to you, what I am trying to say to you is that a reader reads a book in order to remember it and a writer writes a book in order to forget it. For that reason a writer, after he has got the whole thing off his chest, wants to forget it utterly, and yet he wants fame, too. He wants people to read his book, to like his book, to admire his talent as a writer. This is the thing he writes and sweats for, and yet when he meets people, and they tell him they have read his book and praise him for it, he has a terrible feeling of embarrassment and constraint and wishes that they would just say nothing about it and does not know what to say himself.

It's a strange situation, isn't it? It seems very complicated and difficult, and yet it is quite simple at the bottom, and I know that a man of your experience will understand it. I suppose it boils down to this: you want to be a famous man and a great writer, and yet you want to lead an obscure, simple, and plain kind of life like other men. I have told you all these things just to indicate—I can't do anything more but indicate them because if I ever started explaining the whole thing, I could go on until tomorrow morning—but just to indicate the kind of difficulty that arises when a man tries to tell how he felt when he wrote a book, and how when a man tells how he felt when he read one. Now, having said all this, I would like plainly and frankly to admit something—something which I have already mentioned—I do think that, as you say, there may have been something of the bitterness and intolerance and hot temper of youth in "Look Homeward Angel." And yet may I say to you—it is pretty difficult to say this because no man likes to be put in the position where he must seem to defend his own book or to point to the praise and success which it may have had—may I say to you that although the youthfulness and a certain intemperance in the book was recognized by critics elsewhere, these imperfections were on the whole considered only incidental to a book which was read, I assure you, not as a savage and vitriolic attack upon the citizens of Asheville, North Carolina, but as a young man's vision of his childhood and his youth and the world from which he came —a world which in its general humanity could have been as true of Peoria or Spokane or Berlin or any place as it was of Asheville. Anyway, Asheville and I got off on the wrong foot with each other because of that book. I think there may have been some bitterness in it but not as much bitterness as Asheville thought there was, and as for this book, which is also finished, over, published, and out of my system as the first one was, I think I can really assure you that no matter what its many faults and imperfections may be, so far as Asheville is concerned, there is no bitterness at all.

I just ask you to believe this, and if you cannot believe it, I would hope that you have time to go back to the book and examine it for yourself. This is all I can write you at present, and I know you will understand I am writing this out of my heart because you and I come from the same town, the same people, and because I want to answer your kind and friendly letter in a way that will, I hope, bring about a better understanding between the people of my native town and myself.

I am certainly coming home to see you all some day. I don't know when that will be. I have much work to do, many things to learn and to experience, but when I do come home, I hope you will all understand that I am a man who, whatever errors he may have made, has tried to grow and learn and increase in strength and wisdom and humanity, and who will have grown beyond malice and resentment in the end. Certainly I hope the last is now true and that all of you will come, in time, to understand it and believe it.

Meanwhile with all my best and friendliest wishes, and with thanks again for your good letter, I am

Sincerely yours,
Tom Wolfe

The sequel:

Tom Wolfe died in 1938. He left two novels that were published posthumously, *The Web and the Rock* (1939), and *You Can't Go* *Home Again* (1940). His published writing also includes plays, poems and short stories.

GEORGE C. MARSHALL

". . . I was not a shining light in your sections."

ON a spring day in 1935, a colonel of infantry already marked by General Pershing as a future great military leader, sat down to write a note to one Colonel Hunter Pendleton.

Colonel Pendleton was about to retire from Virginia Military Institute—from which the then-Colonel Marshall had been graduated in 1902. At this point, Marshall's service as an aide to General Pershing had probably reached its high point. Then he served as Chief of Staff of the Army, master strategist in World War II, and in subsequent posts as Secretary of State and Ambassador to China. Now, his name is best remembered as author of the Marshall Plan.

The great bulk of correspondence resulting from his long career is still under study by the George C. Marshall Research Foundation, but this study in human relationships was specially released for this volume.

Alumni of V.M.I. will remember Colonel Pendleton as a dedicated "Mr. Chips" who spent his entire teaching-career lifetime there, and who was considered a "perfect" teacher by most of the cadets. In this letter, "Lily" is General Marshall's first wife, and "Mrs. Coles" her mother.

April 8, 1935

Colonel Hunter Pendleton
Lexington
Virginia

My dear Colonel Pendleton:

I have just read the notice in the Alumni News of your retirement in June. Your departure from the faculty will mark a great change at the V. M. I. I fear that with you will go the last trace of the atmosphere I grew up in as a young man.

A "dub" in Chemistry, and not a student at any time, I was not a shining light in your sections. But I carried away with me some very precious, though intangible, assets gained through your example. Later on, from Mrs. Coles and Lily I learned to know you better and to appreciate you more at your true value. Lily admired you tremendously, and with her mother, had a deep affection for both you and Mrs. Pendleton, which I came to share.

I hope you both enjoy good health and that your plans will make for an agreeable and happy period in your retirement. There must be a profound satisfaction in completing an active career, clean in the knowledge that you have exercised a beneficial and a beneficient influence over the lives of thousands of young men, and that you had stood a little higher each year in the admiration and regard of every person with whom you have been associated.

My affectionate regards to you both.

Faithfully yours,
G. C. Marshall
Colonel, Infantry

JOHN BARRYMORE

". . . I who now need some consideration . . ."

OF all the Barrymores, the most brilliant, the most mercurial and certainly the most tragic, was John.

His own life provided as much drama as any in the thousands of performances that marked his theatrical reign, whether in the classics of Shakespeare, modern dramas or films.

In 1935, although only 53 years of age, John Barrymore was becoming an old man, partially from over-drinking, partially from the prodigal manner in which he expended his energies in living, but probably most of all from the unbelievably complicated pattern into which he had twisted his life. He was beset with troubles, trying to put into order his affairs with an estranged wife, while fighting, through lawyers, over claims made by a recent sweetheart, and all the while watching his formerly large bank balance shrink, after a year and a half of idleness.

In the midst of his perplexities, he sat down and wrote a letter, quoted by his biographer, Gene Fowler, to his daughter Diana, first of his children, whom he had not seen for years.

Dearest Diana—

It's a long time since I have seen or heard from you, although I suppose you know that some weeks ago I tried my best to see you—or didn't you know?

This letter may seem a little odd to you, but believe me it is of great importance to us both, and you know we love each other so much that we can talk perfectly frankly with one another.

You probably know I have been having some "domestic trouble" and that, mixed up with it, I have not earned anything for about the last year and a half. Therefore, as you can well imagine, my funds aren't what they were. However, even all through this lean period, I have done my best to see that you should be well provided for.

My best recollection is that for the last ten years or so I have paid for your use something approximating one hundred and eighty thousand dollars. Don't you think that in view of that and of the fact that it is I who now need some consideration, that you could do without any further payment from me, at least until I can get to work again and begin to earn once more?

As you can imagine I have felt very reluctant to write you in this fashion, but I am sure that if these amounts I have paid you have been properly taken care of, you need not want for anything.

I hope you will understand the spirit of this letter, my dear baby, my own dear funny thing, and that you will—as they say in the classics—"drop me a little line, saying that you do."

This will mean a great deal to me, and I know damn well this is all I need to say to you.

All my love—fuzzy dear one.

Daddy

The sequel:

No reply ever reached Barrymore. John Barrymore died in 1942. Eighteen years later, Diana died, a few months after publishing an autobiography described by critics as perhaps the most shocking self-revelatory book of its decade.

FRANKLIN DELANO ROOSEVELT

"I do not claim the magician's wand."

IN 1935, after the first two and one-half years of President Roosevelt's "New Deal," great and irrevocable changes had taken place in the pattern of national government. Many strides had been made toward recovery from the Great Depression, but likewise many sincere and sober Americans who had given the President their support were becoming nervous, even frightened, at the evidences of change.

In that atmosphere, Roy W. Howard watched from the vantage point of an outstanding editor, up to that point in full sympathy with the aims of the New Deal, and one who then enjoyed the President's full confidence.

On August 26, 1935, Howard sat down and wrote to the President a plea to do something to "undo the damage that has been done by mis-interpreters of the New Deal."

A few days later Mr. Roosevelt dictated his reply.

The White House
Washington, D.C.
Sept. 6, 1935

My dear Mr. Howard:

I appreciate the tone and purpose of your letter, and fairness impels me to note with no little sympathy and understanding the facts which you record, based on your observations as a reporter of opinion throughout the United States. I can well realize, more-over, that the many legislative details and processes incident to the long and arduous session of the Congress should have had the unavoidable effect of promoting some confusion in many people's minds.

I think we can safely disregard the skeptics of whom you speak. Skeptics were present when Noah said it was going to rain and they refused to go into the ark. We can also disregard those who are actuated by a spirit of political partisanship or by a willing-ness to gain or retain personal profit at the expense of, and detri-ment to, their neighbors. Then there were those who told us to "do nothing." We had heard of the do-nothing policy before and from the same sources and in many cases from the same indi-viduals. We heard it when Theodore Roosevelt and Woodrow Wilson proposed reforms. The country has learned how to meas-ure that kind of opposition. But there are critics who are honest and non-partisan and who are willing to discuss and to learn. I believe we owe, therefore, a positive duty to clarify our purposes, to describe our methods and to reiterate our ideals. Such clarifica-tion is greatly aided by the efforts of those public-spirited news-papers which serve the public well by a true portrayal of the facts and an unbiased printing of the news.

However, experience is the best teacher and results are the best evidence. As the essential outline of what has been done rises into view, I am confident that doubts and misapprehension will vanish. I am confident further that business as a whole will agree with you and with me that the interests of what we broadly term business are not in conflict with, but wholly in harmony with, mass interests.

I note what you say of the hostility emanating from "financial racketeers, public exploiters and sinister forces." Such criticism it is an honor to bear. A car with many cylinders can keep running in spite of plenty of carbon—but it knocks. When it is overhauled an important part of the job is the removal of that carbon.

In the large, the depression was the culmination of unhealthy, however innocent, arrangements in agriculture, in business and in finance. Our legislation was remedial, and as such, it would serve no purpose to make a doctrinaire effort to distinguish between that which was addressed to recovery and that which was addressed to reform. The two, in an effort toward sound and fundamental recovery, are inseparable. Our actions were in conformity with the basic economic purposes which were set forth three years ago.

As spokesman for those purposes I pointed out that it was necessary to seek a wise balance in American economic life, to restore our banking system to public confidence, to protect investors in the security market, to give labor freedom to organize and protection from exploitation, to safeguard and develop our national resources, to set up protection against the vicissitudes incident to old age and unemployment, to relieve destitution and suffering and to relieve investors and consumers from the burden of unnecessary corporate machinery. I do not believe that any responsible political party in the country will dare to go before the public in opposition to any of these major objectives.

The tax program of which you speak is based upon a broad and just social and economic purpose. Such a purpose, it goes without saying, is not to destroy wealth, but to create broader range of opportunity, to restrain the growth of unwholesome and sterile accumulations and to lay the burdens of Government where they can best be carried. This law affects only those individual people who have incomes over $50,000 a year, and individual estates of decedents who leave over $40,000.

Moreover, it gives recognition to the generally accepted fact that larger corporations enjoying the advantages of size over smaller corporations possess relatively greater capacity to pay. Consequently the act changes the rate of tax on net earnings from a flat 13¾ percent to a differential ranging from 12½ percent to 15 percent. No reasonable person thinks that this is going to destroy competent corporations or impair business as a whole. Taxes on 95 percent of our corporations are actually reduced by the new tax law. A small excess profits tax is also provided as well as an intercorporate dividend tax which will have the wholesome effect of encouraging the simplification of overly complicated and wasteful intercorporate relationships.

Congress declined to broaden the tax base because it was recognized that the tax base had already been broadened to a very considerable extent during the past five years. I am aware of the sound arguments advanced in favor of making every citizen pay an income tax, however small his income. England is cited as an example. But it should be recalled that despite complaints about higher taxes our interest payments on all public debts, including local governments, require only 3 percent of our national income as compared with 7 percent in England.

The broadening of our tax base in the past few years has been very real. What is known as consumer's taxes, namely, the invisible taxes paid by people in every walk of life, fall relatively much more heavily upon the poor man than on the rich man. In 1929, consumers' taxes represented only 30 percent of the national revenue. Today they are 60 percent, and even with the passage of the recent tax bill the proportion of these consumers' taxes will drop only 5 percent.

This Administration came into power pledged to a very considerable legislative program. It found the condition of the country such as to require drastic and far-reaching action. Duty and necessity required us to move on a broad front for more than two years. It seemed to the Congress and to me better to achieve these objectives as expeditiously as possible in order that not only business but the public generally might know those modifications in the conditions and rules of economic enterprise which were involved in our program. This basic program, however, has now reached substantial completion and the "breathing spell" of which you speak is here—very decidedly so.

It is a source of great satisfaction that at this moment conditions are such as to offer further substantial and widespread recovery. Unemployment is still with us but it is steadily diminishing and our efforts to meet its problems are unflagging. I do not claim the magician's wand. I do not claim that Government alone is responsible for these definitely better circumstances. But we all know the very great effect of the saving of banks, of farms, of homes, the building of public works, the providing of relief for the destitute, and many other direct governmental acts for the betterment of conditions. And we do claim that we have helped to restore that public confidence which now offers so substantial a foundation for our recovery. I take it that we are all not merely seeking but getting the recovery of confidence, not merely the confidence of a small group, but that basic confidence on the part of the mass of our population, in the soundness of our economic life and in the honesty and justice of the purposes of its economic rules and methods.

I like the last sentences of your letter and I repeat them: "With all its faults and with the abuses it has developed, our system has in the past enabled us to achieve greater mass progress than has been attained by any other system on earth. Smoke out the sinister forces seeking to delude the public into believing that an orderly modernization of a system we want to preserve is revolution in disguise."

Very sincerely yours,

Mr. Roy W. Howard,
New York City

The sequel:

This letter did not still the criticism, or stop the "misinterpreters," but it had a temporary alleviating influence. More importantly, it set forth in perspective a phase of President Roosevelt's ideas that make it a type of testament and a letter that is revealing, in retrospect.

IRVIN S. COBB

". . . I want no long faces and no show of grief at
the burying ground."

WHILE the public laughed with Irvin S. Cobb for more than forty years, during which he held the spotlight as one of the world's great humorists, he was proving that the line between folk humor and realistic philosophy is so thin as to be almost nonexistent.

In December, 1943, the 70-year-old Kentuckian was notified by his physician that he would soon lay aside his broad-brimmed hat and cigar, and take his last journey.

Cobb thereupon wrote a letter to the editor of his home town newspaper, the *Paducah Sun-Democrat*, with instructions that it remain sealed until his death.

Cobb died on March 10, 1944, and when his last letter was opened, it turned out to be—even when read in less-emotional perspective —one of the great examples of American writing.

TO WHOM IT MAY CONCERN:

In death I desire that no one shall look upon my face and once more I charge my family, as already and repeatedly I have done, that they shall put on none of the bogus habilments of so-called mourning. Folds of black crepe never ministered to the memory of the departed; they only made the wearers unhappy and self-conscious.

I ask that my body be wrapped in a plain sheet or cloth and placed in an inexpensive container and immediately cremated— without any special formality or ceremony. If anybody tries to insert me into one of those dismal numbers run up by the undertaker's dressmaking department, I'll come back and ha'nt 'em. Nor do I crave to make my mortal exit in a tail-coat with white tie and artificial pearl studs. I'll be done with after-dinner speaking forever so why dispatch me hence in the regalia of the craft. When a man dies with his sins let the sins die with the man. That's what I say and it sums up such speculations as I might ever have had touching on the future state, if any. For me a suitable epitaph would be: "Anyhow, He Left Here." But never mind that. It might offend some of the pious and I hate to go on giving offense after I've quit living.

When convenience suits, I ask that the plain canister—nothing fancy there, please—containing my ashes shall be taken to Paducah, and that at the proper planting season a hole shall be dug in our family lot or elsewhere at Oak Grove and a dogwood tree planted there and the ashes strewn in the hole to fertilize the tree roots. Should the tree live that will be monument enough for me. But should my surviving relatives desire to mark the spot further, I make so bold as to suggest that they use either a slab of plain Kentucky limestone set flat in the kindly earth, or a rugged natural boulder of Southern granite bearing a small bronze plate with my name on it and, if it seems pertinent, the year of my birth and the year of my death, which appears to be the custom although I could never understand why a gravestone should carry mention of the only two events in the career of the deceased with which he had absolutely nothing to do—unless he committed suicide. Also on the bronze tablet or the stone slab as the case may be, and provided it doesn't cost too much, I'd like to have inscribed certain lines from the epitaph which Robert Louis Stevenson wrote for himself, to-wit as follows:

> "This be the verse you grave for me:
> Here he lies where he longed to be;
> Home is the sailor, home from sea,
> And the hunter home from the hill."

I'm quoting from memory. If I'm wrong will somebody kindly correct me?

Or, if a simpler single line bearing the same imprint seems desirable, I offer this one as suitable: "I Have Come Back Home."

And, thank you, no flowers. Does anybody feel moved to send flowers, I'd prefer that they give the money they'd spend there to some local non-denominational charity. Cover the spot with leaves—Christmas berries from the flat-lands and cedar from the friendly low McCracken County ridges if it be winter, and leafy boughs from native hickories or hackberries or wild crab-apples if it be in other seasons.

Above all I want no long faces and no show of grief at the burying ground. Kindly observe the final wishes of the under-signed and avoid reading the so-called Christian burial service which, in view of the language employed in it, I regard as one of the most cruel and paganish things inherited by our forebears from our remote pagan ancestors. In deference to the faith of our dear mother who was through her lifetime a loyal though never a bigoted communicant of that congregation, perhaps the current pastor of the First Presbyterian church would consent to read the Twenty-third Psalm, which was her favorite passage in the Scrip-tures and is mine since it contains no charnel words, no morbid mouthings about corruption and decay and, being mercifully with-out creed or dogma, carries no threat of eternal hell fire for those parties we do not like, no direct promise of a heaven which, if one may judge by the people who are surest of going there, must be a powerfully dull place, populated to a considerable and un-comfortable degree by prigs, time-servers and unpleasantly ag-gressive individuals. Hell may have a worse climate but undoubt-edly the company is sprightlier. The Catholics with their genius for stage-management, handle this detail better. The officiating clergyman speaks in Latin and the parishioners, being unac-quainted with that language, are impressed by the mystery and the majesty of the rolling, sonorous periods without being shocked by distressing allusions and harrowing references.

As an aside I might add that my notion of an ideal religion would combine the dignity and the beauty of the Romanist ritual with certain other ingredients; the good taste and the ability of the Unitarians and Episcopalians—a trait not too common to some of the Evangelical groups—to mind their own business. (I'm proud that I never set myself up to be My Brother's Keeper, hav-ing been sufficiently occupied by the job of being my own keeper.) To these add the noble ethics and the splendid tolerance ex-pressed in Reformed Judaism; the sturdy independence and the good business principles of the Mormons; the gentle humility and orderly humanity of the Quakers, plus the militant zeal and un-selfish devotion of those Shock Troops of the Lord—the Salvation

Army, who fight in the trenches of Sin's No Man's Land to re-
claim the tortured souls and clothe the naked bodies of those
whom the rest of a snobbish world forgot. If, based on this combination, there was a determination to practice the sectless preach-
ments and the teaching of Jesus Christ who was the first true
gentleman of recorded history and the greatest gentleman that
ever lived, I might not have joined the fold but certainly I'd have
stood on the side lines and cheered for it. By the way, have you
ever noticed that in time of war not the most passionate partisan
dares to ask the Prince of Peace to bless his bloody arms and forward his bloody deeds? He invokes the aid of the God of un-
justified battles as created by the ancient Hebrews. All Hitler
needed to do was let his whiskers sprout and sit on a nest of
thunderbolts and naked swords, thinking up plague and pestilence
and rapine and slaughter and slavery for the vanquished, to be
a fit understudy for the vengeful murderous Jehovah of the
forepart of the Old Testament. For Brother Joe Stalin, our present
beloved ally and, secretly, the everlasting enemy of our institutions, the job would be easier. He already has the whiskers. (One
advantage of dying is that it affords a fellow opportunity to say a
lot of things that have been curdling in his system all these years.
Frankly, I'm enjoying myself.)

But getting back to what I was talking about: I am a life member of Paducah Lodge, No. 217 B.P.O.E. But I'd prefer that the
burial program of the order not be read. Like most burial pro-
grams it needs editing. However, if the members desire to turn
out, either as a body or singly, I'll be very glad to have them
present. Judging by my latest visits to the basement of the Elks'
Club it wouldn't do them a bit of harm if some of the habitues
there got out in the open air if only for a trip to a cemetery.

For the wind-up I'd be grateful if some of my colored friends
sang, first "Swing Low, Sweet Chariot" and then "Deep River."
I think I could count on Mattie Copeland of Jones Street, who
for so many years was a loyal, loving servant of my family, to
recruit the singers from the choirs of our colored churches.

I was almost overlooking one item: I take it that there will be
no need for pallbearers, as the trade term goes. Pallbearers are
another surviving relic of heathen practices. Recalling how this

pair of my friends could cuddle to their bosoms three of a kind in a dollar limit game, I'd nominate either George Goodman or Will Gilbert as a dependable custodian of my mortal remainders on the trip to the burying-ground. Anyhow, properly rendered down my ashes shouldn't much more than fill a Mason's fruit jar.

Among others I'd like to invite to go along for the ride—provided they promise to be cheerful and bright—I think of Colonel Gus Thompson, Fred Neuman, Herbert Wallerstein, Jim Smith, Douglas Bagby, Ed Paxton, Captain Louis Igert, Fletch Terrell, Ed Scott, Jim English, Henry Weil, A. R. Meyers, Dr. Warren Sights, Dr. Frank Boyd, Linn Boyd, Roy Nelson, Tom Waller, Jack Fisher, Roy McKinney, James D. Langstaff, Morton Hand, Henry Ward, Leo Keiler, Elliott Mitchell, Rev. Custis Fletcher, Luther Carson, James Langstaff, Charley Vahlkamp, Wade Sowell, Bob Moshell and Charley Beard. If I have overlooked any suitable candidates I beg their pardon. Ladies also welcome with or without escorts.

I rather figure some of my fellow-townspeople might favor memorial exercises of sorts, either in connection with the funeral or elsewhere. Personally I have no objection, only desiring that no dismal note be permitted to ooze into the proceedings. Keep the thing cheerful, boys and girls. If somebody feels called upon to speak, I'd like to suggest for the job—well, say, Tom Waller. He could be depended upon to be neither verbose nor lachrymose. Or if Waller isn't available there's Jack Fisher or Jim Wheeler or Roy Shelbourne. Only, make it snappy.

Well, I reckon that will be about all except that I extend, in passing, my affectionate and grateful regards to the gracious and generous folk who make up so overwhelmingly the dwellers in my home community, and my native section. You've been mighty good to me and I appreciate it. Much obliged, you-all, and good-bye and bless you and prosper you.

(Signed)

Irvin S. Cobb

At New York
December, 1943

ROBERT FROST

"Each knows his own discernment best."

IF America had an official poet laureate, only one towering (in a literary sense), dignified and self-effacing poet would be so acclaimed. As evidence of the fact that it could be none other than Robert Frost, witness the unforgettable picture of the bare-headed 85-year-old gentleman standing on the steps of the national Capitol on January 20, 1961, reading a message composed for the occasion of the Inaugural of John Fitzgerald Kennedy as President of the United States.

Part of the immediate humanity of Robert Frost is evident in the number of poems he has written as personal messages, warmly intimate, humorous and indicative of the simple truths he injected into his own songs of America. He wrote one such poem in 1944, as a smiling message to his old friends Frederick G. Melcher, the publisher, and Marguerite Melcher, who in turn printed it privately for their friends as Christmas greetings, under the title, "An Unstamped Letter in Our Rural Letter Box by Robert Frost."

December 1944

Last night your watchdog barked all night
So once you rose and lit the light.
It wasn't someone at your locks.
No, in your rural letter box
I leave this note without a stamp
To tell you it was just a tramp
Who used your pasture for a camp.
There pointed like the pip of spades
The young spruce made a suite of glades
So regular that in the dark
The place was like a city park.
There I elected to demur
Beneath a low-slung juniper
That like a blanket to my chin

Kept some dew out and some heat in,
Yet left me freely face to face
All night with universal space.
It may have been at two o'clock
That under me a point of rock
Developed in the grass and fern,
And as I woke afraid to turn
Or so much as uncross my feet,
Lest having wasted precious heat
I never should again be warmed,
The largest firedrop ever formed
From two stars' having coalesced
Went streaking molten down the west,
And then your tramp astrologer
From seeing this undoubted stir
In Heaven's firm-set firmament,
Himself had the equivalent,
Only within. Inside the brain
Two memories that long had lain
Now quivered toward each other, lipped
Together, and together slipped;
And for a moment all was plain
That men have thought about in vain.
Please, my involuntary host,
Forgive me if I seem to boast.
'Tis possible you may have seen,
Albeit through a rusty screen,
The same sign heaven showed your guest.
Each knows his own discernment best.
You have had your advantages,
Things must have happened to you, yes,
And have occurred to you no doubt,
If not indeed from sleeping out,
Then from the work you went about
In farming well—or pretty well.
And it is partly to compel
Myself in form a pauper is
To say as much as I write you this.

ROBERT OPPENHEIMER

". . . proposals on which a sound solution can be sought "

FROM the instant that the first atomic bomb was exploded in 1945, the question of international control of this frightening energy has been widely discussed. At this writing, fifteen years later, a horrified world has seen the offspring of that first bomb mushroom into an ever-spreading cloud of lethal development—a destructive instrument now owned and used by the contending political halves of the globe.

The vast enterprise resulting in the first nuclear explosion was guided by Dr. Robert Oppenheimer, now director of the Institute for Advanced Studies, at Princeton, New Jersey.

The future of the creature he helped bring into being obsessed him even then (when, as yet, the United States alone held the secret) as it was evident that the time would come when atomic energy would no longer be a monopoly of any nation or group of nations.

His thoughts, as of that date, were set down in a private letter to his friend, David Lilienthal, Director of the Tennessee Valley Authority—a form of private brief, arguing the needs of a humanity that had small conception of what the unlocking of atomic power could mean.

Washington, D.C.
February 2, 1946

In these notes I shall write down some of the non-technical things that have seemed to me relevant to the establishment of effective international control of atomic energy, and make, in rather broad terms, proposals on the basis of which a sound solution can in my opinion be sought. I shall write these notes against the background of our discussions in the past days, and with the thought in mind that the technical basis of many of the judgments will be provided in a separate report.

1. It is probable that the main desire of our Government is

the achievement of safety and protection against the threat of atomic warfare. Even if it were possible to achieve this without considering such positive features as the extension of knowledge and its application to constructive purposes, it might be argued that such a course should not be followed. It is my belief that quite apart from its desirability, the provision for constructive development of the field of atomic energy will turn out to be essential for the operation of any system of safeguards. You have seen in the last days evidence of the enthusiasm, inventiveness, and intelligence that has gone into the development of the field in this country, and that has manifested itself even in such relatively peripheral matters as the exploration of raw material resources. I believe that just these elements must be brought to bear on the problem of control if there is to be any chance for a real solution. In particular, it has become clear to us that not only politically, but scientifically and technically as well, the field of atomic energy has witnessed very rapid change and very rapid progress. I believe that this will be the case in the future, too, and that no organization and no proposal can be effective which does not have a flexibility adequate to these changes. I further believe that any proposed organization must itself reflect the changing character of the problem and the constructive purposes which are a complement to control. It is clear that quite apart from any organizational details, the objectives here outlined will require a genuine cooperation and not a mere acquiescence on the part of the participating powers and agencies. As I understand it, the primary function of the United Nations Atomic Energy Commission must be to lay the basis for such cooperative approach to the problem.

2. The position of the three powers, the United States, the United Kingdom, and Canada, that have in the past collaborated in the development of atomic energy, is a rather special one, and that of the United States perhaps the most special of all. There are two parts of this: our technical advantage put us in a position to exercise disproportionate influence in shaping the proposals made, and our greater scientific and technical mastery of the problem should give us greater insight into the implications of a

proposed solution and the character of the steps necessary to achieve it.

It has, from the first, seemed important to balance our technical superiority insofar as possible by allowing the proposals to be formulated as a result of multilateral discussion, rather than through acceptance of a plan elaborated unilaterally by us. It would seem to be inevitable that differences of opinion similar to those which appeared in the Panel, but far more profound, would be expressed in approaching the organizational problems of control. Here again it would seem to me neither desirable, nor in any long term practical, to avoid a discussion of these issues in an attempt at their constructive reconciliation. Just this possibility is in fact my ground for believing that the negotiations we are now discussing may provide a prototype for more difficult future problems.

I have a somewhat different view of the situation arising from our sole possession of the technical and scientific insight necessary to sound judgments. This problem is in part technical, since many of the facts at our disposal, but not now generally known, are indeed relevant to questions of feasibility, adequacy, and safety. It is also in part a psychological problem in that insight depends not only on having facts available, but on having a sense of assurance that relevant facts have not been withheld. I believe that it is premature to discuss the precise extent to which basic scientific information should be made available to the Atomic Energy Commission. It is clear, on the other hand, that such information neither must, nor with propriety should, include detailed engineering specifications for plants and for weapons; on the other hand, our experience would indicate that the Smyth Report as it stands is probably far from sufficient. We shall be in a better position to judge this at our next meeting.

3. In order to evaluate the proposals that I should like to make, it may be well to consider extreme examples, which have been suggested from time to time, of proposals that I regard as unworkable. Almost everyone has, at one stage or another in his acquaintance with this problem, considered prohibiting further work on atomic energy, and devising a system of inspection adequate to insure that this prohibition is carried out. It is not only that

this proposal would make impossible the application of existing knowledge to constructive ends; it would be so contrary to the human patterns of exploration and exploitation that no agreement entered into by heads of state could command the interest or the cooperation of the people of the world.

An apparently less radical solution would be the separation of the functions of development and of control according to which the only responsibility of an international authority would be the inspection of work carried out under a purely national or private initiative, and the possible prohibition of some of this work. The negative approach to the problem of control would leave the inspecting agency with inadequate insight, both into the technical state of the subject, and into its motivation and the organic characteristics of its growth. It would provide inspectors who are less informed and less enlightened than those whose evasions they were trying to prevent; it would provide inspectors with a motive pathetically inadequate to the immense and dreary task which such inspection would involve, and who would no doubt be in a poor position to apply to their work the technical ingenuity and inventiveness which alone can make it an undertaking of finite dimensions and some prospect of success. One sees these difficulties most clearly if the problem is considered as it may appear in the almost immediate future. On the one hand, I believe that no one would be willing to wait for the institution of a system of controls until such time as many nations had a flourishing atomic energy industry, and no doubt a flourishing atomic armaments program; on the other hand, it is probably true that at the present time there is pitifully little to inspect in any countries but the United States, the United Kingdom, and Canada. It is just this circumstance which would make the task of inspection so unenlightened and so vast as to be prohibitive. It is also clear that this approach to the problem would sacrifice almost wholly whatever advantages there are in the fact that atomic energy developments are nowhere else in the world an established and flourishing activity, representing a vested interest and a living organization.

4. Against this background of the difficulties of control as an isolated and negative function, I have thought it essential at least to consider combining the functions of development and of con-

trol in a single agency. It is fairly certain that there are now, and will increasingly be, activities having to do with atomic energy which are not vital to control and which, for human, or organizational, or political, reasons should not be included among the functions of the controlling authority; but there are certainly several such functions which, as matters now appear, should be so included among them: the development of raw materials, the exploration of atomic weapons, and the application, in its more dangerous forms, of atomic energy to power and technology.

a. I thus propose that the international authority have a monopoly on the study, development, and exploitation of uranium. That this could be an interesting activity some of our discussions of last week clearly showed, and apart from considerations of security a coordinated attack on a worldwide scale is the more appropriate way of exploiting the raw materials. An agency which was well informed about the location of deposits and the most highly developed means of working them, and their relation to each other, would be in a strong position to detect and discourage illegal enterprises of a more private nature. It would also be in a position to provide the basic accounting and material control for an ingredient which is at present, and probably will remain for a long time to come, uniquely necessary. Technical arguments suggest that the same machinery should be applied to the exploitation of thorium.

b. A second activity of the international authority, which is doubtless far less urgent, but for which provision must ultimately be made, is research and study of atomic explosives. You will remember from our discussion that this is a field in which we are by no means confident of the facts; it is, of course, possible that such atomic explosives may be useful to the peacetime economy of the world, but quite apart from this it is only by their exploration that any agency can have a reasonable chance of insuring that developments beyond its control are not of great danger to the world.

c. It would be an essential function of the international authority to develop atomic energy for industrial purposes and as a source of power, and to carry out the technical advances necessary to make these developments practical, and to extend their range.

In conducting this program, it is clear that economic, technological and even sociological considerations will be as important as purely scientific ones, and it is further clear that the solution of the resulting conflicts will involve compromise and good will which only an agency with authority and adequate technical competence can bring to the problem.

d. As we pointed out, there are a number of potential applications of atomic energy which can be made relatively safe, either by denaturing procedures, or because plants are involved which destroy, rather than create, atomic explosives; or because the scale of the operations is small enough to be immaterial for atomic weapons. There may be strong arguments (and there probably are) for conducting these developments under a license system, with nations or with more private organizations, but the line between safe and dangerous activities should not remain fixed where we would draw it today, so that I should be reluctant to make a final a priori definition at this time.

e. It would seem to me desirable and, in fact, essential, that the international authority cooperate with scientists, engineers, industrialists, and others who are not members of their organization but who have an interest in, or a contribution to make toward, the work of the authority. This openness would contribute in an important way to making the authority subject to enlightened criticism and to making its findings available for more private exploitation wherever this could be done effectively and safely.

5. There are a number of questions which probably should be discussed in connection with the above proposals, although I do not feel qualified to discuss them. In particular, the organizational structure of the international authority, whether it be a commission or a corporation (or take another form), will have to be settled in the light of conflicting views as to the best methods of providing initiative, responsibility, and integrity. The machinery set up for providing a reasonable, forward-looking allocation of atomic power and atomic products, the machinery required for financial undertakings, many of which in the earlier times may not be economically profitable, and the contributions that might be expected in the form of labor, technical competence, and raw

materials, all would need a fairly prompt discussion. Other questions on which there will be differences of opinion are the appropriate scale of development and the priorities that should attach to various phases of the work. In all of these matters one will have to draw both on the technical ingenuity of those familiar with the field of atomic energy, and on all useful precedents of effective organization.

6. There are a few questions which it seems to me not very profitable to discuss at present. One has to do with the complex of problems that would arise should there be abrogation of agreements by a nation or a group of nations, or activities in serious violation of these agreements. Such discussions will inevitably bring one to the problem of sanctions, which seems to me essentially separable from the questions we have been asked to consider. Related to these questions is the provision of an adequate physical security for installations operated by the international authority but susceptible to diversion for military use, and the question of whether any useful purpose can be achieved by stockpiling atomic weapons to facilitate the application of sanctions. It is inevitable that all these questions will be asked; in my opinion their discussion cannot contribute in a constructive way to the solution of our primary problem.

Robert Oppenheimer

Mr. David Lilienthal
Knoxville
Tennessee

EDNA ST. VINCENT MILLAY

". . . I am very proud of Aria da Capo."

WHEN Edna St. Vincent Millay was fifty-five, in 1947, she had achieved a world-wide and sometimes controversial reputation. She was compared by some critics with the great Elizabethan romanticists and was acclaimed as a master of the sonnet; more particularly Miss Millay had shown a range of achievement from witty verse reflecting the mood of the "roaring 1920s" to the writing of poetic plays.

A request for publishing rights to a collection of her plays brought forth from her pen a letter of self-criticism and appraisal rare in the fields of the arts, and all the more dramatic because she was at that time plagued with monetary problems and suffering from illnesses that would cause her death only three years later. True poet that she was, she turned down this otherwise easy means of adding to her earnings.

The letter, here quoted in part, was written in reply to one from Cass Canfield, then and now head of the publishing house of Harper and Brothers, to whom Miss Millay expressed thanks for some recent financial assistance, before taking up the assessment of her own work.

Steepletop
Austerlitz, New York
October 1947

Dear Cass:

. . . As to your proposition that Harper's publish my Collected Dramatic Works, I am afraid I must disappoint you here, although I hate most dreadfully to do so. The fact is, I have too much pride and too much faith in myself as a dramatist, to permit the publication in one volume of seven dramatic works of mine, of which only three—Two Slatterns and a King; The Princess Marries the Page; and Aria da Capo, are good plays, and only one of these, Aria da Capo, of any significance.

Two Slatterns and a King does exactly what it sets out to do.

It is very light and slender, but it is carefully constructed and plays well.

The Princess Marries the Page is romantic and sentimental. This, too, is well constructed. It is easy to act, and pretty to watch and listen to. It is a good little play, but of no importance.

Aria da Capo, of course, is something else utterly. It has its own imperfections, but they are not heavy enough to drag it down. A person reading it might think it too complicated for the stage, but he would be mistaken. It was written for the theatre, and on the stage all its intricacies move into place in a clear and terrible pattern. (Aria da Capo is being played all the time, in little theatres, colleges, high schools, clubs, all over this country and Great Britain and in other countries. I saw it a few years ago in Paris, done in French, of course. . . . You have no idea how good this play is, until you see it on the stage. I hope you will see it someday.)

Well, as you have gathered, I am very proud of Aria da Capo. I wish I had a dozen more, not like it, but as good. Then we could bring out a book!

The King's Henchman is a bad play. It was written in the first place as the libretto for an opera. Later, I tried to make it into a play. But it was hopelessly contaminated. It smells of libretto; and has other great faults as well. . . .

The Lamp and the Bell was written as an occasional piece, and shows it. It was written to be played at Vassar, on the fiftieth anniversary (I think) of the founding of the college. It was written to be played by girls, and shows it. The play is well constructed. It is not, like The King's Henchman, diffuse, crowded with detail, and verbose. But whereas The King's Henchman, considered not as drama but as narrative poetry, is often full and rich, the blank verse of The Lamp and the Bell seldom rises above the merely competent. Five acts of uninspired writing, with only here and there a line, or two or three lines at most, to light up the page—and by no means every page—this is not good enough.

The Murder of Lidice, of course, was and is merely propaganda. I tried to make it as good as I could in the time I had. It has some good lines, but not very many, and not very good. This piece should be allowed to die along with the war which provoked it. . . .

Conversation at Midnight is an interesting book: I like it. But the published version is not nearly so good as the original manu-script, which was destroyed by fire. I was able to remember the greater part of it, but there were many passages which I had to re-invent, and others which I was forced to leave out entirely, so the result is patchy and jerky. . . .

We are left only with Aria da Capo, one really good, serious play, and two other one-act plays, both skillfully wrought, but both inconsequential. We have nothing to work with. We have no book.

I am very sorry to disappoint you. . . .

I am writing. I have not many poems finished, but those that I have are good. The effort of writing so much propaganda during the war—from the point of view of poetry, sloppy, garrulous and unintegrated—is to make me more careful and critical of my work even than formerly I was, so that now I write more slowly than ever. But there will be a book.

Sincerely

Edna

DWIGHT D. EISENHOWER

". . . that such an expression would smack of effrontery."

AFTER Dwight D. Eisenhower had completed two honored terms of service as President of the United States in 1961, very few persons remembered that, in 1948, he had unequivocally declined to be con-sidered as a candidate; that his ac-ceptance of the nomination, in 1952, represented a break with his former convictions achieved only after some years of experience as a civilian.

As long ago as 1945, former President Truman had in effect of-fered to support General Eisen-hower for the Presidency, being quoted as saying at Potsdam that there was nothing the latter might want he would not support, and, as Eisenhower wrote in his book *Crusade in Europe,* "That definitely and specifically includes the Presidency in 1948."

By 1948, however, the image of the Presidency loomed before General Eisenhower as a Republican Party symbol, not a Democratic Party one, and President Truman, while affirming his former state-ment, no longer welcomed an Eisenhower candidacy in a year when he was determined to seek election in his own right.

It remained for a relatively obscure newspaper publisher—Leonard V. Finder, of the *Manchester* (New Hampshire) *Evening Leader,* to ask the question that evoked General Eisenhower's 1948 disclaimer, and incidentally shed much light on the high concepts he would take later to the Presidency.

I have hitherto refrained from making the bald statement that I would not accept nomination, although this has been my intention ever since the subject was first mentioned to me . . .

This omission seems to have been a mistake, since it has inadvertently misled sincere and disinterested Americans. But my reticence stemmed from cogent reasons. The first was that such an expression would smack of effrontery . . . A second and even deeper reason was a persistent doubt that I could phrase a flat refusal without appearing to violate that concept of duty which calls upon every good citizen to place no limitation upon his readiness to serve in any desired capacity . . .

It is my conviction that the necessary and wise subordination of the military to civil power will be sustained, and our people will have greater confidence that it is so sustained, when lifelong professional soldiers, in the absence of some obvious and overriding reasons, abstain from seeking higher political office . . .

Politics is a profession; a serious, complicated, and in its true sense a noble one. In the American scene I see no dearth of men fitted by training, talent and integrity for national leadership. On the other hand, nothing in the international or domestic situation especially qualifies for the most important office in the world a man whose adult years have been spent in the country's military forces. At least, this is true in my case . . .

In any case, my decision to remove myself completely from the political scene is definite and positive.

OGDEN NASH

"I'm a very happy daddy."

MANY parents have written notes to their children when business forced them to be absent on birthdays or other noteworthy occasions.

But only one little girl was forced to celebrate her tenth birthday while her father, Ogden Nash, the famous poet, was absent from home.

Therefore only one little girl, Isabel Nash (the present Mrs. Frederick Eberstadt) has among her keepsakes a letter such as the following one.

My sweet, although you were divine
When you were just a child of nine,
I'd be the happiest of men
If I could see you change to 10.
I do not like to be away
On such a stupendiferous day.
Now that you're old enough to caddie
I'm a very happy daddy.
Many happy returns and
I love you.

HERBERT HOOVER

"Thank you, Miss Gray."

IN 1959, the Reader's Digest addressed an inquiry to an 85-year-old man of considerable distinction, asking him to do an article on "the best advice I ever had."

The recipient of that request was Herbert Hoover, former President of the United States, organizer of relief for the distressed and impoverished populations of Europe after World War I, internationally famous engineer and the holder of numerous other distinctions.

Mr. Hoover was neither a "retired" elderly gentleman nor the occupant of a lonely pinnacle basking in his sunset years. He was—and is at this writing—an active head of an empire of research from which have come the significant "Hoover reports" for reorganization of America's governmental structure, a gregarious man of many public interests and appearances, and a continuing student of politics and social problems in many fields.

When he received the request, he wrote—he has never employed a "ghost writer"—not an article, but an open letter in reply, expressing his thanks in retrospect to a woman who guided his thinking seventy years earlier, when "I left school to practice the profession of an office boy,"—his thanks to Miss Gray.

New York, July 1959

I have received a request from The Reader's Digest for "the best advice I ever had."

There is another method of changing the shape of things to come than just raw advice for both kids and grownups. And that is the field of tactful suggestion.

At 15 years of age I left school to practice the profession of office boy in a business firm in Salem, Ore. One day there came into the office a Miss Gray. She was a tall lady in her 30's, with agreeable manners, kindly eyes and a most engaging smile. I was alone in the reception office. She announced that she was a schoolteacher and asked me about my schooling. I told her I had to work, but I hoped to go to a night school that was soon to open in town. Later I found that Miss Gray's extracurricular occupation was advising—or just being interested in—the young working boys in Salem.

She asked if I was interested in reading books. She must have thought some wider scope in book reading was desirable from my replies to her questions as to what I had read. As a matter of fact, under my austere Quaker upbringing my book reading had been limited to the Bible, the encyclopedia and a few novels which dealt with the sad results of demon rum and the final regeneration of the hero. As office boy, I read only the morning paper, when my superior finished with it.

I also mentioned that outside my office hours I had duties with sandlot baseball and fishing. Notwithstanding this, Miss Gray asked me if I would go with her to the small lending library in town. At the library she said she wished to borrow a copy of Ivanhoe, and she gave it to me saying I would find it interesting. I read the book at the office between chores, and in the evenings. It opened a new world filled with the alarms and excursions of battles, the pomp of tournaments, the tragedy of Rebecca's unrequited love, the heroism of the Black Knight and Locksley, and the destiny of Ivanhoe. Suddenly I began to see books as living things and was ready for more of them.

A few days later Miss Gray dropped in again and suggested David Copperfield. I can still remember the harshness of Murdstone, the unceasing optimism of Micawber and the wickedness of Uriah Heep. I have met them alive many times in afteryears.

And so, through books, my horizons widened, sometimes with Miss Gray's help, sometimes on my own initiative. I devoured samples of Thackeray and Irving, biographies of Washington, Lincoln and Grant.

At the night school the principal introduced me to textbooks on mathematics, elementary science and Latin. They were important, of course; but, looking back, I realize that the books inspired by Miss Gray also had great importance. While textbooks are necessary to learning, it was those other books which stimulated imagination and a better understanding of life. They made the whole world a home. They broadened my scope and made me feel a part of the mighty stream of humanity.

At 17 I went to Stanford University to study engineering. My time was occupied with the required reading and the extracurricular duties of managing the baseball and football teams and earning my way. But occasionally Miss Gray wrote to me and suggested certain books to read.

Miss Gray's influence widened when I began the practice of my profession as an engineer, and it extended over the 18 years which followed. In that work I had long days of travel, and many hours of waiting for things to happen on ships, railways and canalboats all over the world—from the United States to China, to Burma, to Mexico, to Australia, to Africa, to Canada and to Russia. On one journey, thanks to Miss Gray's inoculation, I armed myself with paperbound volumes of Defoe, Zola and Balzac; on another, with such less exciting books as those of Herbert

Spencer, James Mill and Walter Bagehot. Another time I took along Carlyle's French Revolution, Gibbon's The History of the Decline and Fall of the Roman Empire, and some popular histories of Greece and Egypt. I also read books on Mohammed, Buddha and Confucius, as well as more American history.

With the coming of World War I and with official duties devouring my time and energy thereafter for many years, my book reading slackened. Nonetheless, Miss Gray's influence penetrated even as far as the White House. When I arrived at that residence in 1929 I found it was mostly bare of books except for the published papers of former Presidents—incomplete at that. One day I mentioned this famine of representative American literature in the White House to John Howell, an old friend and a leading bookseller. Under his leadership and with the cooperation of the American Booksellers Assn., some 500 books were selected. Most of these I had read long ago, but they were much enjoyed by the many other inhabitants of the White House.

To me they were always a reminder of Miss Gray, and of the words of John Milton: "A good book is the precious lifeblood of a master spirit, embalmed and treasured up on purpose to a life beyond life."

I repeat the title of this article—"Thank You, Miss Gray!"; thank you for guiding me to the rich world of wonder, beauty, wisdom and imagination that can be found in books.

JOHN F. KENNEDY

"I think I know a little about how you feel."

AMONG the earlier major appointments by President Kennedy was that of J. K. Galbraith, Harvard professor and one of his biographers, to the post of Ambassador to India. Among the unexpected repercussions was the report that Peter, second son of the Ambassador designate, was upset at the idea of leaving his normal associations and going with his family to this faraway land.

Despite one of the busiest schedules ever faced by a President,

Kennedy took time to explain the parallel in Peter's new experience with his own background and to emphasize his deep-seated belief that American youth abroad could do much for understanding of the United States in a crisis-torn world.

This letter is included here by express permission of the White House.

THE WHITE HOUSE
Washington

March 28, 1961

Dear Peter:

I learn from your father that you are not very anxious to give up your school and friends for India. I think I know a little about how you feel. More than twenty years ago our family was similarly uprooted when we went to London where my father was ambassador. My younger brothers and sisters were about your age. They had, like you, to exchange old friends for new ones.

But I think you will like your new friends and your new school in India. For anyone interested, as your father says you are, in animals, India must have the most fascinating possibilities. The range is from elephants to cobras, although I gather the cobras have to be handled professionally. Indians ride and play polo so you will come back an experienced horseman.

But more important still, I think of the children of the people I am sending to other countries as my junior peace corps. You and your brothers will be helping your parents do a good job for our country and you will be helping out yourself by making many friends. I think perhaps this is what you will enjoy most of all.

My best wishes,

Sincerely yours,
John F. Kennedy

Mr. Peter Woodward Galbraith
30 Francis Avenue
Cambridge, Massachusetts.

ALPHABETICAL LISTING OF WRITERS

EDDY, MARY BAKER (1892) To a new congregation
EDISON, THOMAS A. (1888) His first "phonogram"
EISENHOWER, DWIGHT D. (1948) Declining the Presidential nomination
ELIOT, CHARLES W. (1865) On Lincoln's assassination
EMERSON, RALPH WALDO (1855) Hailing *Leaves of Grass*

"FABIUS" (JOHN DICKINSON) (1788) On the Constitution
FITZGERALD, F. SCOTT (1933) A fatherly letter
FRANKLIN, BENJAMIN (1745) On choosing a mistress
  (1784) The newly invented balloon
FREEMAN, B. (1776) Political tensions and a botanist's pension
FROST, ROBERT (1944) To his friends

GALLATIN, ALBERT (1808) On softness in American life
GIBBONS, JAMES CARDINAL (1887) Catholics and socialism
GOMPERS, SAMUEL (1905) Labor's honorable course
GRANT, ULYSSES S. (1864) Hurrying General Thomas
GREELEY, HORACE (1872) To western colonists

HALL, FRANK (1861) A pioneer in Colorado
HAMILTON, ALEXANDER (1800) Denouncing Aaron Burr
HANCOCK, JOHN (1775) A love letter delays Washington's commission
HEARST, WILLIAM RANDOLPH (1885) Asking his father for a newspaper
HOLMES, OLIVER WENDELL, SR. (1851) The author plans a poem
HOLMES, OLIVER WENDELL, JR. (1919) On socal change
HOOVER, HERBERT (1959) Thanks to a boyhood teacher
HOUSE, EDWARD M. (1919) To President Wilson on changes

IRVING, WASHINGTON (1802) Satire on "modern" manners
  (1836) Inviting William C. Bryant to dinner

JACKSON, WILLIAM HENRY (1866) Adventures of a young bullwhacker
JAY, JOHN (1794) Temporary farewell to wife
JEFFERSON, THOMAS (1783) Advice to his 11-year-old daughter
  (1789) Accepting the job of Secretary of State
  (1819) His vigor at 75 years of age

KENNEDY, JOHN F. (1961) Sympathetic advice to an Ambassador's son
KENT, JAMES (1842) Reflections in his old age

LAFAYETTE, MARQUIS DE (1826) Admiring his adopted country
LANE, FRANKLIN K. (1918) A test of economic philosophy

LEE, ROBERT E. (1861) To his wife in the first year of war
LINCOLN, ABRAHAM (1835) The hurt feelings of a young postmaster
  (1858) Challenging Stephen A. Douglas to debate
  (1864) To a bereft mother
LITTLE PRINCE (1818) An Indian asks for justice
LONGFELLOW, HENRY WADSWORTH (1826) His desires to be a writer

MADISON, MRS. JAMES (DOLLY) (1814) Burning of Washington
MARSHALL, GEORGE C. (1935) To an old teacher
McQUAID, BISHOP BERNARD J. (1876) Defining catholicism and patriotism
MILLAY, EDNA ST. VINCENT (1947) On her plays
MONITOR (ANONYMOUS) (1862) A sailor's letter after battling the Merrimac
MONROE, JAMES (1805) A diplomatic protest to Britain
MORRIS, GOUVERNEUR (1806) The limitations of democracy

NASH, OGDEN Birthday greetings to his daughter

OPPENHEIMER, ROBERT (1946) The control of atomic development

PERKINS, MAXWELL (1914) A young man shows promise
PERRY, OLIVER HAZARD (1813) The Battle of Lake Erie
POE, EDGAR ALLAN (1848) His grief and confusions

ROGERS, WILL (1926) Letter of an "unofficial ambassador"
ROOSEVELT, FRANKLIN DELANO (1935) No magician's wand
ROOSEVELT, THEODORE (1905) On the rigors of diplomacy
RUSH, RICHARD (1837) Queen Victoria's popularity

SCHURZ, CARL (1864) The stature of Lincoln
SEEGER, ALAN (1916) On the supreme experience
SHERMAN, WILLIAM TECUMSEH (1880) Plight of the Indians
SHIRLEY, DAME (1852) A woman in the gold fields
SMITH, JOHN (1608) Report from Jamestown Colony
SMITH, MRS. SAMUEL HARRISON (1801) On life in Washington
STRICKLAND, WILLIAM (1844) The architect visits Washington
SVENDSEN, GRO (1865) A pioneer woman's letter to Norway

TANEY, ROGER BROOKE (1857) On the Dred Scott decision
THOREAU, HENRY D. (1843) A letter to Emerson

TONG, THE GEE KUNG (1888) Letter hiring a hatchet man
TRAVIS, WILLIAM B. (1836) "Victory or death!"

Udall, Morris · On Conservation

VAN DORSTEN, RUDOLPH (1789) On the first Inaugural of an American President
VANZETTI, BARTOLOMEO (1927) To Sacco's son just before the execution

WADE, W. B. (1846) A soldier's letter from Monterey
WARD, MATTHEW F. (1849) On Victorian England
WASHINGTON, GEORGE (1776) Advice to his stepson
   (1782) Refusal of a crown
   (1793) Acceptance of Thomas Jefferson's resignation
WEBSTER, NOAH (ARISTIDES) (1800) Alexander Hamilton's "shame"
WEEMS, MASON LOCKE (1800) Outlining the *Life of Washington*
WILLIS, NATHANIEL PARKER (1830) On manners and morals
WILSON, WOODROW (1922) Tribute to William E. Borah
WIRT, WILLIAM (1805) On matrimony
   (1822) On the practice of law
WOLFE, THOMAS (1935) A plea for understanding

YOUNG, BRIGHAM (1857) Defiance of the government

LETTERS
BY CATEGORIES
(*In Chronological Order*)

I. INSPIRATION AND EXHORTATION

311

II. HUMOR

WASHINGTON IRVING (1802) Satire on "modern" manners
WILLIAM WIRT (1805) Advice on matrimony
WILLIAM CULLEN BRYANT (1821) On his marriage
WILLIAM STRICKLAND (1844) A visit to Washington
OLIVER WENDELL HOLMES, SR. (1851) The author plans a poem
MATTHEW WARD (1849) On Victorian England
WILL ROGERS (1926) Report of an unofficial ambassador
OGDEN NASH (1958 publication) Birthday greetings to his daughter

III. BY WOMEN

ABIGAIL ADAMS (1800) The new President's Mansion
MRS. SAMUEL HARRISON SMITH (1801) Life in the Capital
MRS. JAMES (DOLLY) MADISON (1814) Burning of Washington
ELLEN BIGELOW (1835) A winter trip by water
EMILY DICKINSON (1847) A school girl's letter home
DAME SHIRLEY (1852) A woman in the gold fields
GRO SVENDSEN (1865) A pioneer's letter to Norway
SUSAN B. ANTHONY (1872) After voting illegally
JANE ADDAMS (1879) On sincerity
MARY BAKER EDDY (1892) To a new congregation
EDNA ST. VINCENT MILLAY (1947) On her plays

IV. TRIBUTES AND EULOGIES

RALPH WALDO EMERSON (1855) Hailing "Leaves of Grass"
CARL SCHURZ (1864) The stature of Lincoln
CHARLES W. ELIOT (1865) On Lincoln's assassination
ANDREW CARNEGIE (1910) Tribute to Booker T. Washington
WOODROW WILSON (1922) On William Edgar Borah
GEORGE C. MARSHALL (1935) To an old teacher
HERBERT HOOVER (1959) Thanks to a boyhood teacher

V. WAR

OLIVER HAZARD PERRY (1813) The Battle of Lake Erie
MRS. JAMES (DOLLY) MADISON (1814) Burning of Washington
LITTLE PRINCE (1818) An Indian asks for justice
JAMES BOWIE (1836) From the Alamo
WILLIAM B. TRAVIS (1836) "Victory or Death"
W. B. WADE (1846) Letter from Monterey
BRIGHAM YOUNG (1857) Defiance of the government

THE AUTHORS
AND THEIR
BOOK

THE AUTHORS AND THEIR BOOK

CHARLES HURD, *author, journalist and public relations consultant, was born May 11, 1903, in Tonkawa, Oklahoma. He received his boyhood education from tutors and was an extension student at Northwestern University, Evanston, Ill., from 1918 to 1923. He began his writing career during his college years as a full-time reporter for The Associated Press in Chicago and then in New York City. He became an associate editor of Liberty magazine in 1926 and left three years later to join the staff of The New York Times in their Washington bureau. Until 1949 he remained there, having served as White House correspondent at various times and having been a London correspondent specializing in international politics during 1937 and 1938. He has since been actively engaged in the public relations field doing industrial promotion work through his own firm, Charles Hurd Associates. He was also a news commentator and has contributed to many magazines including Life, Reader's Digest, and American Magazine. He wrote a regular feature on personalities for Redbook and has had material published in anthologies. His books are* The White House *(Harper, 1940);* The Veterans Program *(Whittlesey House, 1946);* Washington Cavalcade *(Dutton, 1948);* The Compact History of the Red Cross *(Hawthorn, 1959);* A Treasury of Great American Speeches *(Hawthorn, 1959);* U.S. Mail, *in collaboration with Postmaster General Arthur E. Summerfield (Holt, Rinehart, Winston, 1960); and* Cavalcade of Europe, *with Lowell Thomas (Doubleday, 1960). He was married to the former Eleanor Branson of Washington, D.C., in 1934, and they make their home in Washington, D.C.*

ELEANOR HURD *was born in Washington, D.C., of parents whose families had lived in the Tidewater Country of Virginia and Maryland for almost three centuries. After attending Gunston Hall in Washington and Goucher College in Baltimore, she won an honors degree in library science from George Washington University in Washington. The joint "by-line" on this book recognizes a collaboration in research and writing that antedated Charles Hurd's first book in 1940. She has organized and done much of the research into the cumulative story of America embraced in these books, as well as some of the editing. When business required her husband to visit East Africa and Europe late in 1960, she helped in the selection, organization and writing of the introductions.*

A TREASURY OF GREAT AMERICAN LETTERS *(Hawthorn, 1961) was designed by Sidney Feinberg, and completely manufactured by American Book–Stratford Press, Inc. The body type was set on the Linotype in Times Roman, originally designed for use by The Times of London.*

A HAWTHORN BOOK

816
H 93

T 621053

HURD
Treasury of great American letters.

WITHDRAW

Plainfield Area Reference Center
PLAINFIELD PUBLIC LIBRARY
EIGHTH STREET AT PARK AVENUE
PLAINFIELD, NEW JERSEY 07060

DEMCO